Glass Slippers Shatter

Janet Britton

Glass Slippers Shatter
COPYRIGHT 2021 by Janet Britton

Cover Art by Storyteller Photography, Rebecca Nieminen
(Original photo of Maus Castle by Helen and Jerry Heimann)

Paperback Edition ISBN 978-1-43488-179-3
Electronic Edition ISBN
Published in the United States of America

Foreword

To the reader, especially if you are a friend or relative of the author:

Okay, here's the issue. A novel is fiction—make believe, pretend, not real—got it?

On the other hand, a basic rule of writing is, "Write what you know." Writers do that, of course. What else can we write about except things we've either experienced or researched?

So, I based *Glass Slippers Shatter* on the most formative time of my life, my time in Turkey. The historical events of 1967-68 are accurate, what I remember from my life and from my research, and the setting real, our apartment building in the city of Adana. Those details came from letters I sent Mom, especially after Dad's death, and from letters Rex wrote me. He spent over 30 months in Incirlik AFB, half of that time as a K-9 handler of a German Shepherd named Lux. I tapped into stories about the dogs of that unit.

But we are not Steve and Cindy. Of course, many of you know I don't have a sister with Down syndrome and didn't grow up in a multi-generational home, etc. And just to make it clear, there was no romantic encounter on a Turkish toilet floor, no black-market crisis, no mad drive through a Turkish city to save a child from kidnapping—well, you get the idea. As I said, the story is fiction.

All of the other characters are fiction, too, though I hope they seem very real to you, the types of people you've met: the abusers, the partiers, the struggling parents, the dreamers, the precious children. Only the character of Pam is based on a real person, Rex's little sister. The events surrounding her death are fictionalized, but all too real.

So, sit back and read. And remember. It's fiction.

Janet Britton

Prelude—2009

"I've had it! I'm kicking him to the curb." My girl's fist struck the table. "I know you expected me to stay married forever like you, Mom, but it's not a Brady Bunch world anymore."

No, it's a world where over half the marriages end in divorce, I didn't say. She wasn't listening anyway.

"You flower children with all your talk about peace and love don't have a clue what it's like today."

I sipped tea in silence. She didn't need a history lesson about the obvious similarities of our decades—young people dying in unpopular wars, the threat of nuclear weapons, racial tensions. She saw only the glaring differences. As she talked, I remembered.

"He thinks because he's the man, he's always right," she said. "It's like he's never heard of women's lib."

I thought, *Betty Friedan didn't change our world either. Edinboro State with its housemothers and sign-out sheets. Hippies wearing tie-dye and frayed bell-bottoms while we put on our nylons and skirts and went to work. In fact, more of us stuffed our bras than burned them. And free love? If we "got in trouble," we got married and raised a baby. Ask my sister-in-law. No bathtub abortions for us.*

"He says he needs to unwind with a beer because he works all day. Like I don't know what else goes on at The Inn. Toking and sniffing, shooting up."

The drugs of Haight-Ashbury and Greenwich Village hadn't touched Hartstown, PA, yet in the '60s. Our rebels drove to Ohio and smuggled 3.2 beer, what we called "near beer," behind the grills of big, old sedans. Guys got drafted for Vietnam at eighteen but couldn't drink until twenty-one.

"But if I stop after work, even for a cup of coffee, he's singing a different tune."

Tunes. The Beatles on the Ed Sullivan Show in '64, though in our house, we sang Irish ditties, hymns, oh, and kid's songs for Tee.

"I bust my butt doing everything while he sits doing nothing. Just scrolling or flipping."

We didn't have modern technology to contend with. Our skinny local newspaper and half-hour report on one of three fuzzy black-and-white channels held the madness of the world at arm's length. Truthfully, before the Kent State Massacre, a little over an hour away, even Nam was irrelevant. Until a friend got drafted.

She squinted those black eyes. "Can't you see, Mom? It's over! Finished! Kaput!"

After less than two years? But then, her generation viewed life through the shadow of the collapsing Twin Towers, mine through the beacon of JFK's moon challenge. We believed civil rights laws would end prejudice, Green Peace would solve pollution, the Peace Corps would bridge cultures, and debates over politics really mattered. Even God was alive back then.

"Don't be so quick, dear," I said. "What is it you think you can't work out?"

"Don't ask if you don't want to hear some really bad stuff." The disillusionment in those black eyes broke my heart.

"I'm listening, dear," I said but found myself drifting off to the "really bad stuff" of my own life as an Air Force bride—the rages, sordid deals in Turkish toilets, three-day drunken break parties, my terror of cancer (in the '60s, it truly was a death sentence) ... and finding out that drunk drivers murder dreams.

I'd air-brushed those stories. I'd said, "The hardest thing I've ever done was leave your Aunt Tee"—my sister Charity, born a Mongoloid, what we call Down Syndrome today—but never mentioned my greatest guilt, abandoning a baby boy as blond as Aunt Pam. I'd said, "Faith is the answer," but never confessed I'd watched our Turkish neighbors bow toward Mecca and questioned who God is.

I'd talked about the Six Days' War, the burning of draft cards and American cities during the Long Hot Summer, and the assassinations of Martin Luther King, Jr. and Bobby Kennedy. But not that I'd prayed one of these political crises would get me evacuated back to the States, away from *my* monster husband.

She sucked in a breath and threw down the challenge. "After all that, you can't still think there's any hope for us."

I set down my teacup and steeled myself. "Yes, actually I do. If we could make it through our problems that first year in Turkey, you can make it, too. And be stronger for it, like us."

My girl sniffed in open defiance. "Yeah, right." But she uncrossed her arms. And I began—

Chapter 1

Torn—May 13, 1967

I began where novels usually end. After the wedding. After we got home from State Line Church, the last place the McNeilly-Aldens (some just faces in old family photos now) were all together—

"You're your mama's last hope for a child with a happy marriage," Grandpa said, holding me so tight my head crushed the snuffed-out cigar in his jacket pocket. "Don't disappoint her, Baby Girl. Doc says *it* could come back."

That familiar blend of Old Spice and cherry tobacco. Tee tap-tap-tapping on my back. "Dee, Dee."

"Cindy." The squeak of the screen door opening to the porch. Then Steve stroking my neck and murmuring, "Don't you think you should go with Tee?"

I nodded. Hesitated. Grandpa's calloused hand brushed my cheek. And I stooped down, gazed into Tee's wide almond eyes, and smiled. "I know, Tee, I know. Tree house." I didn't cry.

Squealing, Tee clutched Raggedy Ann and shuffled off. Etched in my mind forever is the image of her in pink organza, looking kind of like an upside-down tulip. Miracle, the lamb Grandpa bottle-fed in a box behind the Franklin stove, trotting along behind.

Tee paced circles at the base of our gnarled maple until I caught up. She tugged my skirt and grunted. "Dee."

I smiled wider. "Yes, Tee, but be careful. Climbing's hard in a dress." I nudged her up the wide-railed steps onto the rough-planked platform.

"Zul! Zul! Zul!" she begged, squirming to the porch edge.

As tradition demanded, I wiggled over beside her, chanted, "Rapunzel, Rapunzel, let down your hair," and shook my brown tresses through the protective railing Grandpa had built us. As always, Tee imitated me.

Then we flopped over for the mandatory survey of our kingdom—the red barn, the white farmhouse, the lush alfalfa, the newly planted oats and corn, and the great woods behind the hilly pasture (ten acres of which Grandpa had just deeded Steve and me for a wedding gift). When my folks moved here for my grandparents' help with infant Charity and Sean (a two-year-old then), Grandpa ran out and painted "Alden" under "McNeilly" on the milk co-op sign by the mailbox. But no one ever called our place anything but the McNeilly Farm.

Tee's forehead bumped mine. Squinting through the bangs of her Dutch boy haircut, she said, "Dee"—her first word had been "Dee" for Cindy. Mine had been "Tee" for Charity.

My eyes stung. Blinking back the tears. *Mongoloid, retarded. That's what most people see. Me? I see my beloved other half.* Cradling her round shoulders, rocking and rocking.

"Cindy," Steve interrupted from below. "It's two hours to Pittsburgh. Planes don't wait."

Rocking ... and rocking ...

"Cindy," Steve said, a little more softly, a little more urgently. "We have to go."

I knew he was right. I had to face what I could no longer avoid. So, my shallow breath puffed out the words.

"I'm ... I'm going away, Tee. I told you when the prince came I had to leave for my happily-ever-after. Remember?" I fixed on those wide eyes. "Steve's the prince."

Haunting eyes stared back, unblinking. Suddenly, I had trouble comprehending, too. *When did I stop waiting for the mysterious handsome stranger on a white charger? When did I settle for the cute neighbor in a blue '55 Ford Fairlane?*

I swallowed hard, started again. "Remember all the pretty places jets fly to?"

She snorted on cue. Maybe this time some of it might make sense to her.

I pointed to a white trail vanishing into wistful clouds. "A jet's taking us to the land of Aladdin. We'll zoom past flying carpets." My arms swooped like wings.

Her arms, imitating mine, landed around me. We rocked and rocked.

"Steve will bring me back. I promise." I gasped in a great gulp of air before confessing, "But it'll seem like a long time, Tee. For me, too." Squeezing her tight.

"Cindy?" Steve repeated, almost in a whisper.

My head nodded, my feet ignored him, I almost made the mistake of asking myself if I could ever love him as much as I loved my Tee.

"It'll be okay," Steve said, "I promise." His deep ocean-blue eyes argued, *Trust me.*

I hesitated a moment longer, then took the plunge off the ladder into his arms. Tee, maybe a little wiser, balked, perhaps truly understanding our leaving was different this time.

But Steve was prepared. He popped the lid off a bottle of Coke. Tee slid to the edge, and he helped her down.

She slurped the sweet syrup. I patted her perennial cowlick. Grandpa called it an "Alfalfa sprout" after that cute character in *The Little Rascals.* Steve winked at me and mouthed, "I love you."

"Uh!" Tee poked Steve with the empty Coke bottle, and he grinned. "No more, Tee. Don't want you getting sick."

"Uh!" Tee pouted and tucked her moon face under my arm.

"Aw, Tee, don't be mad." Steve tickled her neck.

I think he fell in love with Tee long before he did me.

"I can't leave unless you give me a big smile," he said.

She pulled deeper into my skirt. Part of me hoped she'd never smile.

But Steve had a reputation for never giving up. "Watch this, Tee." She peeked. He flipped into a handstand. She snorted out laughter. That trick never failed. "That's my girl."

Air Force blue wrapped pink organza, and I knew. *It's time.*

I fumbled for the button I'd ripped from my wedding dress. Tee still carried the marble I gave her the first day the big yellow school bus took me away. But when I pressed the new pearl button into her soft fist, she latched onto my finger instead. Bewildered eyes condemned me.

Lord, help! One more second and my feet would've turned to stone. In fact, I'd probably still be standing there if Grandpa hadn't intervened. "Show me your treasure, Angel."

"Uh!" Tee clapped, and that pearl button launched into the gravel. Grandpa spotted it right away. Years of practice had made him an expert in calculating the trajectory of flying objects.

The others stepped forward. Tee clutched my skirt. "Dee."

My dad, the phantom who'd worked second shift all my life, tucked me under his lanky arms first. Probably to get it over with, like a plunge into an icy pond instead of the dipping-a-big-toe-in method. "We raised you for this day. Enjoy your time alone." One of his shirt buttons scratched my nose, but I didn't stir a fraction of an inch. I knew he'd rehearsed over and over for this rare talk. I didn't want to interrupt a single word.

"Dee, Dee," Tee tapped and tugged.

Mama traced my face, as if to memorize every feature. Her weak right arm trembled. *Why didn't I push her harder?* After her mastectomy two years before, I'd tried to be a good exercise coach. I really had. I'd say, "Reach for the moon," and our fingers would creep up the wall side-by-side. But then she'd grimace and suggest a snack, and I'd cave, every time. Off we'd go to the kitchen to munch on warm sticky buns or meringue pies.

"Dee. Dee." Tap-tap-tap.

"Write every exotic detail, Princess," Mama said. All of Hartstown was in a tizzy about my flying into a war zone, "The Middle East's a tinderbox," they said. But not Mama. "It's going to be so much fun, Princess." A single telltale squeak betrayed her. She scooted back.

"Dee. Dee." Tap-tap.

Nana. Vanilla scent and husky alto voice. "Don't forget, children. Marriage takes work and prayer." (I'd labeled the "It's work and prayer, not fantasy" lecture as Chapter 14 of Nana's *Advice for Marriage* series.) Kisses as fragile as the flickers of a firefly pressed against my skin. "I'll pray, my dears." (The worn spot from Nana's knees in the carpet by their four-poster bed proved those weren't just pious words.) Silent tears baptized us.

"Dee. Dee." Tug.

"Remember your mama," Grandpa mumbled. Then an Irish blessing: "And until we meet again, May God hold you in the hollow of His hand." One last time I rubbed my cheek on the coarse serge of his navy marrying-and-burying suit.

"Dee. Dee." That soft sing-song voice.

Steve nuzzled Tee. "We have to go now, Big Sis."

She grunted, tugged my finger.

Me stooping. Looking into wide almond eyes. I felt like I was aiming a rifle—at half of myself.

"Here, Angel. Let's go put your pretty in your collection. Come on, Angel."

Grandpa's calloused finger prying Tee's stubby finger from mine. Him striding off with Tee and Nana and Laddie, collar decked out with scraps of bridesmaid's material. Mama and Dad following. We'd all agreed an airport good-bye would frighten Tee.

I can't believe I didn't run after them like I always had before. I've often wondered how things would've turned out if I had.

But Steve grabbed me. "We're out of here, Mrs. Carmine."

He sprinted us to his Ford, stopped to yank the traditional pair of old shoes off the rear bumper, heaved them at the culprits. "Don't forget, guys. Payback."

Merle and Denny, home on leave from Ft. Benning, ducked into the back seat, sandwiched my best friend, Jill, between them. Pammy, Steve's sister, claimed "shotgun." I slid under the steering wheel to my spot beside Steve.

I'd imagined at this point I'd have to muzzle myself to keep from shouting, "I'm free. Free at last!" In a decade of revolution and change, our farm was a haven of stability, as in "boring and predictable"—ball games, church picnics, scavenger hunts, charades, upset the fruit basket, and an occasional contraband game of spin the bottle. I'd dreamed of more.

But facing reality, I clung to Steve and scolded myself. *Toughen up. You're twenty years old. It's time to leave home.*

Steve's Ford sprayed gravel all the way from the mailbox down to Flochs' driveway. There he whipped it into reverse, roared back, and—even though Grandpa warned, "Boys, someone's going to get hurt messing around"—executed a perfect brody, sliding around the curve and into the end of our lane.

"Copacetic!" Merle and Denny shouted the ultimate compliment. Pam and Jill cheered. Steve said, "Had to do that one last time." Everyone was laughing. But I didn't open my eyes for one last look.

***

The loudspeaker blared, "All those boarding Flight 319 to New York, please proceed to Gate 36 at this time."

"That's us, Cindy." Steve grabbed me under the arms and swung me around and around like a pinwheel. I must've been quite the sight. Mouse-brown flipped hair soaring. Thunder thighs twirling out from under my pink seersucker going-away suit.

My feet touched down and Merle and Denny grabbed Steve in a bear hug. Since elementary school, they'd agreed on almost everything, except Fords and Chevys.

"Watch your backsides at Jump School," Steve warned.

"No sweat," Merle said. "A piece of cake after all those hurdles out of the haymow."

"Give our regards to Lux," Denny said. Together Steve and Lux guarded the perimeters of the ammo dump, airplane hangars, and the not-so-secret pad where four planes loaded with nuclear bombs pointed toward the Soviet Union. Steve had sent home so many stories about his German Shepherd that the guys acted like that dog was one of them. They slapped backs and punched triceps.

Jill slipped me a pack of Necco Wafers. "A color for your every mood until we can share them again. Avoid the black ones." Willowy arms and bright orange love beads entwined me. Then green eyes snapped. "This is all a real bummer. You should've stuck to the plan"—a double wedding for double best friends, a perfect idea until the draft ruined everything.

I shrugged, like she usually did. "Just making a political statement. I'm off to make love, not war." My cheeriness sounded phony even to me.

"Not very original, Madam Comedian. But you could've waited." She had her usual crooked smile. But her tone sounded like it did when we argued whether her long auburn hair was, as I said, the "permanent glow of a sunset's kiss" or, as she said, "ugly Ronald McDonald hair."

"Pammy." Steve's voice distracted us. "Pammy, Grandpa McNeilly and I made a deal." He clenched her shoulders. "I take care of Cindy for him and he takes care of you for me." His jaw tightened as it always did when he was thinking what to say. "Promise you'll head for the farm fast if Ed flips out." Steve never called their dad anything but Ed. "Same thing for Michael." Their brother had that out-of-control temper, too. "Promise me, Pammy. No chances."

Winner of the Most School Spirit Award, known for soaring mid-air in a bucket jump with her cheerleader's skirt flared, Pam stared down at her brother's gleaming low quarter shoes. Her crisp navy A-line never twitched.

Steve, eerily serious, repeated, "Promise?"

Her oat-blond pixie cut nodded ever so slightly. She burst into tears.

My soul sobbed, too. For them. For myself. I longed to hug Tee one more time.

Jill held me upright.

Steve mumbled something in Pam's ear—I couldn't hear what he said—and she quieted into sniffles. He wiped her cheeks and nose and teased, "Don't laugh now."

She sniffed and raised her chin. "Only ... only if you promise me something, big brother." She did that dramatic pause thing. "Promise me you'll bring me back a new niece."

I remember her giggle sounded like a tiny silver bell. I remember their blond heads rested together one last time before he turned and said, "No more stalling, Mrs. Carmine. Time to beat feet." I remember Jill nudging me toward him.

I remember Merle and Denny looked so strange in their GI haircuts, like a bald John Lennon would. And Jill—paisley miniskirt, bright orange love beads dangling over her shoulder— the seasoned traveler, reassuring me, "Flying's the bomb. You'll have a blast." I remember her flashing the peace sign and her voice echoing as through a tunnel. "We'll all be here waiting when you get back." I remember she sounded so confident of that fact.

Steve never loosened his grip on my elbow.

Like a butterfly fluttering from its cocoon, I watched my old world drop away through the tiny round window of a Pan Am 707. Green Pennsylvania forests faded into wispy clouds.

He's whisking me away. He's whisking me away. Not away from a wicked stepmother and stepsisters but away from a godly family, as clannish as our Amish neighbors. *He's whisking me away. He's whisking me away.* Not away from friendlessness but away from Tee and Jill and Pam. *He's whisking me away.* The pronouncement of a mild-mannered country minister, not the flick of a fairy godmother's wand, had changed my life forever.

"I love you, Mrs. Carmine." Steve drew my head onto his strong shoulder.

I stared straight ahead, my mind racing toward sights I'd only read about—New York City's skyline as we flew into Kennedy Airport to transfer for our transoceanic flight. Paris, perhaps a glimpse of the Eiffel Tower. Rome where we'd stretch our legs just miles from the Coliseum and the Sistine Chapel before flying over the Dardanelles to Istanbul, the gateway to the East. Then Ankara, Turkey's capital in the mountains, our final stop before landing in Adana, our new home. With time changes and layovers, we wouldn't arrive there until the next evening when city lights would sparkle like diamonds on black velvet.

Twisting my shiny new wedding band over my moon-shaped birthmark, the one Mama called my "promise of forever romance," I repeated Elizabeth Barrett Browning's lines. The ones she wrote before leaving her family in England to go to Italy with Robert: "If I leave all for thee, wilt thou exchange/ And be all to me?" I tried to believe her question was rhetorical.

Chapter 2

He Swept Me Away to What?

When I vowed "until death us do part," I had assumed I'd get to enjoy a real honeymoon first—

Turka Hava Airline's turbo prop thumped and rattled to a safe stop a few short miles from the borders of Syria and Iraq. Steve lifted my quivering chin. "See? I told you *most* flights clear the mountains. How could you doubt me?"

I unclenched my eyes, just a slit. His blue eyes twinkled over a grin. It took me a minute, but I had a comeback. "Prayer landed this death trap, not Turka Hava." We'd boarded the scrap heap in Ankara. Any logical person would've clawed her way out before the steward used something like baling wire to secure the passenger door. But, stupidly, our wedding song, "Whither Thou Goest I Will Go," kept my clammy hands gripping the armrests. The wings flapped to get us airborne with inches of runway to spare. The fuselage brushed the mountaintop as we leveled off. I chanted the 23rd Psalm, Cindy version, "Yea, though I *fly* through the valley of the shadow of death, I will fear no evil."

"Actually, I prayed a few times myself." Steve whispered. "Mostly to keep my hands off you 'til we get to our apartment." He strode purposefully down the aisle.

My face flushed warm as I marveled at this great miracle. Out of all the girls in the world, Steve had chosen me—plain, covered with freckles, too small at the top, too big at the bottom. "You need a bride for a honeymoon," I grumbled to his back.

My wobbly legs scrambled after him. As far as the exit, that is. There, a blast-furnace heat sizzled my lungs. A blaze of sunlight seared my eyes. *No cloud cover from Lake Erie.* But "Whither thou goest I will go," and Steve had gone to Turkey, to a valley in the Taurus Mountains where Noah's ark rested on Mount Ararat. I crawled down the shaky metal steps onto the steamy tarmac.

Steve opened the terminal door for me. To a wall of piercing black eyes. I froze.

"Relax," Steve said. "It's boring around here. Watching foreigners get off a plane is a big deal." It was as if he hadn't written me about all the riots. The one in November involved 2000 plus Turks on a rampage, destroying anything American in Adana—cars, buses, the Red Cross Center, the American Consulate building.

Quaking, I went along with the joke. "It would've been a big deal back home, too, if we had an airport." Hartstown, PA, was so small it didn't even have a stoplight.

He grinned. "Stick close. And keep your eyes on the ground."

Guiding me through the crowd by my elbow, he nodded hello, "*Marahaba,*" as if greeting old friends. A few hesitantly dropped inscrutable expressions and responded, "*Marahaba.*" Most glared invisible daggers.

I felt so white, so American.

At the back of the crowd, Steve gloated, "See? All in one piece."

And I believed him. Until the pressure on my thigh. "Steve?" I hoped for a calloused hand at the end of Air Force blue.

It wasn't. It was a small gritty hand attached to a barefoot child wearing patched peasant pants, kind of a ragged version of Joseph's coat of many colors. Black mournful eyes drew me like magnets. I stooped and bowed my head to hers. Tiny dark fingers traced my white arm, perhaps to soak up some of my good fortune. She huddled close and implored, "Lira?" I reached for my purse.

"Cindy, there'll be no end. Don't you know we'll be lucky to feed ourselves?"

I skewered him with Nana's disappointed look. He glanced away and said, "I'm under orders to ignore beggars."

"Beggar?" I let my indignation echo. "She's a helpless child. I can't say no."

"Well, I can." Steve said to the child, "*Yok,* no," then lifted me up. "Let's go find our luggage." He steered me firmly away.

Tiny dusty feet shadowed us—hopefully, futilely—out into the oppressive heat.

"She'll be okay, Cindy. C'mon." Steve gestured toward a dark blue school bus. "Your chariot awaits, Princess." An obvious attempt to charm me with his Mama imitation, but I ignored him.

He ignored me ignoring him. "See that T-U-S-L-O-G painted on it?" He didn't wait for an answer. He explained the acronym stood for Turkish-United States Logistics Group, the NATO unit attached to Incirlik Air Force Base, his duty station nine miles away.

The little girl tagged along behind us, tugging on my skirt. *Just like Tee.*

I turned and looked into those mournful eyes. I shouldn't have.

With a nod to the mustached driver, Steve nudged me onto the blue bus. It reeked of tobacco—not like Grandpa's cigars, more like burning strips of rubber tires—and rancid sweat. Turks don't wear deodorant and enlistees were issued only two summer uniforms for a two-year hitch. Steve threw open several windows. "That'll make it smell better." Temporarily, at least.

"Okay?" the driver announced. We jolted forward. And the air turned noxious. I almost barfed. "What's that?" I'd shoveled hundreds of spreader loads of manure in my time, but this? It'd gag a maggot!

"Raw sewage. You'll get used to it." He grinned and handed me his handkerchief. "Hold this over your nose. It'll help."

I buried my face in English Leather.

Clonk! My forehead hit the seat ahead of us. The driver had slammed on the brakes. A ragged shepherd and his scrawny flock blocked the road.

My head jerked back. The driver had gunned it in a game of chicken with a dump truck brimming with workers. Our bumpers almost scraped. Beads of nervous sweat glued me to the vinyl seat.

"Relax, Madame." Steve used an exaggerated Turkish accent and twisted an imaginary mustache. "If Allah wills our deaths, no safety precautions would help."

"Not very reassuring," I said and punched him. I guess my reactions hadn't changed much since junior high. Two soldiers gawked back in disapproval. Clearly, Turkish women treat their men with less impertinence.

I lowered my eyes to the window. Workers, aged four to eighty-four, combed bleak brown fields. I bounced and pointed out each camel, each water buffalo. Okay, most kids go to the zoo. Believe it or not, I never had. In fact, my most exciting adventure to that date had been the senior class trip to the Pittsburgh planetarium and the Heinz factory with its "57 varieties."

Then, I spotted a massive medieval stone structure encircled by a village of lean-tos. Emaciated children scrounged through a garbage dump. I'd never imagined such poverty, not even with all those missionary slideshows and MLK speeches.

"It's a prison," Steve said. "Families of inmates live in those shanties. Prisoners have no rights here, not even to enough food."

I grew very quiet.

But a mile or so down the road, I leapt up. "Steve!"

A scrawny peasant writhed on the ground, clutching his ears as a policeman clubbed his head, shoulders, head. A second cop booted the peasant's ribs, torso, ribs in the same cruel metronomic rhythm.

"Shhhh! Don't point." Steve inched me back down.

"Someone should do something!" *That nightstick. Those steel-toed boots. The pain.*

Steve set his jaw. "They're the authorities," he said, as if that explained it.

The bus slowed. My tears stung. I repeated, "Someone ought to help that boy."

He scowled. "What do you want me to do? Cause an international incident?" He'd written me about Turks trashing a TUSLOG bus, but not what caused it. "Or maybe you'd like to see what my butt looks like in a sling?"

I answered his questions with silence.

"Besides, he's probably a grown man." He ran his fist through his curls. "You can't tell age by size. Too much malnutrition." His eyes softened. "We're not in the States anymore, Cindy. There's no due process here. It's not just prisoners who don't have rights."

His matter-of-fact tone echoed as foreign to me as the tan landscape. *Who is this Steve?*

I pressed his aftershave-scented handkerchief more tightly over my nose but couldn't block the stench of injustice.

"It's just you and me now, Cindy." He gently raised my chin. "I'm not going to jeopardize us before we even have a honeymoon."

I sat rigid. We crossed a stone bridge where a hunched older girl, observably mentally handicapped, huddled against a ragged little beggar girl. I started trembling and couldn't stop.

Steve held me close. "You had to leave Tee sometime, Cindy." I'd always known that. "Remember Old Blue?" Once Tee fell directly under the front hooves of Grandpa's workhorse. Unbelievably, Old Blue stood perfectly still, hoof suspended in midair like a circus elephant, long enough for me to tug Tee to safety. Nana explained it. "God's angel."

That memory made me smile a little. Steve knew it would. He knew much more about me than my shoe size. I relaxed a little.

"I've had eighteen months over here to adjust," he said. "You'll get used to things in Turkey, too, right?"

I shrugged yes but suspected I might be lying. I leaned against his knotty shoulder.

Eventually, we arrived in Adana, a labyrinth of cobblestone and dirt streets crowded with horse-drawn wagons, bicycle carts, a few old-dilapidated cars, and *arabas* (buggies used as taxis, not Amish style, but more like Wild West stagecoaches with drivers on top).

The late afternoon sun blazed over huts, cardboard shacks, and modern buildings alike. Mosques sprouted towering minarets. Partially veiled women, carrying baskets on arms and heads, inspected vendors' wares, pastries, and vegetables. Men, some in baggy-seated trousers and others in Western pants, walked hand-in-hand and arm-in-arm.

"You said Muslims don't believe in public affection," I chided Steve.

"I meant between opposite sexes," he said. "It's perfectly normal between the same sex."

We slowed for a wagon piled high with long crusty loaves of bread. The horse's scraggly tail swished back over the unwrapped bread, then swished forward. The flies on the horse's back rose and settled in a perfect countermelody with the flies on the bread.

"How could anyone eat that? It's crawling with germs."

"It's cheap and people are hungry," Steve said.

On a paved palm-lined street, we passed a statue of Ataturk, Turkey's great military leader. A Turkish flag—God's thumbnail moon and a single star on a passion-red background—waved us on toward our apartment. And romance.

Steve started wiggling, "Almost there." He inched forward, then charged down the aisle. "*Dur!* Stop!"

"Okay." The driver braked and sat revving the engine while we hauled off our luggage. Then he popped the clutch and lurched away, leaving us alone on a foreign street in a foreign land.

Turks openly stopped to stare. I'd followed the guidelines for this secular Muslim country ("discreet" dresses, no shorts or blue jeans or sundresses) and chosen a seersucker suit, very conservative in my estimation. But the color, Mama's pink, looked wildly flamboyant beside the dark outfits of the few escorted women. My drab brown hair appeared almost blond against theirs. For the first time, I knew how Merle's mother, a Japanese war bride, felt in our white community with her yellow skin. I felt what it's like to be "other."

Thud! I dropped my suitcases to the sidewalk and seized my waistband, usually my move to shorten a skirt with a waistband roll and an under-the-bra tuck. This time, I squeezed my thighs tight and yanked my skirt down as far as it'd go.

Steve turned. "Hey, what's holding you up? Suitcases too heavy?"

"I lift milk cans," I snapped. "I'm fine." Though, to be honest, my farm girl's arms ached from typhus and typhoid shots. I hoisted bags and, at a trot, caught up with him near a *lyceum.*

"Not far now, Mrs. Carmine." Steve pointed across from the school. "That lane there." He took off in a sprint.

I scurried along behind him toward our honeymoon bed.

Unfortunately, I jeopardized the mission. In my defense, in northwest PA you smile at everyone whether you know them or not. Unless you're stuck up. But in Turkey, smiling at males gets you branded a brazen American hussy.

A gang of guys was lounging against the chain link fence around the school. The corners of my lips curled into an automatic smile of greeting. And those innocent-looking teenagers exploded. "Yankee, go home! Yankee, go home!"

Steve picked up speed, ordering, "Ignore them."

I frowned confusion at his back. At home, he never went looking for fights, but he never backed down either. *My* Steve could intimidate those kids with a look. I'd seen him defy Ed's doubled-up fist with a stare that said, "I wouldn't try it, if I were you." And his dad, nicknamed the godfather of the Hartstown Mafia by people who'd had dealings with him, just walked away. These punks were no match for *that* Steve. He had guts.

But *this* Steve tucked tail and ordered, "Get a move on it, Cindy! Now!"

"Yankee, go home!" The chanting got louder. *Riots against Americans!* The pack stooped, almost in unison. Pebbles like hailstones pelted the sidewalk. Out of reflex, I turned to grab Tee. A rock nailed my ankle.

Steve sheltered my back. "Move, I said!"

My body turned clammy, my mind crystal clear. *We didn't get this far for nothing.* Suitcases, stuffed with lead, banged against my legs as I staggered into the gait I'd perfected running for hay wagons, bales in hand, to beat the rain.

"Faster, Cindy!" Steve waved me into the lane. "Run. Run." He cheered me toward a two-story building. "Run. Run. Almost there."

My mouth dried, my throat constricted, I cried to God, *"Don't let me die a virgin."*

We darted between two parked cars, slid onto a cement sidewalk and huddled, panting. The echoes of running feet receded.

Silence. Steve gulped, glanced back, broke into that sheepish grin of his. He ruffled my hair and said, "Look."

My head was practically wedged in his armpit. My heart pounded in my throat. I couldn't quit shaking.

"It's really okay, Cindy. They stopped back at the street. Probably having a good laugh at us wimpy Yankees beating feet." He pushed strands of hair over my ear. "Don't you believe me?" He sounded insulted. "Look for yourself. The lane's empty."

He lifted my chin. I peeked. On the right, several dilapidated shacks and barbed wire tacked to scraggly orange and lemon trees to fence off a cotton field. On the left, an elegant estate surrounded by lush gardens butting up to a patchy yard with a picnic table. The "haves" and the "have nots." The lane and both sides, empty. Really empty.

I swallowed my heart back into my chest and whispered shyly, "Thank you, God, for answering even embarrassing prayers."

"Got your breath?" Steve asked.

"I'm fine," I retorted. "I've told you for years I need more excitement than an evening stroll by Pymatuning Lake." Nothing ever changed back home, except an occasional new owner's name on an old building.

He grinned. "Do I know how to pick a wife or what?" He shifted back and forth, then answered what I hadn't asked. "Sometimes it's the wrong thing to stand and fight. Over here, avoiding the problem is usually the smart thing. Understand?"

I nodded, only partly understanding.

"Now let's find us a bed, Mrs. Carmine." He seized his suitcases and whirled—straight into the husky chest of a massive Turk blocking the foyer.

I grabbed Steve. My suitcases clonked back onto cement.

"*Bush bush?*" A row of gold teeth flashed. *A smile? A sneer?*

Steve said, "*Yok!* No!"

The Turk, expression of a gargoyle, loomed over us and repeated, "*Bush bush?*" His bass voice rumbled like a threat.

Steve stood taller, broader, as in the guidelines for facing a bear. The set of his jaw, the timbre of his voice, the steel in his eyes, his grizzly stance looked feral. He simply repeated, "*Yok!*"

A horse nickered on the street. Someone coughed upstairs. My eyes stung from not blinking. Hours passed.

At last, the Turk grumbled, "*Gule gule,*" and turned away down the path.

I exhaled the breath I'd gulped in when his fangs first flashed —and wilted.

"Everything's fine," Steve insisted. "That tough guy had to back down. He'd be out of business without us Americans." He explained that *bush bush,* literally the word for "junk," was code for black-market agents. "They deal in cigarettes, blue jeans, paper products, things like that."

I'd read about World War II trafficking in silk stockings and chocolate but didn't know black-market still existed. Obviously, college texts don't teach it all.

"Turkey's crawling with *bush bush*. They're *all* bad news. Stay away from them *all*." He drew me against his muscular pecs. "And stay close to me ... forever."

My gaze drifted up the stairwell behind him. My spine tingled. *Honeymoon time.* He'd sweep me away to satin sheets, caress me with tender words, arouse me with gentle hands....

He bolted down cavernous musty stairs, pulled a chain to a dim light, gestured to the left. "Our first home, Mrs. Carmine."

It's a dungeon! He'd described every piece of furniture bought from a lieutenant rotating Stateside, every room of our two-bedroom apartment across from an American couple, so I'd have company. But he'd left out one pertinent detail. He'd booked subterranean accommodations.

I gripped rough cement walls to steady my descent. He stabbed his fist through the bars of a formidable iron gate guarding the apartment to the right and hammered. "Sophie. Ray."

"Please." I almost groaned. "Can't I meet the neighbors tomorrow?"

"No, they have our key." Steve pounded. "Sophie, Ray!"

"Key?" No one in Hartstown ever locked anything. I gazed longingly at our door. Behind it lay "privacy," a concept as foreign to me as "key."

"Besides, I need an update on Lux." I suspected that dog and I would be in competition for Steve's time and affection.

I perched on a suitcase, twisted my hair off my neck, my carefully cultivated flip long since limp. Sweat trickled under my sore arms, not a whiff of my apple blossom cologne left. I wanted to rip off my clothes, jump into a tub of icy water, lie naked on a cool sheet. Instead, I pointed to the gate, strong enough to protect Fort Knox itself, and asked, "Why the barricade?"

"We're American." *The simple answer.* He squinted at our door with its three simple bars over a small smoked-glass window. "I'll get our gate as soon as Finance straightens out my pay." Again, he yelled, "Sophie, Ray!" Then rapid-fire, machine-gun style, "Sophie! Ray! Ray!"

Footsteps, clanks, rattling chains, the creak of the door, and a shadowy form like a troll under a bridge peered out. Then, "Blam!" The door smashed open against the block wall.

A Yogi Bear creature sucking on a cigarette, paws struggling to snap Bermuda shorts under a sagging belly, openly inventoried me through the bars. I felt like a zoo specimen. The creature belched a disgusting laugh—"guffaw" might be a better word—"How about that honeymoon?"

I must have been wearing a billboard announcing, "Virgin!"

It fumbled open a padlock and motioned us in. I kicked off my shoes. It growled, "Keep those on if you know what's good for you," and gave Steve a lascivious wink and a jab in the ribs. "Honeymoon get Elly May all flustered? Tell her she ain't in the States anymore."

I wanted to say that, unlike him, I'd been taught not to tromp dirt into other people's homes. Steve pulled me close and said, "Sophie, Ray, this is Cindy."

Sophie, a pudgy brunette, jerked a little nod of her razor-cut short hair but never lost her focus—poking a rag under the exterior door, saturating our tracks in with bug spray.

I cast furtive glances at the crumbling cratered walls and single bare bulb. Ceilings low enough to send a claustrophobic running, wobbly aluminum table with six yellow swirl-print vinyl chairs, a fan, frayed curtains tacked shut, crossed-off wall calendar advertising Aroostook State Bank, Aroostook, Maine. *This can't possibly be a preview to our place.*

"Hey, broad. Knock it off with the bugs. Hustle up some grub."

Sophie buzzed off to follow orders while every fiber of my body screamed, *No, we don't have time.* Well, every fiber except of my stomach, that is. It whined about its last substantial meal being from the picnic basket Nana packed us for the ride to the airport.

My stomach won. Steve pulled out a chair. I sat. Under the table, his fingers slowly ran up my thigh as he asked, "How's Lux?"

"Missing you for sure." I knew the feeling. "Garza ain't had nothing but trouble getting that kennel cleaned. Only got it done once since you left."

"In six days?" Steve yanked his fist from under the table and drove it into his palm. My stomach flipped. "That's how dogs get sick."

"Hey, back off," Ray simpered. "Lucky for him, he got out once. We been pulling double shifts since you left. We're nothing but a bunch of pack mules." Steve had told me that on alerts K-9 units added gas masks and M-16s to their regular equipment. "The Arabs and Jews are heading for the big one," Ray grumbled.

Steve and I have better things to do than listen to this twit. I popped up from the table and trailed Sophie and the scent of bologna. At first she waved aside my offer to help, but then said, "Well, you could get glasses. Up there. I can't reach. I might be pregnant, you know."

I found glasses, flicked on the faucet, tried to hurry things up.

Sophie shrieked, "Don't drink that water!" My heart almost crashed out of my chest. "One unboiled drop and you'll be in Ankara. They fly you there for anything bad. The base dispensary is about worthless."

Her heavy French accent mixed with the muffled clack of dentures, though she seemed surprisingly young for false teeth. She babbled on about Incirlik's dentist drilling good teeth and about a male nurse who made women strip down for complete physicals under the pretense of saving the doctor time. "He's a pervert."

Like the one you're married to, I thought, then drifted off to images her story had provoked—of me stripping down for Steve.

A putrid odor blasted me back to reality. I gagged.

Unfazed, Sophie said, "Sewer gas. Someone upstairs flushed a toilet." *Bathrooms. I need a shower before ... Did I pack my peignoir in the black or brown suitcase? Oh, my kingdom for a key.*

The tyrant roared, "Beer! Now!"

Sophie snatched up a stack of sandwiches and a beer. *Pour it over his head,* I wanted to say but just grabbed ice made from "carefully boiled" water.

He sneered. "What kind of dame did you get yourself, Carmine? Any retard knows ice don't go in no beer."

I stiffened. I might not know much about beer, but I knew about the word "retard." Kids yelled it from the school bus as Tee pulled her red wagon down the lane. Steve squeezed my hand.

The Neanderthal grabbed the thickest sandwich. "Uncle Sam don't pay nothing or we wouldn't be eating no bologna."

"Eat as many as you want," Sophie insisted, apologetically.

Steve linked my foot with his and tore into a garlicky slab iced with mustard on mushy white bread. He'd given fair warning that I'd need all my strength when we got to our apartment, so I forced a bite down. I tried not to think about my family sitting around the great oak table for a Mother's Day feast of roast beef and mashed potatoes swimming in rich brown gravy. The bologna tasted surprisingly good to my empty stomach.

Geisha-like, Sophie repositioned her husband's fan, emptied his ashtray.

He yapped, spitting food particles onto Formica. "That dog of yours is one high strung animal. By the time Garza got that menace out of the kennel, he was cussing up a storm and told him to go to hell"—I suspected I knew where this was going. Steve had told me Lux's command to dig straight down was, "Go to hell."

"That black menace dug a hole a foot deep. I'd lay bucks he'd have made it to hell if Garza hadn't got back and stopped him." Ray scratched his belly button.

Will he ever shut up and give us the key?

Steve flashed me a "time-to-be-alone, Mrs. Carmine" grin and faked a noisy yawn. "Long trip. We'll take our key and get out of your hair." I almost giggled. Steve's never been a very good actor.

Ray drained his beer, then dropped the bomb obliterating my dreams. "Ain't got no key."

Steve's fist hit the table. Its puny aluminum legs bowed. "You better be joking. The landlord said he'd give it to you."

"Don't know what was said. Just know what was done. Ain't got it, and the Turk ain't home."

Steve slumped back as if he'd taken a bullet. He'd fought the bureaucracy and won—extended his tour of duty in Turkey, got approval for our marriage from the commander, arranged immunizations and visa, flew me across an ocean to the Syrian border—only to be thwarted by a tiny piece of metal.

"You don't have no electricity." Sophie chirped in. "You're better off here." I didn't believe her. "Raymond's going to post, so you can sleep with me, Cindy. Steve can have the couch."

I swallowed the lump threatening to choke me. *This can't be happening.*

Steve hunched over like an ancient seer. I could see him reviewing the options, a picnic table under the stars in a city of Yankee haters or accepting Sophie's invitation. I dreaded the answer I knew he'd give. "Thanks for the offer, Sophie. Sorry to put you out."

The clank of the iron gate behind Ray sealed our fate. "Here's a pillow. Don't have no sheet," Sophie said and twittered off to the bathroom.

Steve grabbed me tight and whispered, "I'd give a year's salary for a motel room right now."

"You already gave a year's salary for plane tickets," I joked, suppressing a moan. *I'll never smile again. I'll be listed in the Guinness Book of Records as the saddest bride in history.*

Then like all great martyrs, I marched unswervingly toward my destiny—Sophie.

Chapter 3

The Honeymoon Just Keeps Getting Better

My bridegroom sprawled in rumpled Air Force blues on a rough rayon sofa. Wearing his X-Large white T-shirt, I slunk alone into the honeymoon suite. My sleeping partner wore the skimpy nightie, a hot pink one that exposed massive bruises cowering on her thighs—

"Get comfortable." Sophie jimmied the door closed, and with the precision of a plumber caulking a leak, restuffed the rags in the crack under it. The room sealed like a tomb.

"I hate bugs," she said, redundantly, and I thought, *How ridiculous.* I'd spent a lifetime collecting dragonflies and lightning bugs for Tee. I couldn't relate to bug phobias.

But one glance up showed me Sophie would never relate to *my* greatest phobia—the fear of flawless female bodies. On the wall over the footboard of the rusty iron bed, a *Playboy* centerfold flaunted gargantuan breasts at me.

I shuddered and twisted away. On a small crucifix, the only other wall hanging, Jesus also averted His eyes. I mummified my flat chest with a clammy sheet.

Armed with flyswatter and spray can, Sophie initiated an intense search-and-destroy mission, crawling to saturate every inch of the baseboards, dancing on tiptoes to spray walls and the shrouded window. She would've loved the DDT bombers we used for barn flies. One blast covered a Holstein cow, back to front.

The silence grew awkward, so I finally pried open my lips and asked, "How did you two meet?"

That's all it took to activate an eternal fountain of chatter from Sophie. "I worked at a drive-in movie in Quebec. Right across the border from Loring Air Force Base. One night Raymond pulled up to pay, and I fell hard. That neat black hair, those clean fingernails."

Of course they were clean. He's probably never done a real day's work in his life, I thought, but Nana's teaching seemed to chide, "Now, dear, if you can't think of anything nice, don't think anything at all," so I spaced out, just interjecting an occasional "Oh" or "Uh-huh."

Some details managed to permeate my brain, though. Like her description of their second date—a moonlit evening at Fort Kent Reservoir. A "rock" of a ring. He "begged" her to marry him. At her yes, "He picked me up and ran, laughing, down the beach."

Sophie waited for my, "Uh-huh," but I'd been struck mute trying to imagine Ray running anywhere, except maybe for a beer.

(To be fair, my engagement story pales in comparison—a drizzly afternoon at Jill's dorm. Steve, with a stiff sort of Gomer Pyle expression, asked Tee, "Think your little sister would have me?" I answered, "Sure." He sprang a back flip. Tee squealed. Jill said, "Let's have a double wedding." Diamond chips glittered under fluorescent lights.)

When the room dripped insecticide, Sophie declared, "No bugs," and fluttered under the sheet.

I adhered leech-like to my edge as she continued non-stop about her Raymond, a local home on leave, not stationed at Loring as she'd assumed. Her in-laws, "as rich as those people on TV," owners of a big potato farm near Presque Isle, Maine, "wanted us to get married right away to keep Raymond out of trouble." She giggled.

She went on ad nauseam about Fortiers flying the family to Turkey for a chapel wedding "with a real priest" and buying the Nova so they didn't have to ride the bus and setting up their apartment. "My Raymond says basement apartments are cooler in the summer and warmer in the winter. And cheaper."

She paused. "Course we get more bugs and all the sewer gas every time someone flushes upstairs. But my Raymond said it's good enough for Turkey."

She glanced at the frayed curtains. "In Maine, he says, everything will be perfect. His sister said that, too."

She burrowed into the mattress like a robin into its nest and chirped, "My Raymond says the only thing his parents expect back is a Fortier grandson. He says I better get pregnant fast. He says he owes them for a few things."

She considered that statement a moment, then pulled the chain on the seemingly standard bulb protruding from the wall, said "Good night" in one breath, and was snoring the next. "Bzzzzz." Sawing logs as Grandpa called it.

I teetered on the brink of the mattress. *I deserted Tee and Mama for Steve, not a half-naked French woman.*

Sophie's snore stuttered, "gasp," then started again.

Jet-lagged, long past the point of sleep, I stared up into the darkness. Jagged memories flashed like snapshots—

Deep teasing blue eyes peeking under my veil. Lips. As reverent as a soldier kissing the ground after combat. (Not the dramatic kiss of the Western hero before he rides off into the sunset like he'd threatened.)

Clapping hands. A ticker-tape parade of lilac blossoms. Tee's "Me! Me!" Steve laughing. "I could never forget you, Tee." Him dipping her in that kiss. Sunlight through the old stained-glass window making a rainbow on the floor by her organza hem. Oval eyes scrunched shut, mouth gaped, flashbulbs flashing.

Sophie's snore whistled softly.

Creaking pews. Guests swarming like fans around a State Championship basketball team and sweeping us downstairs. Tiered cake decorated with sugar bells and pink snapdragons. Nana's Missionary Circle serving punch. The smell of Stout. "Love ya, little sister." Thinking, "Then why couldn't you stay sober for me today?" Knowing the answer. Sean could never keep a promise to have "just one." Jo muttering, "When you come back, Cin, I'll be your ex-sister-in-law."

Sophie's thigh encroached on mine. I squirmed away.

Tee, filmy organza dangling over candle flame. Me, gown hiked to hips, dashing across church basement. Jill and Pam close behind. Sean and Michael stumbling over each other. Ed thinking they were fighting (of course anything looked like a fight to Ed). The guys collaring him to stop a rumble. Tee crying, "Dee. Dee"

Rev. Minnow's throat clearing. "Let's pray a blessing on this special couple." Bowed heads. Held hands. Jill's and Pam's organza shoulders bouncing like ping pong balls (to their credit, they didn't laugh out loud). Me counting pink and white mints floating in red punch on the floor. Holding Tee close. Her crying, "Dee. Dee."

What if someone forgets whipped cream holds heat? Tee loved hot Ovaltine smothered in whipped cream. *What if she chokes?* When I left her for prom, she gagged on a peach. *What if she falls?* The tree house was too high for her to climb alone…. *"Dee. Dee."*

What if she refuses to sleep like when the nurses separated us after our tonsillectomies? Tee and I had always slept together in a double bed. *I didn't even leave her for that weekend peace march. Will she accept Jill and Pam in my place?* They'd promised to alternate nights sleeping with Tee…. *"Dee. Dee."*

Sophie's tethering arm flopped over me. I inched it away.

"How can I survive being away from Tee for over a year? Or from Mama? "Your chariot awaits, Princess." … *"It"* can't recur. "Don't disappoint her, Baby Girl. Doc says *it* could come back"—in our family, saying "breast cancer" would've been like shouting a truck driver's obscenity.

If I leave all for thee, wilt thou exchange/And be all to me?"

"Dee. Dee." … *"Princess."* … *"Baby Girl."* … *"Dear."* … *"Little Sister."* … *"Cin."* … *"Dee."* …

"Bzzzzz." The snores of the stranger in the strange bed in the strange land. With an eight-hour time difference from PA to Turkey, dawn glimmered in Adana before I finally dozed off.

Smoke! I jumped, "Tee? Where are you?" My eyes flew open.

Ray Fortier, my newest nightmare, smirked at me over a cigarette. "Mmm! Elly May."

My hands shot over the nubs of my breasts, standing at attention under Steve's white T-shirt. I lunged for the door.

The creep blocked my escape route. "What's your hurry? Room for three here. I get the top." Sophie giggled.

I squeaked, "Steve," expecting him to stomp to my rescue like he did at a rude statement to his Pammy. But he'd already bolted upstairs to the landlord's. I managed to shove myself out of the danger zone just as Steve returned, waving a key and grinning wide.

I threw myself into his arms. "Ooh, hold that thought," he whispered, then announced, "Electricity won't be on until tomorrow, but the landlord said we can move in now."

Deliverance!

We grabbed our things, and I held out my hand to be swept and carried over the threshold. I'd dreamed of this moment since I was too little to know Grandpa could never be my husband. But, apparently, Steve hadn't read the novels.

He *dragged* me across the hall, yanked open the door, and gasped. "Incoming!" He covered his head as soldiers do on the artillery field. "Someone upstairs flushed again." He waved the door back and forth, declared, "All clear," then *tugged* me over the threshold of reality.

Flies, gnats, and mosquitoes bombarded us. *What filth!*

"The landlord said they had a little to clean up yet." ("*A little?*" I wanted to say. It was a minefield of debris.) "But I said we'd take care of it. ("*We?*" I wanted to say. He'd never done a minute's cleaning that I knew of. Even hired a houseboy in the barracks.)

And pink walls? Pink, the color Mama'd smothered me in since my first bunting. Only flowered wallpaper could've been worse.

Steve's eyes followed mine to the wall. He flinched as if hit with a bucket of cold water. "Sabotaged by the language barrier. I told him *anything but* pink. Honest." He ran his hand over the powdery surface. "And it isn't even paint. It's like the whitewash in the barn, only tinted, right?" His lower lip pouted. "I wanted things perfect for you. See what happens when I get my hopes up?"

I felt so bad for him. "It's really fine," I said, then made the situation worse.

A centipede, longer than most garter snakes, came sliding out from under a building block. Curious how they keep all those hairy legs in sync, I leaned down to check it out. And he freaked. "Not so close! They're poisonous, you know."

I really *didn't* know, but what I did know is "poisonous" requires death. I vaulted onto it with both feet. Black ooze seeped over the cement. Its head hung out from under the left side of my shoe, its tail out from under the right—unless it was running backwards? It's kind of hard to tell the difference between the ends of creatures like that.

Steve, all offended, huffed like I'd attacked *him* or something. "I would've done that if you'd given me time. Aren't you always saying I'm supposed to climb mountains and kill dragons for *you*?" He had a point.

I made excuses. "You know, with Tee and all.... I'm not used to you handling things yet."

He punted a chunk of concrete. "What next?" He clenched that jaw. "The furniture! Some Turk probably ripped it off. You'll be stuck in this armpit of the world forever"—the resale of furniture was a major portion of my return airfare to the States.

Mumbling words I probably didn't want to hear, he kicked open a door. I braced myself ... but he grinned kind of sheepishly. And I relaxed.

"The landlord must've put the fear of the wrath of Allah in the workers. Now where's that bed?"

A green tarp wrapped with so much rope it looked like a spider's work. Much unwinding. One great yank ... and that romantic white French provincial headboard he'd written about.

"Finally." He sighed. "We've waited so long." He dipped me back in that passionate kiss he'd threatened me with at our wedding. I bent, limp as a willow branch. My foot lifted.

Snickers erupted. Steve whirled and almost dropped me.

Outside our propped-open window squatted two black-eyed peasant girls, gawking and tittering. Steve bowed grandly. "*Marahaba.*"

The giggling little ones covered their faces. Gold bracelets jangled. I giggled with them. "Tee and Pam probably hired these little spies to take their places."

"Cindy, you make the simplest things mysterious." He ruffled my hair. The spies snickered again. Steve shrugged. "This audience calls for Plan B."

He pulled me back down the hall. "Hey, finally, good news!"

"No windows?" I craned around his shoulder at a bathroom overflowing with trash.

He grinned that grin I love so much. "It's not pink, and it's not that whitewash stuff."

"Yeah!" I played along, though it had to be the world's second most ugly color, a slightly yellowish shade of Army green.

The little peasant girls peeped in. "I'm not giving up yet." Steve towed me back into the hall. "Let's try *your* bathroom."

"Mine?"

"Didn't I tell you?" His eyes sparkled. "We have his and hers bathrooms."

On the farm, seven of us shared one. "My own bathroom? Where I can soak in a tub with no one banging on the door?" He knew I'd be impressed. "I can't believe it!"

"Right this way." Like the doorman of a grand hotel, he motioned to the door by the entry. I grabbed the handle. But at the last second, I caught that "Gotcha" grin of his.

And I remembered. Turkish toilets. He'd written about them after a trip down the Mediterranean coast. "You squat on cement, wipe with your fingers, use a faucet near the floor to wash them off, then pull a cord to flush."

He'd almost duped me. But no way was I giving him the satisfaction of knowing it. I slowed and nonchalantly stepped into the bare room, cement floor as rough as a barn's.

Four black shiny bugs, the size of corncobs, chose that time to parade to the drain in the middle of it. I guess I should've screamed and thrown myself into his arms to make up to him for killing the centipede, but I chose to pretend I didn't see these carapens.

I smiled. "You're right. No windows, but lovely ambient light from those glass blocks."

"And private, too." He tweaked my cheek. "Consider it yours. You can squat in here and no one will bother you, not even me."

I faked an even-more-exaggerated smile. "You're *so* generous. I've always wanted exotic, and it's certainly more exotic than the outhouse."

He kind of scrunched his face, questioningly. "I'm joking, you know. Americans don't use Turkish toilets."

"Well, in that case, it'll make a lovely storage area," I said.

"Only you, Cindy."

His succulent lips kissed my hair, my nose, my mouth. "Alone at last," he murmured and unbuttoned my blouse.... He unbuttoned his pants.... He sighed, retreated with the reluctance of a satellite leaving the earth's gravitational force, held me at arm's length.

"I-I-I promised your grandpa to be ... to be good to you." He glanced away. "The floor of a Turkish toilet probably doesn't fit that promise?"

It has no windows. It's debris free. It appears to have been mopped within the last year. I answered not a word. I smiled and ran my index finger in circles down his arm.

He shivered. "Maybe we should wait to cover the windows and make the bed up with those satin sheets?" He didn't sound convincing. "Maybe we should wait for the right time?"

I'd waited a lifetime plus several days for the "right time." "Whatever *you* want, dear husband," I said, confident of what he'd choose.

Flushed, he stripped off his T-shirt and fanned it out on the floor. His firm tanned shoulders, glistening with beads of sweat, looked wide enough to build a life on. He approached me with the hesitation of Moses nearing the burning bush.

My head whirled, my heart pounded, I prayed I wouldn't faint—possibly he'd studied a book like the one Nana slipped me, circa 1948, outlining the groom's proper approach to the virgin bride. More plausibly, he used our own history as his reference.

He held me with the care given to a priceless museum treasure. "In a way it seems I should leave now, before someone catches us." He wrestled the words into submission. "But in another way, it seems like we've been here like this forever. Know what I mean?" I nodded, and he kissed me.

I tingled like Sleeping Beauty, newly awakened to life.

Okay, so I was no beauty and it was a cement floor and we were inexperienced—not the stuff of the world's great romances. But we had something special.

He knew me. He'd seen me with hay dust stuck to my bubbling sweat, with candied apple stuck to my teeth, with briar scratches mapping my legs after a heifer chase. He'd seen me with blotched distorted face when kids taunted my Tee, "Retard, Retard." He'd seen me with nose dripping as I sobbed out, "Mama has it ... breast cancer."

We'd shared our first time on ice skates, first proms, my first roller coaster ride. Now we shared this first. Vanilla love. Not bland like some people think of vanilla but vanilla like in Nana's scent, the scent of security and family.

I was truly Mrs. Carmine. The two had become one.

***

Later, I caught my reflection in the mirror, and I saw it. Something in my eyes—no longer dull brown, but glistening hazelnut—said Steve had transformed an old country fiddle, fit for playing Virginia reels, into a priceless Stradivarius, ready for grand symphonies.

Chapter 4

Two Worlds Collide

"Quite the appetizer, Mrs. Carmine. Ready for the main course?" He patted my bottom. "We'll need a real bed and some privacy for that, right? I'll find a broom."

I laughed. Nana used to say, "Don't wait for a fairy godmother to dress you for a prince. Choose a man who grabs a broom and helps you sweep out the fireplace." She'd be happy to hear I'd followed her advice. Even though this man griped—

"We could plant a garden in this dirt." Steve sputtered, swatting a mosquito. "It'll take forever to get this place cleaned enough to set up the bed."

I twisted my hair into a ponytail, chafing at the challenge. Guess it's a woman thing. "It'll take no time at all," I said, hoping I wasn't lying. But really, the rooms were the size of calf stalls.

Grandpa says any shack is home if the ones you love are there. Guess this will test that theory. Equipped with Sophie's cleaning supplies and our elbow grease, we started in, to the entertainment of those black-eyed gigglers following us from window to window.

Dust whirled in funnel clouds and turned us into ashy mimes. I paused to wipe my forehead. Steve sneaked up from behind. Bushwhacked my ticklish spot until I was gasping for breath. "Stop! Stop!"

He gloated, "You're so defenseless."

Later, though, he made the mistake of dropping *his* defenses, and as he loves to say, "There's always payback." Sophie's mop made a perfect shot to that muscular *gluteus maximus* of his.

He retaliated, of course. "Hey, Cindy." A geyser of water caught my face dead center.

"Cowardly ambush," I snapped and darted off in a serpentine path. That squirt gun was small but a real soaker, actually quite refreshing in the Turkish inferno.

By the time his ammo ran out, we'd made a narrow maze-like trail through the trash. I blocked the sink to prevent reloading and demanded, "Where'd you get the weapon?"

"Merle and Denny, of course. We guys stick together."

Now that part was true. Wherever you found one, you found the other two. Under the hood of a car, in Pop Coe's Diner playing pool, in the woods hunting, trapping, spear fishing, building a cabin, skinny dipping by the beaver dam so much that Grandpa insisted they must've been born with snorkels for noses.

"Where's mine then?" I'd fought as many water battles with his pals as he had.

"Musketeers never arm the enemy."

Now that part was a lie, The guys had packed me my preferred weapon, too—an empty syringe for injecting cow teats. Probably a peace offering for their knotting all the clothes in my suitcase. But my sneaky husband had confiscated it before I saw it.

So I resorted to guerilla tactics. Caught him hunched over, scraping tar, his defenses totally down—and struck. Foamed him with shaving cream. He looked like a snow sculpture with blue eyes.

"Hey, we're not millionaires. Do you know how much that Burma shave costs?"

"Ooh, better write Grandpa. Maybe he'll spot you a loan."

He flicked a great gob off his arm at me, dead aim. But I ducked in time. It splattered all over the screen, and over those two little gigglers with their noses pressed against it.

And so it went.

End in sight, we called a truce, covered the bathroom window with a towel Mama embroidered for my hope chest and took an icy dip. "I'll buy a water heater after we get our iron gate," he said.

Then, with the gigglers blocked out with pink cotton sheets from Nana, and white satin sheets from Jill setting ready, Steve beamed. "As I was saying a bit ago...." We heaved the mattress onto its springs.

Together at last. And in love—but as Robert Burns said, "The best-laid plans of mice and men often go awry."

A banging on the door. "Head 'em up, Tex."

My groom contracted like a centipede at first hit. "This one won't be easy," he said and yelled, "Cindy's got jet lag. How 'bout tomorrow, Sarge?"

Oh, Sergeant Cole. Three-day-break parties for the K-9 handlers. So "tomorrow" was perfectly reasonable, especially for newlyweds.

The hammering silenced. Steve made the okay sign and did his puff-out-the-chest thing, unfortunately, a little too early.

"Today, cowboy! Move it!" *An edict, not an invitation.*

Steve moaned, his breath warm on my cheek. Iron clanged against blocks. Sarge barked, "Brewski, Fortier," then, "Carmine, you got ten minutes to get in that car."

Steve sighed and drew back. "It's like the Welcome Wagon at home. But instead of an elderberry pie or warm rolls, Sarge hands out fifths of whiskey."

I grabbed the white satin sheets. "But we have plans." Our initiation on the Turkish toilet floor had been like a handful of M&M's that sends you racing to the store for a pound bag.

Steve jerked his side of the fitted sheet tight. "Sarge waits for no one."

This is unheard of. A little friendly teasing, decorating a car, messing with suitcases, I get those things. Even a belling. But dragging a couple away from their honeymoon? Unbelievable!

Steve slid around to my side, traced my spine. I shivered, shook out the top sheet. He asked, "How long will it take you to get ready?" He made a hospital corner.

I stroked the satin. "For that second helping?"

He moaned again. "You heard Sarge. Ten minutes. If we had a choice, a forklift wouldn't get me out of this bed, but—" His sad eyes implored me. "Besides, there'll be food."

How could we have no choice? I couldn't comprehend that thinking. But food? Steve knew my weak points. "So, what do women wear to these things?" I asked sadly.

He ruffled my hair. "Never paid much attention, except Garza's wife, Barb, wears way too much goop."

Lipstick? I couldn't remember if I'd packed any.

"Besides, you look good in anything." His lips brushed the tip of my nose. "Or, better yet, nothing."

My cheeks flushed. Steve saw me so differently than I see myself. I'm built like Dad's side of the family—small breasted and big hipped, an anemic pear shape. I always wished I could have Mama's heart shape—full bosomed and small waisted, like Marilyn Monroe.

I slipped on a hand-me-down from Jill, a lime-green princess-style dress. My hips showed every sticky bun I'd ever eaten. I wanted to cry. "I look like an over ripe honeydew."

He laughed. "You're goofy!"

I scowled down at Casper-the-Ghost legs. My only hope for a tan was if all my ugly freckles joined forces. I fished out a pair of nylons. They glued to my sweaty hand.

Steve patted me. "Gorgeous long legs," he said. "Be a shame to cover them."

I twitched. The stockings, shocked too, flicked off my fingers and onto the floor.

Fortiers' gate clanged. A baby cried. Steve said, "Sounds like Sarge sent Garzas over." He'd told me Rod Garza had a three-month-old. "Timmy's real cute. As blond as Pammy."

He picked up the key. "I'll keep the guys busy to give you a few more minutes, okay?" But he didn't leave. He watched me spray my limp flip into shape. His warm sigh tickled my neck.

"Your nana'd say we'll laugh at this someday. But I'm not laughing yet."

I wasn't either.

Ray and Sophie sprawled in the front of their red Nova. Steve slid me onto his lap in the back beside Garzas and slammed the door, precipitating an earthquake of rattles. *This junker's definitely ready for the boneyard.* The broken spring leaned us all to the right.

The baby bawled. Barb's frosted lips mouthed, "Sorry." Her shyly lowered eyelids were shadowed blue and lined feline-like. *So that's what Steve meant by "goop.* Rod, well over six-foot tall with dark wavy hair and a muscular tanned body, said, "Hangin', man." He tapped out a cigarette, rolled the pack back up in his sleeve.

Steve described the Garzas well. "Kind of hippies. California beach bums."

A pop of the clutch and off we went, Steve sneaking sly pinches on my bottom as we bounced and slid toward base.

At Incirlik's main gate, Steve leaned out the window and motioned at me. "My wife." The guard snapped a salute and a smile.

Steve proudly pointed out the AFEX [the Air Force Exchange] and commissary, the library, the Airman's Club, the dispensary, the runway allegedly used by the notorious spy (Gary Powers) for his U-2 missions over the Soviet Union, then he tapped Ray. "Hey, Fortier, stop at the kennels. Cindy and Lux need to meet."

But we weaved on by. "Flake off, Carmine. Brewski waitin'."

"The booze is not going anywhere," Steve grumbled and shrugged to me. "Next time."

We rattled past rows of prefab houses, then trailers with attached paper-thin cabanas, certainly not built to hold up to north winds and snowstorms. Ray braked to a stop and barged into a cabana, Sophie several paces behind him, like all good subjects with their sovereigns. Garzas followed.

But Steve drew me close, ran his hands down my neck, my shoulders, stopped a millimeter from my butt. Music pounded through thin trailer walls. He sighed. "CCR"—his favorite band. "Let's get this over with." He guided me into ear-bursting din. Apparently, too much alcohol anesthetizes auditory nerves.

The place reeked of stale booze—maybe oozing from pores, maybe fermenting in rugs and furniture—and smoke so thick it looked like someone forgot to close the chimney damper. *Definitely not a birthday party or youth group scavenger hunt.*

A sophisticated woman, brandishing a cigarette like a voluptuous Statue of Liberty with her torch, emerged out of the haze. She pushed back a platinum strand of a Jackie Kennedy hairdo and fixed me with an imperious gaze. I slouched.

Steve said, "Cindy, this is Mrs. Cole, our hostess."

Aglitter with diamond earrings so heavy they elongated her earlobes and a ring closer to two carats than one, Mrs. Cole raised a disdainful brow at my left hand. I seemed to hear the hum of "Twinkle, twinkle, little diamond." I sheltered my beloved rings and resorted to Jill's formula (a female's I.Q. measures in inverse proportion to her bra size), calculated Mrs. Cole's IQ to be only slightly higher than Tee's, and stretched taller. "It's a pleasure to meet you," I said.

"Hey, wife," thundered a mountain of a man. *That bass voice from outside our apartment just a bit ago.* "Bring 'er over." A room of perspiring shirtless GIs turned and checked me out. The ogling of Turks on the street had been less disconcerting.

"Sarge, this is Cindy, *my wife.*" Steve sounded proud, though I didn't know why. I was back to feeling dowdy and pear-shaped.

Sarge stared. Eons passed. "So, this is what kept you out of the Pound, Carmine?" He took a swig. "Interesting."

"Pound?" I mouthed to Steve. I could tell Sarge didn't mean sixteen ounces. Steve shook his head, "Later," and turned to his comrades' congratulations.

One said, "Enjoy her while you can, Carmine. Captain says dependents are outta here at first whiff of local danger"

Nooo! I just got here.

The other guys jumped in. "What's the big deal? Turkey's not involved."

"Syria's in the thick of it. What do you think that means for us?"

"That's not Turkey."

"How far do you think Incirlik's from Syria, numb nuts?" They argued, "60 miles," "70 miles." Agreed on, "Less than 100," and that the tensions between the Arab world and Israel were serious.

"Trouble's not goin' away."

"Ain't a matter of whether war will break out again, just a matter of when."

"Israel should make a preemptive strike."

"If the other Arabs are as tough as the Turks, Israel better think twice about messing with 'em."

"No matter how it starts, we'll end up being the staging base. Like with Lebanon"—

No one but Jill and Merle sits around discussing things like this. Oh, and Professor Gowdy. "Postpone your wedding," he'd said. "The whole Middle East is about to erupt." I told him if we waited for peace in that region, we might be waiting another 2000 years. Guess it wasn't a joking matter.

Steve whispered, "Don't sweat it, Cindy. It'll be fine."

"Forget the Arabs and Jews. Let 'em all kill each other." Sarge raised a glass. "Let's party." *What an attitude. Rev. Minnow calls special prayer meetings for the Jewish problem.*

Sarge jabbed Steve's chest with a glass. "Take a swig. Lion's milk." I learned later it was *raki,* colorless until you add water, then milky white. "It'll test your manhood." As if Sarge had a clue what a real man is.

Steve waved it aside.

Sarge cursed. "Then what's it to be, Panty Waist?" Obviously, the expected answer was alcohol of some type.

"Ginger ale," Steve said.

"No way!" Sarge dumped vodka into tumblers, topped them with a dash of ginger ale, and poked them in our faces. "All my men are drinking men or they're not my men for long."

The glass slipped in my sweaty hand. Elvis boomed out "Ain't nothing but a hound dog." Nana censored those vibrating hips for us better than CBS did for Ed Sullivan. *Booze and Elvis. What next?*

I stared at the turntable of the automatic record player, round and round. *Wonder what that cost?* It'd taken months for Mama to save up enough tips for the cheapest manual one. *Mama'd have a conniption if she saw Sarge's records strewn all over like this.* Our precious few stayed safely in their jackets until removed by only clean hands.

Sarge grabbed the arm of the record player and raked the needle across poor Elvis. "Enough of that howling. Need some real music." He yanked the adaptor off, threw the 45s on the floor—I'll bet he cracked them all—clicked the speed dial, shoved on a 78, and hit the rejection switch. Tex Ritter dropped onto the turntable. "Do not forsake me, oh my darlin'."

Then Sarge leapt onto the sofa. *Standing on the furniture?* Pushed the thin plywood ceiling up like a barbell. *Ooo, big man!* And started singing along. Well, "sing" is probably not an accurate word, but he knew the lyrics.

"Church key," someone shouted. "Think fast!" A bottle opener zipped past my nose.

"Another #*! Ace? You *!@ cheater."

Real men don't talk that way with women around.

"Listen up, loser. Don't be screwing up again. You let those Flight A pansies beat us."

"Me? You the Melvin."

Quite a few new wrinkles over here. Grandpa joked that Hartstown was so small everyone knew every wrinkle of every person in town.

A pudgy guy downed a shot of whiskey with a beer chaser, then ran to the kitchen sink and puked. "First you take a drink, then the drink takes you," Nana warned. Sean didn't listen and lost himself and now probably his whole family.

Anyway, an obscene joke about a traveling salesman and a Doberman distracted Sarge, and Steve dumped our glasses and refilled them with straight ginger ale. Living with Ed Carmine had taught Steve to bend to immovable powers, but only outwardly.

Rod Garza, circling the room with a boda bag, slurred, "In your mouth or on your shirt." A red fountain of wine squirted out. Steve's white T-shirt stained pink. My fresh apple blossom scent wilted into the stench of fermented grapes. "Groovy, man," Rod said to no one in particular. I suspected he was the winner of the "See Who Can Get the Drunkest the Fastest" competition, or at least a definite contender.

Someone put on the Righteous Brothers, "Unchained Melody," and Rod halted mid-cycle. "My pretty little Barbie doll. I need your love, my pretty little Barbie doll."

Barb turned to me and held out Timmy—wide-eyed, squirming to avoid my arms—"Would you mind?"

A swish of hip-length hair. A Mona Lisa smile. She twirled off, her hair undulating at the waistband of her mini skirt. *A definite contraction to Nana's "big hips for beautiful babies" theory.*

Steve wrapped Timmy and me in a moist embrace. "Don't you think it's our turn, Mrs. Carmine?" We hadn't even danced at prom. "We'll be sleeping in the same bed tonight, Cindy. There's nothing immoral in putting your arms around me in public."

Beside us, Barb swayed like a palm tree on the beach.

I'll probably look more like a pear tree shaking in a hailstorm.

I leaned into Steve, Timmy cocooned between us. The cheek of my new "other half" quivered on mine. He shuffled us around the room.

"Now I know how to define 'copacetic,'" he whispered. I waited. "It's being your husband."

In that moment, for the first time ever, I truly knew how Cinderella felt at the ball.

But then, the clock struck midnight, as it always does.

"Hand grenade," Sarge yelled. An Oriental vase smashed against the refrigerator. Guys ducked flying shards. Steve glanced over. "Typical Sarge. Ignore him." Rod never lost a beat of his "groovy" dance.

"Yee Haw!" Dry reeds held over the gas stove burner. "Whoosh." Flames licked up the kitchen curtains—*Singed organza.* "*Dee. Dee*"—I quaked. "Steve!"

He sighed, unwound himself from us and stiffened into the notorious Carmine intimidation stance. "Toss it, Cowboy," he yelled. And Sarge "Yee Haw!"ed and heaved.

The reed torch flared brighter in flight. Steve caught it with the finesse of a circus stuntman, flung it to the street, and did a Mexican Hat Dance on the flower flambé—"*Dee. Dee.*"

Two official blue pickups roared down the street. *The law!* Debating whether to run away or hide, I rocked Timmy frenetically—"*Dee. Dee.*"

Mrs. Cole doused the curtains with the sink sprayer, then in the "chicks up front" technique of political demonstrators, glided outside. Steve cut her off. "I'll handle this." He strode confidently toward the trucks. Pink Floyd pounded on.

"What's the trouble here?" The Air Policeman tightly gripped his M-16. "Got complaints things are getting out of hand."

Nervous sweat glued me to Timmy.

Steve leaned against the vehicle. Gave that casual grin of his. "No problem. Just horsing around."

I jiggled Timmy—"*Dee. Dee.*"

"Disturbances cannot be tolerated on base." The other Airman's voice cracked.

Steve nodded agreement. "You're right, man. Disturbances can't be tolerated."

Steve commiserated with them about the problems law enforcement had with wild parties, segued into a story, told a joke, then cooperatively herded drunks toward the trailer.

Ray plopped down in a one-man protest. "Not comin' in." Steve leaned in the cabana door, waved a bottle of whiskey. "Need freshened up, Fortier?" Ray lumbered in like Tee following a Coke.

It didn't take long, less than ten minutes, before the APs were apologizing for the misunderstanding and slapping each other on the back. Their military uniforms made them look tough, but they were as wimpy as Hartstown's cop, Officer Herrick. Everyone called him Deputy Fife after Barney in the *Andy Griffin* show.

Snuggling Timmy, I relaxed back into swaying.

He cinched my waist and gave me his protective look—Steve had spent a lifetime icing down fat lips and listening to, "You should've seen the other guy." Carmine drunken brawls were notorious for counties around. Guess those exciting tales were one thing that attracted me to Steve ... and the belief I could heal his hurts—"You and Timmy okay?"

I nodded. "You really know how to handle things, Steve."

"All in a day's work," he said dismissively, but stretched an inch taller. "I'll collect my reward later, if we ever break loose from here." He surveyed the area. "I better check on Sophie."

With her head stuck in the wastebasket, she looked like the Headless Horseman.

I escaped to the bathroom with Timmy—he was sopping—and washed him down with Johnson's No More Tears and let him kick naked on a towel on the floor. We both needed to air out some of the stink of that party.

Someone pounded on the door. "Hurry up in there."

I coated Timmy's little red bottom with baby oil, rubbed some into his cradle cap, wiggled his plastic pants and sweaty outfit back on him, sang, "I love you a bushel and a peck." He squealed when I did falsetto for the "hug around the neck." *Just like Tee.*

The pounding on the door picked up again. *No more stalling.* I turned the knob. A fidgeting GI almost bowled us over getting in.

Steve was waiting. "Better now?" He knew I always ran off to wash up Tee when I was upset. He pecked my cheek. "Give me Timmy. We'll go corral his daddy." The Beatles sang, "Yesterday, all my troubles seemed so far away."

I drifted into the tiny kitchen and dove into second helpings of Vienna sausages wrapped in dough and popcorn dripping with butter. I needed comfort food.

"Not used to the party scene, are you?" Mrs. Cole said.

My neck warmed as I shook my head no. I knew hayrides and PJ parties didn't count.

Mrs. Cole moistened yeast, measured out flour. I washed my hands, thumped out my frustrations kneading dough.

"Oh, you've done this before." Mrs. Cole sounded almost approachable.

"We feed a lot of people on the farm, too." *Maybe she isn't as phony as her roots.*

She nodded. "Where's the farm?"

"Pennsylvania. Amish country."

"How quaint. Must be beautiful."

I nodded.

She mixed another batch of dough. "Have you known Steve long?"

Unsure if she expected a fill-in-the blank answer or a short essay, I said, "Since grade school. We went to church together. He hayed for Grandpa. We have the same best friends and kind of adopted each other's sisters." I felt like a student struggling to pass.

"He has a level head," Mrs. Cole evaluated tersely, and I knew she'd wanted the short answer.

Still, I couldn't resist adding, "He's a good guy."

"I hope marriage doesn't change that opinion," Mrs. Cole said, almost to herself. I followed her gaze to where Sarge was lighting another cigarette over the gas burner.

Finally, about 3:00 a.m., after the great Sarge passed out on the floor and long after the footmen and horses had turned back into rats, Mrs. Cole began rousing bodies and gathering shoes. I shackled my feet to keep them from dancing a jig.

"Nice meeting you all," I lied and balanced Sophie to the door. Steve wrestled Ray for the keys. "Hand them over, Fortier." But, as I said before, that slime was a slippery one. He wedged himself behind the steering wheel. "My car! Don't be buggin' me."

Steve crawled over Sophie and co-piloted us precariously down muggy deserted roads. I'd read once that Turks cut off your fingers if you have a drunk driving accident. Or maybe it was a thief's hand. Not sure which. Anyway, I was afraid to imagine the penalty for accessories to the crime. But I told myself as long as Steve kept the car between the ditches, the swerving would be okay. No one would notice one more bad driver in Turkey.

I was right. We made it to Adana without incident. Well, except for Rod almost ripping off his sleeve in an attempt to retrieve his last mangled cigarette.

Ray fell out the driver's side. Barb, Timmy on her hip, steadied Rod down the path. Steve lifted Sophie.

"You don't have no electricity," she said. "You can't see no bugs."

"Mmm huh, we'll be fine." Steve practically carried her.

"You can't see no bugs. Sleep with us."

I'd rather sleep with a passel of bugs rather than the vermin you're going to crawl into bed with, I thought, feeling quite morally superior to both of the Fortiers. At this point, Nana would've said, "Be careful lest you fall," but her bits of wisdom were continents away.

A blast of sewer gas greeted us. "Welcome to the Sugar Shack." Steve said, slid the last lock, and pulled me close. "Guess we ended up with a Carmine reception after all. The best. The first to bring in U.S. troops." He smelled like a stranger, red wine and cigarettes. But his calloused thumb on my cheek, scarred from prom night, was so familiar. "You okay?"

A high-pitched squeal from across the hall. "I tell your parents and they don't send no more money." I stiffened.... A bellow of curses ... A faint squeak ... Silence ...

I squirmed away. "I'm okay but Sophie isn't. She needs help."

"Forget them!" Steve sounded irritated. "Butting in just makes things worse."

And you're the supposed great protector of women? A doubt sprinted past.

The tyrant's roar, "Shut up, broad." ... A little whimper.

"Steve, that guy's a monster. You've seen Sophie's arms and legs."

I could feel him shrug. "Don't you think she might just bruise easy? Like Pammy?"

And people call me a dreamer. I shook my head in disbelief. "He totally degrades her. The perv even has a Playboy centerfold staring right at their bed."

"To tell the truth, I haven't spent much time in their bedroom." I could feel his grin. "Haven't spent much time looking at pinups either. Too top heavy. A little wind would knock them on their faces. I like solid women like you." He patted my bottom.

I felt myself blushing.

He repeated, "Forget them. By morning, they'll be all lovey-dovey."

I hesitated. *He's probably right.* He was the expert in the world of domestic violence, not me.

He stole a peck on my nose and dared, "Beat you to bed," and took off. We stumble-ran down the pitch-black hall, hit the bed with so much force we slid to the other side. "Whoa! Hazardous area!" Those satin sheets always bugged him, but I loved them.

A ray of moonlight through a tiny gap at the window showed his eyes flashing like a lion on the hunt. "I promised myself at the party, if I ever got you into this bed, I'd never let you out again."

I wasn't sure if that was hyperbole or not, but my suspicion was that he was sincere.

***

Later, with Steve spooned against my back, I thought, *Now for my ultimate fantasy*—to lie in bed straight through the night.

Chapter 5

A Castle Under Siege

Over and over, I dozed, then woke. A cry ... *Tee?* No, a Turkish baby somewhere across the field. A murmur ... *Nana?* No, a Turkish mother upstairs. A high pained voice ... *Mama! I'm coming!* No, Sophie across the hall. A spasmodic cough ... *Tee's choking!* No, a tubercular Turk. A touch on my shoulder ... *"Dee, up. Dee, up, Dee."* No, I sleep with Steve now. A wail ... *Tee?* No, the muezzin at the mosque. Loud speakers echoing through Adana ... *Grandpa, "Co' Boss, Co' Boss." The lows of Holsteins.* No. Then—

"Get a move on, Carmine. You can't sleep all day."

At that bellow from across the hall, Steve sprung up like a released diving board. Our bodies, fastened together by the sticky heat, separated with a "pop."

"Me and the ole ball and chain going to the AFEX and the Club 'fore the party. Garzas going, too." Ray slurred. "Lighten up on the honeymoon to give your little wifey a look-see 'round. Said yourself she needs to meet that black menace of yours."

I whispered, confidently, "You promised if you got me into bed, you'd never let me out."

"Well, that was the plan." Steve's rough hands meandered along my farmer's tan lines. "But we need groceries." He'd stocked up on flour, sugar, canned goods, things like that, but we needed more. "And I have to check on Lux."

I wanted to see why they called Lux the Black Menace, so I quit arguing.

The AFEX and commissary had aisles as long as cornrows and prices through the roof—like milk (we settled for powdered) and butter (we chose oleo) and fruit and vegetables (looked gross. I stuck with the canned goods). The price of meat seemed outrageous, but since we butchered our own on the farm, I had no price reference. I settled for two pounds of hamburger to tide us over until Finance sent my check. (I could stretch it for days, I knew.) Steve said we could buy more "cheap" at the meat market downtown. That sent Sophie into a frenzied description of sides of beef hanging in the heat on the street. "Flies. No refrigeration. Pale and slimy. Who would eat that?"

The same people who eat ekmek, I thought.

Anyway, after Garzas and Fortiers ate lunch at the Airman's Club while Steve and I made peanut butter sandwiches on a bench beside the base library, we were off for me to meet the "menace."

The kennels' door warned, STOP/DUR, in both English and Turkish—Off Limits, Sentry Dog Area, Danger. Steve pushed it open. The deafening yelps and howls of thirty sentry dogs forced me to read Steve's lips as he lectured:

"Sentry dogs are the Four-Footed RADAR. A dog's nose is a hundred times more sensitive than a human's. A dog bites with 750 pounds of force per inch." He pantomimed each sentence. "If a dog attacks you, your only hope is to throw your forearm up and let him rip. Otherwise, he'll go for your throat or groin."

I wished everyone back home could see Steve, so professional, so confident, the Middle East so much more secure, resting on his strong shoulders.

We walked down the long corridor, kennels on both sides. Ray's dog, Rex, lay in the corner of his cage and yapped without bothering to get up.

Like master, like dog, I thought. *Probably waiting for his woman to bring him a beer.*

Rod's dog, Gunner, jumped up and barked as we passed.

He's kind of cute.

Then Steve stooped. "Hey, buddy, how's it going?"

Even if this hadn't been the only solid black dog in the kennels, I would've known Lux by the way he licked Steve's hand through the bars, like Laddie greeting Grandpa.

I stepped up. "Hi, Lux." And that lap dog froze, ears in picture-perfect alert position, throat rumbling like a volcano about to erupt. I grasped Steve's arm, that touch a trigger.

Lux detonated. Lunged. Clamped onto the chain-linked door. Ripped with Super Dog force. The cage clanged, rattled, clanged. The latch strained.

I sweated and prayed…. The latch held. *Thank you, Lord!*

"Out!" Steve ordered over his shoulder and ran his finger under my trembling chin. "It's, okay, Cindy. Really." His calming blue eyes convinced me to ease down the forearm I'd instinctively thrown up to save my throat.

Focused back on the killer, Steve repeated, "Out, boy!"

Still Lux gnashed chain-link. His growls vibrated my chest.

"Cindy, you need to step away." Steve slid me a few feet. "Lux doesn't let anyone near me, Cindy, see?" Steve pried loose my claws and marched back. "Out, Lux!"

Lux's ears twitched. His throat rumbled, his jaws frozen, his teeth clamped.

Steve, his finger an inch from Lux's nose, repeated, "Out!"

Lux's jaws slackened. Reluctantly, his teeth released the door. His snarls quieted into a kind of gargle. He edged into a crouch.

"Good boy," Steve crooned. "That's my boy."

Tensed to spring, sinews under black fur quivering, eyes beaded on me, Lux licked Steve's hand

"The government considers Lux a piece of military equipment, but I never got this attached to my boots or transport truck, right, partner?" Stroking Lux, Steve smiled up at me. "Not even you, Cindy, could sweet talk him. A good sentry dog has to stay a little high strung."

"A little high strung?" *A gross understatement.* But then, Steve grew up a Carmine, and as Grandpa said, "Those Carmines will rip you apart if you look at them cross-eyed."

Back in the Nova, the guys reported the scuttlebutt from the Club—the Turks might join an Arab military agreement. If so, that would put Incirlik in the thick of it. So, unsure what was going down, Sarge had canceled that night's party.

Steve's wandering fingers gave me a celebratory pinch.

"How about some cards to kill time? We've got the drinks." Ray's invitation sounded so cordial. I should've suspected something fishy.

Rod exhaled a plume of smoke. "We're in." Steve made excuses—those satin sheets almost in our grasp—but Rod argued, "Six-handed is better, Carmine," and Steve caved. "Only a couple of hands then."

When we piled out of the car, Barb said she had to go to their apartment first to "freshen her makeup," although her blue eyeliner and frosted lips looked perfect to me. She returned shortly, admittedly looking even more radiant, without Timmy.

"You were lucky to find a babysitter on such short notice," I said, and she lowered blue lids in sort of a royal dismissal. About then I dubbed her the Azure Princess. Sophie ignored Barb who looked lost without Timmy to hide behind.

Rod put "California Dreaming" on the turntable. Ray thumped an empty tumbler down. "Whiskey, broad!" Sophie ejected from her chair, poured his glass full, then perched on alert like Lux. Ray chugged, belched, picked up a deck of cards, and demanded, "Hit me again." I wished Sophie would take him literally.

Steve mouthed, "Pinochle." I peeked at my index card of rules—hearts, spades, pinochle—I was a novice. There were no cards on the farm.

Sophie, with the lead, studied her hand. Steve and I played footsie. Rod took deep drags on his cigarette. Barb drew figures on the tabletop. The creep swirled his whiskey and glared.

Finally, Sophie spoke. "And what's trump?"

The guys moaned and answered simultaneously, "Clubs." She might have been a ding-bat, but I felt sorry for her. She looked totally confused.

"Oh, guess I have this one," she said and scraped up the cards.

Anyway, that's the way the game went. She'd fumble around as if she didn't have a clue. "I can't decide. Is it better to lead with trump or save them?" and Steve would say, "Play your hand and don't worry," and she'd scrape up the trick with a manicured claw.

It was the strangest thing. I couldn't decide if she was the dumbest person in the world or the smartest for pulling off the dumb act.... I counted minutes until Steve and I could be alone.

Two barely perceptible taps interrupted it all.

Ray dropped his cards and rocketed to the door. I'd never seen him move so fast.

The clank of chains and bolts. Muffled voices. The stink of Turkish tobacco. The guys exchanging knowing glances.

The gate squeaked, then clanked. Ray reappeared, stalked by a bulky Turk with gold eyeteeth. *The man from the foyer. Bush bush.* "Stay away from them all." Steve had warned.

I tensed, ready for Steve to lead the charge to the exit. But he just sat there, tapping his fingers in the distinct rhythm of a ticking time bomb.

Ray kicked open the Turkish toilet door. My bulging eyes made an escape attempt at the sight— a mini-commissary of rationed items.

Gold-Tooth turned full-face to us and glowered down. I felt like we'd posed for a group photo. The Turkish toilet door banged closed behind him.

Muffled voices. Voices raising, haggling. Counting in Turkish, then English—"Lira … Yok." "Dollars …. No"

Lower your voices, I wanted to scream, afraid a passerby would hear and a bullhorn would blare, "Police! Hands over your heads, against the wall, spread 'em!" We'd be booked and fingerprinted. I'd be the first ever to besmirch the McNeilly-Alden name. Well, maybe the second.

I kicked Steve's foot under the table, our signal for years. Of course he understood me. But this man who'd stood in front of God and witnesses and promised to protect me 'til death mouthed, "Relax," and turned his back.

"So, Rod, I told you about my buddies in Airborne at Fort Benning, right?" Rod blew a smoke ring and nodded.

Clouds of panic mushroomed over me. I appealed to a Higher Power. *Oh, God, save us from a Turkish prison.*

I waited. I couldn't tell if God turned His back on me, too.

The Turkish toilet door squeaked back open. Paper bags rustled. The scuzz waddled out with one bag overflowing with Winstons, another with Marlboros.

No wonder he bums cigarettes. "Toss me a smoke" was the only complete sentence I'd ever heard him manage to articulate. *He saves his to sell.*

Gold Tooth carried a tower of blue jeans—at the AFEX, Sophie had asked me to reach a blouse on the top shelf. "I might be pregnant, you know." Her so-called husband butted in. "Keep moving, broad. Don't be buying stuff we don't need." She waited 'til he left, then freaked out. "I'm in big trouble." Her dentures chattered. "Forgot our ration cards." Steve patted her and handed her ours. "It's okay, Sophie." She'd filled her cart with cigarettes, whiskey, toilet paper, blue jeans—*It was a merchandise run.*

Steve kept talking. "Merle says the thirty-four-foot tower's a piece of cake after our haymow jumps. But I'm the Hayfork Master, and there's no way I'm jumping out of a C-119 dressed like a pack mule."

Rod took another big drag. "Thought those flying boxcars were extinct."

"No, they still use them."

The felons hauled out boxes of toilet paper.

I get it now. Fortier steals that rough stuff from the barracks, so they can sell their ration.

Barb sipped Kool-Aid. Sophie frenetically emptied ashtrays and wiped the table. Steve, ignoring me, jabbered, "Best friends with those guys since grade school. Merle dates Jill. He's got the Amish pacifist gene. Jill's the fiery one like me, right, Cindy?"

I didn't answer the stranger.

Another thud of the Turkish toilet door. The scuzz huffed and puffed by with bags of napkins and paper towels. Gold Tooth was loaded down with blankets. The gate clanked.

What a stupid farm girl I am. No wonder the crud calls me Elly May, I thought.

"Jill told Cindy to stay in college. Cindy's smart. Gave up a fellowship to study in England for me, right?"

He ignored the dirty looks I peppered him with. *If I was so smart, I wouldn't be sitting here.* Sophie stared blankly, clearly unimpressed by my scholastic prowess.

Turkish and English muffled together. A swoosh, like a snake leaving. The clank of iron. The scuzz slithered back, as casually as if he taken a legitimate restroom break. "Oh, almost forgot. Never say I don't get you nothing, broad." He flipped Sophie a ring.

"Turquoise!" She snapped for it like Laddie did for a treat, shimmied it over a knuckle, jumped for a hug.

The scuzz caught her midair. Heaved her back into her chair. My fingers itched to scratch out his eyeballs. Steve wiggled his foot against mine.

"Oh, by the way, Carmine," the felon added, "my man offered $5 for a night with Elly May. Likes them corn-fed." He leered.

I squirmed. Steve sprang up, jaw gritted.

And as stupid as he was, the slime ball shied back. "Chill out! Told him *Yok.*" I guess even jerks with the sensitivity of warthogs have a sense of self preservation.

Steve's hands slowly unclenched, and the pervert gelled back into his old cocky self. "No, for now at least. Might need that $5 before it's over, Carmine."

Steve glared fists and stood. "Let's go home, Cindy."

"Honeymooners!" Fortier smirked, then, not so subtly, dismissed Rod and Barb. "Don't you two got something to do? Like check on a kid maybe?" He snatched up the whiskey bottle.

Blue-shadowed eyes formed slits. Garzas followed us out.

Steve fumbled with locks while I sputtered. "That crook! That coward! That—" I couldn't find the word and probably shouldn't say it if I found it. "He used us to hide behind."

"Shhh! Simmer down." Steve ran his hand through his curls and sighed. "He'll hear you."

"He deserves to hear me." I stormed into the bathroom, grabbed my brush, and practically ripped my hair out by its roots. My nightly hundred strokes had saved me many a nervous breakdown and saved several people some broken teeth.

Steve followed. "I told you it's different over here." He rubbed my rigid shoulders. "Well, not different from my family. Ed hijacked freight and no one cared." He grinned.

"You're old enough to know better now."

"Everyone deals in black-market over here," he said. "Besides, it's Fortier's business, not ours."

I fixed a stare on him. "Ray made us accomplices. That makes it our business." Complicity was against everything I'd been raised to believe in.

"You worry too much." He pinched my butt. "The worst that could happen is that they'd stick us in a cell next to Uncle Louie. It'd be a family reunion."

"Quit joking." I bit my tongue to keep from saying my family got its money by hard work, not illicit activity. Instead, I said, "Grandpa says what we do reflects on the whole family."

"You're not an Alden anymore. Can't ruin a Carmine reputation. Anything we do can only improve it." His grin dissolved. "Theoretically, the Air Police could arrest us all, but not likely. We're K-9, the elite of Security. Besides, every day guys hop the bus for town and come back to the barracks rich. It's no secret why. You're being kind of rough on Fortier. He's got bills."

How can Steve accept this? I pushed aside the obvious signs—tarps stamped "U.S.," the property of the United States government, tools "borrowed from the kennels." My family wouldn't "borrow" a life preserver to save a drowning child—I said, "Crime's no way to fix a budget."

Steve lowered his eyes. *Finally, shame,* I thought, inaccurately. "Maybe it's not," he said, "but it gets Fortier money to take his wife to the Club and to buy an iron gate to protect her. Everyone knows it's almost impossible to make it here on military pay only."

So why'd you bring me over? I wanted to vomit the words at him but only said, "Sounds like I need a job. Any kind." I'd picked berries for eight cents a quart, green beans for ten cents a crate, typed card-catalogue cards at the library for 90 cents an hour, no job too menial.

"A job? An American woman? Where? Not downtown. You don't even speak the language. Not on base. Turkish civilians do those jobs for peanuts. And if I'm wrong and you found a job, how do you think you'd get there? Didn't the guys at the *lyceum* teach you anything?" He ran his hand through his hair. Softened. "Besides, we'll be okay. We don't waste money on cigarettes and booze. You can make a feast out of nothing. Finance just has to get my pay straightened out."

I never got around to asking when he thought that'd be. He tickled my neck and started humming the *Dragnet* theme. "I'm the only cop you'll have to deal with tonight."

He's trying to distract me, I knew. *We have to decide what our values are,* I knew.

He ran his finger along my jawline and drew my mouth to his. And I melted. I couldn't help it. And it was easy to rationalize. After all, Nana said to "never let the sun go down on your wrath."

Actually the sun had gone down already, but the idea seemed to apply otherwise.

I gave him a little shove and began groping my way down the dark hall.

"Madame," Steve crooned. "It's useless to resist the U.S. Air Police. Stop and surrender while you can."

"Never!"

"Then it's hot pursuit."

His feet scratched the floor for takeoff. I fumbled into a sprint.... We hit the bed at the same time. He head-butted me to the edge. I held my defensive position.

"Remember, you were offered mercy," he said.

I somersaulted and braced my feet against the wall. He pushed. A creak. A groan. The box springs, mattress, all landed on the floor—that was the first of many such crashes—our noses smashed against the rail still dangling from the headboard.

"It was inevitable you'd end up behind bars, Madame. You can run, but you can't hide from a trained professional."

He shackled me with his body. Officer and prisoner melted together. Exotic Eastern music from the ice cream pavilion several blocks away provided the soundtrack.

Eventually we drifted off to sleep.

But around 2:00 a.m. a mouth pressed against my ear.

Tee! I flinched to slide her over a little—Tee never understood the concept of a dividing line down the middle of the bed—a muscular arm snapped across my sweaty chest like a safety bar on a roller coaster. *Steve, of course. I forget.*

His faint whisper, "Keep your eyes closed." The s's hissed insidiously. I tensed. "Stay still." Since he had me pinned to the bed, I found it easy to obey.

He garbled his next sentence. All I got was, "Two men ... freeze." Just enough to send my pulse pounding in the hollow of my throat. *Gold tooth? "Yankee, go home" boys?*

I tensed for the jolt when Steve whipped out the billy club from under our mattress. And I discovered your life really does flash before your eyes. In my case a boring mini film featuring Tee in the tree house with supporting characters of Mama and Nana in the kitchen, Grandpa and Dad in the hayfield, the guys in the creek, Pam cheering, Jill and Merle....

Visualizing our slit throats, blood flowing like in that shower scene of Alfred Hitchcock's *Psycho*, I prayed. *Oh, God, watch over Tee*—Tee, moon-shaped eyes wide, crumpled wedding hat askew, pulling her red wagon, searching for me—*Let her understand I never thought I'd die here.* I slowed my shallow breaths. *"Into Thy hands I commend my spirit."* ... Silence.

A mosquito drilled into my clenched eyelid, piercing my piety. Unable to quell the urge, I blinked it. One eye risked a furtive sweep of the room—once, twice ... nothing?

My other eye grew brave and inched open to confirm its partner's findings.... Sure enough, the room totally deserted. Except for Steve, peaceful and still. His arm across my chest, now lying in limp repose. My paralyzed throat began to relax.

How could I forget? Pam had warned me. Steve talked in his sleep when he was upset. *It's the iron gate he's worried about.*

From the beginning, he'd lectured, "Everything of value here stays behind bars." At the kennels, he tapped Lux's cage and said, "Shouldn't my wife have better protection than my dog?" On the bus he pointed to a grocery shack. "See that gate? It protects leftover *ekmek*. You're worth more to me than bread." I had heard nothing but speeches.

I went through my death throes for nothing, I fumed, plotting the perfect revenge. It took me a little longer than usual without Jill's help, but we humans have a great capacity for creativity when it comes to evil.

I'll pluck his chest hairs out ... slowly ... one at a time.

My fingers twitched to execute justifiable torture. My eyes honed in on the victim—his face, so sweet in troubled sleep, like when he dozed off on the farmhouse sofa after rushing Pam away from a Carmine brawl.

He's fretting about protecting me. I sighed. *Okay, pal, you're forgiven ... this time.* Disappointedly, my fingers relaxed.

I flexed to roll away from temptation.

"Snap!" Steve's arm trapped me again. "Hold it," he whispered. "They're by the dresser."

Okay, I'm a little slow, but only a little. This time, skeptical, I up-periscoped one eyeball and reconnoitered the area, wall by wall. The one with the dresser, with the closet, with the cubby hole window at the ceiling. The corridors around the bed.

All empty. As I assumed.

I waited. His arm relaxed. I flopped away. *And guys wonder why we lose faith in them.*

Later in our marriage when I was working full-time with two young kids, I would pummel him myself if he dared to wake me for no reason. But that night I was suffering from new-bride syndrome.

Dawn's call to prayer echoed across Adana. Steve, wearing only his "I'll-save-you" look, catapulted out of bed. "I'll find the money. I'll—" He woke with a sheepish grin.

"My husband," I murmured. "It'll be all right."

"What?" He saw his nakedness reflected in my eyes and crawled back under the sheet. "About that iron gate—"

"Let's talk about it later," I suggested.

We played like two kittens with a new ball of yarn. In a flash, it was afternoon.

The clank of iron gate, the roar, "Carmine, move your *-!"

Steve in green fatigues, blue eyes narrowed. "No more talk. The deal was, Grandpa takes care of Pammy, I take care of you. That means you stay with Sophie while I'm on base."

I stood tall myself, eye to eye. "No way! I will not be babysat by a bug neurotic."

His hands waved surrender. "Then tell me again. What do you do in case of an intruder?"

I sighed and recited back to him for the hundredth time: "Grab a club." He'd stashed them all over the apartment. "Secure the safety strap on my wrist. Crack his shins with everything I've got. When he leans over to grab his shins, go for the back of the neck. Then run!" I know my sarcasm showed, but I was really quite sick of hearing about intruders and iron gates.

"I didn't bring you over here to get your throat slit." He used that authoritarian tone. "And stay away from windows. Got it?"

Uncovered windows. Obsession #2. But staying in the two rooms with curtains—bathroom and bedroom—for nine hours didn't sound doable to me.

"Why? It'd take a contortionist to twist down far enough to see in these windows. Besides, you said yourself Turks don't carry guns. I can dodge a flying knife. No problem."

He didn't smile. I wondered if sometimes I looked at Tee the way he was looking at me. "Why can't you understand?"

I guess of all people I should have. After all, he'd confided, "I promised myself when I was one inch taller than Ed, he'd never hit Mom or Pammy again." And he'd kept that promise, by getting decked himself. Of course, he wanted to protect me.

But I stood strong. "I understand two things, Steve. You're a good man, and I really will be fine. Nana's kneeling by her bed. Do you really think any iron gate is stronger than Nana's prayers?"

Checkmate! He ran his hand through his curls and clomped out. The "Just the two of us" had become "Just one—me."

Chapter 6

Queen of My Castle

To Mama, Turkey was the home of Ali Baba, mosques, caravans, and sultans. To Nana, it was the first Christian church in Antioch, St. Paul's home in Tarsus, and Noah's Ark. To tourists, it was white sand beaches and ancient castles.

But that's all glitter. The cold fact is, no matter how exotic the world is outside, inside, world round, most women are doing tedious chores and waiting for men to return home. I had no idea what to do with the "alone time" I'd always craved—

Nothing to clean. In two days we'd polished every surface. Of course the place was only the size of a postage stamp. Okay, I'm exaggerating. Maybe the size of an envelope.

No phone, no TV, only a tiny AM radio. Turkish music and Armed Forces Radio, playlist from Mama's *Reader's Digest Music Club. Not even a good book.* I'd read my *Sonnets from the Portuguese* a thousand times. And my Bible? Nana'd be thrilled to think of me pouring over it nine hours a day, but only one Scripture interested me. "The two shall be one flesh."

No clothes to wash. We'd washed laundry in the bathtub and hung it in the spare room. "Things outside unguarded get ripped off," Steve had said and put up a clothesline with spikes. By the time he found studs, he'd gouged craters in the walls, some rivaling the Grand Canyon.

Clothes too wet to iron. Normally, a good thing. Nana said she'd know I was in love when I found a man who made me *want* to iron his shirts. That day I would've gladly ironed his T-shirts and boxers to boot.

I can't bake without an oven regulator. "Didn't notice it's a piece of junk 'til too late," Steve had complained.

But No Bakes will keep me busy. I scrounged in the cardboard boxes under the marble counter for cocoa, oatmeal, peanut butter. *I've never mixed dough without Tee sticking her fingers in the bowl.* I wedged the cookie sheet into the squatty refrigerator, its icebox only big enough to hold an ice cube tray and a half gallon of ice cream, if we ever got lucky enough to afford the ice cream.

Still eight hours to go. A short ten feet out the kitchen window, the forbidden cotton field called to me to take a walk.

Four little dusty feet skipped by toward the dirt path, hesitated, skipped back toward the driveway. Back and forth.

I wonder if they're the same cute little girls.

Feet halted outside our bars. I waited.

Wide black upside-down eyes popped down between those bare feet. We all blinked in surprise. Two coal black heads vanished. Four dancing feet and "tee hees" stayed.

Then, two little girls squatted, simultaneously. "Hello," the bravest said.

"*Marahaba* [hello]," I answered.

The shy one pointed at me. "*Chok gazelle.*" Steve called me "*chok gazelle,*" very pretty.

"You *chok gazelle,*" I said, pointing to her. "And you *chok gazelle,*" I said, pointing to her friend.

They giggled and chattered gibberish. *Like Tee.* I used to think Tee's oval eyes proved the hospital gave Mama a Chinese baby by mistake. I pretended someday I'd learn Chinese and translate her every word.

A tea party would be fun. I filled a plate with Chocolate No Bakes, motioned the black-eyed girls in. "*Gel* [come]."

They giggled. Skipped away.

I yelled, "Gule gule [Go with a smile]."

Their feet echoed, "You skipped off to your own adventures and deserted Tee." *I had to go,* I argued with myself.

My Phantom Limb throbbed. I twisted my wedding band. *"How do I love thee? Let me count the ways?"*

I left Tee for you. I fingered the cat's eye marble, Tee's gift. *I left Mama for you.* I ran my hand across my chest. Surgeons had lopped off Mama's breast, left concave bone. Radiation burned her neck black. She almost crawled from exhaustion. *If I leave all for thee, wilt thou be all to me?"*

Quit thinking. Since I was big enough to fetch Tee's diapers, I'd worked. Now I was lounging around while Mama picked up the slack. But she'd given me one final chore. "Write every exotic detail, Princess."

I reached for the stationery on top of the fridge and laughed at myself. *I'm still hiding it from Tee.* Once the school taught her to shred paper as a dexterity exercise. She came home and happily ripped up the whole Old Testament of Nana's King James Bible.

Don't think. Write. I sat at our Formica table and began.

"Grandpa, you were right. The road to happiness wasn't paved with rose petals. It's not paved at all. It's full of air pockets, especially over the Dardanelles. And, Nana, you were right, too. Glass slippers would be useless here. They'd shatter the first time I stomped on a centipede." For Mama, I described the Turka Hava plane. "I expected that overhauled pumpkin to leave us sprawling at the stroke of the clock"—she'd love that line. For Dad and Sean who hated the smoke over Youngstown, I wrote, "With no steel mills here, the stars seem closer and brighter, like fireflies." For Pam, I talked about Timmy. "I found your look-alike."

Then for Tee, I sketched a picture. I'm no artist, but she'd recognize her hooked rug and my Raggedy Ann. *How many Raggedy Anns has Nana sewn?* For twenty-three years, one ragdoll in Tee's arms, another in the wash.

I felt my emotions bleeding out from where Tee'd been ripped from my side. *Do Siamese twins feel like this after separation?*

"If I left all for thee, wilt thou be all to me?"

Six hours and forty-five minutes left.

Jill would be ironing waist-length auburn hair or chording a Joan Baez ballad or on the payphone with Merle. *I can't believe it's the 20th century, and I can't talk to her.* There wasn't a transatlantic cable yet, so I resorted to writing.

"You nailed it, Jill. Life isn't like a romance novel. Sitting side-by-side in those Pan Am seats had all the passion of the Cleavers' single beds. Then it got worse." I described my sleepover with Sophie. I could almost hear Jill laughing. "But that scene in the Turkish toilet?" I lapsed into metaphor. "Miss Youngblood did the topic a disservice in biology class. All those worms and frogs.

But it wasn't fireworks either. More like us on a roller coaster. The higher we climbed, the more Steve loved it. I held on for dear life." (He'd studied me, plain old Cindy, with the awe of the art critic examining his first Rembrandt. Well, considering my crabapple breasts and pear hips, more likely a Rubens.) "Can you imagine, Jill? For the first time in my life, I feel pretty." I knew she'd understand.

I sucked a black Necco Wafers from my sleepover stash and looked around the apartment. *Jill'd be proud of how I used her lessons on scale*—dresser/buffet filled with Mel Mac dishes on the wall between the bedroom doors in front of the tiny table. Brown nylon sofa with plastic legs between two Formica end tables on the far wall. Matching chair under the peep-hole window on the long sidewall. Small green-and-black Turkish rug defining the conversation area.

A refreshingly modern look. So unlike the farmhouse's oak china cabinet, massive sofa, overstuffed chairs, bentwood rocker, great round oak table....

The 4th call to prayer echoed eerily across the dusky city. *I miss normal sounds*—rattling stanchions, Laddie's yip, Tee's chatter, Nana's rhythmic "I love you," Grandpa's "Pshaw," the party line's ring, Mama's car door slam, Dad's lunchbox's clank, the wind chimes on the porch (Mama called them tinkling fairy bells)....

I've got to quit thinking. I dug out that green linen tablecloth Nana bought to teach me to embroider. It'd taken me four years to cross-stitch one small flower, but Nana, always optimistic, insisted, "You might find a few free minutes to work on it over there, dear."

The embroidery hoop seemed to morph into Tee's moon-shaped face. *Her tongue always sticks to the side when she separates strands of floss.* Linen doggy-paddled over the sticky sweat on my legs.

Six out of nine nights of this boredom. I'll go nuts. This isn't the way I imagined it. Grandpa and Nana were together 24/7, 365 days a week. Dairy cows don't take vacations.

I squashed a water bug.

"Yoo hoo!" *Sophie!*

I dashed to the door, fumbled off chains and bolts. "Come on over. I made cookies."

"No!" Sophie's fingers fluttered. "You don't have no gate, no curtains. You come here."

Less than twenty-four hours before, I'd vowed to never again darken the door of that crime scene, but faced with hours before Steve got back, I broke my word to myself. "Sure, Sophie." Talk about desperate for entertainment.

"Wait!" She craned up the stairs and said, "Okay. All clear. Run."

I booked out.

"Key!" Sophie shrieked.

I lunged. Caught our door milliseconds before it latched. Almost fainted.

"Get your key," she cheeped.

I did. And a plate of No Bakes. I suddenly craved chocolate.

"That could've been a disaster." She waved her key wristband. "Buy some elastic. You need to wear that key at all times." She sounded like a salesman for some new kind of jewelry.

I'm a wife, not a prison guard, I didn't say. Just stuffed my mouth with a cookie.

She traced my path in with bug spray, doused my feet under the table. I suspected her bug radar had detected a remnant of water bug carcass on the sole of my shoe. "Have to keep us safe from bugs," she chirped.

Questioning the safety of a toxic dump, I extended the cookies.

"Oh, no, I couldn't!" She sounded like I did when someone offered me a cigarette. "Did you see that centerfold in our bedroom?"

I nodded yes. *How could I miss it? A full view of the Big Rock Candy Mountains.*

"My Raymond said he put it there to remind me not to get fat." She clamped her dentures together with a loud clack, then added, smugly, "But did you notice that slut's *toes*? All twisted! *Mine* are perfectly straight."

Toes were the *only* anatomic detail I *hadn't* noticed. I wolfed down another cookie.

She arranged the fan, poured a glass of Coke. A blast of sewer gas provoked thoughts of running out to say good-bye to Grandpa and Dad before school and Nana warning, "Only go as far as the milk house, or you'll smell like the barn." *Steamy manure, wet cowhide, iodine wash for udders, soybean calf pellets, clover—*

"Garzas' place stinks," Sophie said. "No sewer gas up on their top floor. It's old crappy diapers. Barb looks good, but she's a pig."

"Oh," I said. *Guess Good Housekeeping's not on Barb's reading list.*

Sophie snatched a taboo cookie. "That snooty hussy don't appreciate no baby." She broke the cookie in two, gobbled both halves. "They had to get married, you know."

A minor chord sounded—once Mama overheard that old biddy Mrs. McCormick say, "The Alden boy got Joanne Bates pregnant. How do you think that goody-goody family feels now?" Mama had sobbed for days. *I hope we never disappoint Mama like Sean did.*

Sophie fingered another No Bake. "Use my oven anytime. Do you make brownies? I like walnuts in mine, but the commissary never gets them in." She inhaled the cookie whole. *Finally, something we have in common. Soothing ourselves with sweets.*

I sipped green Kool-Aid, wishing it were a dipper of icy milk from the cooler. Munched another No Bake.

Sophie topped off her Coke with rum. *Guess she needs more comfort than chocolate can give.*

She started rattling off a depressing list of who was sleeping with whom. *Enough of this!* I'd crossed an ocean to escape small-town gossip. Besides, the men in my life would never cheat. Not even Sean, no matter what Jo accused him of.

"And you won't believe the guys that go to the Pound."

Sarge's word from the party. I perked up. "What's the Pound?"

"Your husband don't tell you nothing? It's a whore house. Turkish government runs it. Believe that?" I couldn't. "They call it a Pound 'cause the whores are real dogs. Fat, missing teeth...." She added more details than I wanted to hear. *No wonder Steve avoided the topic.* "My Raymond says any dude who goes there's sick in the head." *He'd qualify then.*

The rum emptied. Sophie's accent thickened. "My Raymond's people bug us every month 'bout making 'em grandparents. Say Fortier men always get a baby first year." She laughed bitterly. "Most of 'em four or five months after the wedding." She drained the final drop. That girl could really guzzle.

"I was sure this month my prayers would be answered. Pope Paul VI comin' to Istanbul soon on his peace pilgrimage and all." She slopped more rum into her glass. Straight. Not a drop of Coke this time. Huge gulp. "I hate gettin' my period."

And Sophie's solo drunk suddenly made sense.

"My Raymond's right," she muttered. "He's too good for me. Lucky he'll have me. Fat. Not even pregnant."

That scuzz deserves a punch in that flabby gut of his. How can she let him make her feel this bad? I didn't know then that the one who sweeps you away has the potential to sweep away your life, your soul, your very identity.

I fled Fortiers'. *Better fortify our marriage before it's too late.*

Ironically, Nana, wearer of hairnets over coiled braids, had provided my resource materials. A tidbit in that yellowed marriage manual: "The wet human body is extremely sensual."

I wound my hair in pink rollers, larger than OJ cans. Smudged Vaseline on lashes and lips. Shortly before Steve's ETA, I poured steaming pans of water into the tub. Dropped my negligee in white swirls. Lowered myself into a mountain of Joy dish soap bubbles and reviewed the script—a week without television had greatly enhanced my graphic imagination.

My role:
Jump out of tub. Leave trail of wet footprints to door.
Coo, "Oh, Steve." Drop just a corner of towel. (My dewy round bottom winks at him.)
Feign innocence. "Oops." (Glisten with watery beads.)

His role:
Fumble off boots. Crush me against massive chest.
Lean back to let towel fall to floor. Carry me gently to bed.
Trace my spine with calloused fingertips. Lick droplets from my shoulders, my clavicle, my throat, my.... Well, you get the idea. You've watched enough movies. Jill gagged at those scenes, but I memorized every detail.

Another blast of sewer gas. I twisted my flip off my neck and plunged my assaulted nostrils to water level like a frog. Inhaled the lingering fragrance of the last lonely Joy soap bubble. Memorized every blue and yellow stitch on the white-embroidered towel tacked over the bathroom window. Even time froze....

Finally. The clomp of boots.

"Sophie, Ray got held up. We hopped the bus. Ray'll be late."

Rap-pause-rap.

Keep your man happy.

I jumped from the strangely icy tub. The heat of my passion should've had it steaming like a sauna by then. My pruned fingertips draped a towel over the very tips of my breasts.

Shivering in the muggy air, I shook my flip upside down. Licked lips. Ran to the door.

The wet human body is extremely sensual.

The curtain rose. Cindy Carmine starring as Coy Seductress—

"Oh, Steve, I lost track of time. Wait. I'll step back."

Slid locks, pirouetted away. The door opened, slammed.

I slipped up from behind and wrapped around him. *The wet human body is extremely sensual.* Purred, "My bed was lonely without you."

"Ew, you're dripping wet." He hadn't read the script. He held me back as if I were a soggy pup.

Undeterred, I delivered my lines. "Oh, I'm sorry. I was taking a bubble bath. To be nice and fresh for you." I rubbed my nubs across his rough fatigue shirt.

His brows furrowed. "We're late, you know. Couldn't get Fortier to get a move on it. Finally gave up and—" My lips interrupted him.

He sighed, leaned back, inspected me closely. "How long were you in there? You're *blue.*"

I looked down. Actually, I wasn't blue. More a light shade of purple. My arm hair stood up like miniature quills. Instead of "My little Portuguese," I seemed to be his little porcupine.

He unlaced his boots. "Fortier will be telling Sophie some cockamamie story about getting mandated to spray kennels for contagious hepatitis. Truth is, he's feeding slot machines another paycheck."

Refusing to be sidetracked, I let the corner of my towel droop. "Oops," I said.

He wrapped me back up like an Egyptian mummy, flicked the lights off, dragged me down the hall and into the bedroom.

"Wait until you see what I've got for you."

Aha, success, I thought until he added, "Put something on and I'll show you."

I sighed, threw on a shift dress, stepped into the kitchen.

He whirled. "Ta da." And flourished ... a pair of vise grips. "Now you can bake."

"Huh?" I didn't get it.

He practically bubbled. "These'll work for a regulator." He attached the vise grips where the knob should be. "Push in and turn." He opened the oven. "Then throw a match down the hole."

As in an infomercial, he pushed, turned, and threw. Unlike the infomercials, flames shot out two feet. He dodged them. "Whoa! Almost got singed." I quivered like Chubby Checker.

His tongue peeked out of the corner of his mouth as he fine-tuned the grips, leveling the flames, then straightened and grinned. "Another fine graduate of the Charles McNeilly's School of Mechanics." Grandpa could fix anything with a twist of baler twine. "Perfect, right?"

I nodded. *Yeah, if I were a Vietnam War protester setting myself on fire.*

To my silence, he turned on Sad Sam eyes. "It's not a turquoise ring, but it's a gift."

I kissed him like I did Tee when she handed me a lovingly picked dandelion. "As Sophie says, it's good enough for Turkey."

He beamed. "I'll find something safer the minute I get some money. 'Til then, get the match down the hole fast. Don't want you blowing yourself up."

On that reassuring note, even though "the wet human body" was dry and the towel-droop thing long past, he gazed at me with wild intensity.

Success! I thought. Again, wrongly.

"Thinking of you with an oven's got me craving your homemade biscuits," he said.

Then I remembered when I'd seen that passionate expression. Right before he devoured an entire extra-large pepperoni-and-mushroom pizza all by himself.

A man and his appetites. I was only slightly amused. *Foiled again.*

Chapter 7

The Best of Times, the Worst of Times

In San Francisco, 1967 was the summer of love. But on Incirlik AFB, it was the summer of high alerts.

Right after Sarge canceled his party, the UN peacekeepers left Syria, and the Arabs formed a military pact. In response, on June 5th, Israel launched a surprise offensive—destroying 400 planes belonging to Egypt, Syria, Jordan, and Iraq and most of their airports. They captured the Sinai Peninsula, the Gaza Strip, the Golan Heights, and the West Bank (areas that had little meaning to most of us then).

As quickly as war began, the UN brokered a ceasefire. I would have liked to write Professor Gowdy, "You almost convinced me to ruin my life for a six-day war." But that would've been snotty.

I had no clue that short war would result in decades of violence. But then, we seldom have a clue about the impact of today's events on tomorrow—

Anyway, the vise grips were the first of a series of return-home-from-work gifts—a dog treat from Lux, a bag of pistachios, a poppy picked on post, a used copy of Michener's *Hawaii*—culminating in the jackpot. A heap of material!

Steve dumped it inside the door.

"An officer rotating Stateside left it on the curb for the *bush bush*. I got permission to take it. Curtain problem solved." The AFEX had really cute curtains, but he'd insisted we didn't have a penny to waste on them. "If anyone can make this stuff look good, you're the one."

I smothered him with kisses, then rifled through the pile.

Gold-and-green antique satin. "I can make floor-length drapes for the living area and our bedroom. The stripes will elongate the … windows." I'd almost slipped and said, "cubby holes."

"And there's enough of this cotton to cover the kitchen window and under the counter, too." I hated the exposed plumbing and cardboard boxes.

"You'd use that?" Steve's forehead furrowed. "Pink?"

Not even Mama would put pink in a kitchen, but I reassured him, "There's enough of it. It'll work nicely."

"I wish I had money to buy you ready-made ones." He pecked my cheek and twirled me to bed to collect his "finder's reward."

Afterwards, a ray of the moon's promise smiling on the foot of our bed, I paraphrased my favorite sonnet: "Oh, Steve, how do I love thee? I love thee for making me laugh. I love thee for always including Tee. I love thee for finding a way for us to have nice curtains."

Today that might sound like much ado about nothing, but back then those scraps meant privacy and, even more importantly, a project to pass time during Steve's double shifts.

By the time tensions between the Israelis and Arabs de-escalated enough for K-9 to be granted a break, I'd sewed thousands of hand stitches and washed and starched those curtains crisp.

Steve stomped in armed with clothesline, Rod's hammer, the landlord's nails, the kennel's level, and a determination to make the curtains hang straight, though nothing else in the building was plumb. "Let's see what these look like up."

And tensions between the Carmines escalated.

Calculations made to the micro-millimeter, he drove the first nail. The porous wall crumbled. He lobbed the nail across the room. "Typical, no stud!"

He picked up a six-penny nail, then an eight-penny nail, then a spike. First divots. Then canyons. I refused to notice how much he looked like Ed Carmine.

In an attempt to save the walls from total demolition, I patted his arm and said, sincerely, "It's just fine, Steve. It doesn't have to be perfect." *After all, I decorate with Tee's "pictures" framed with construction paper.*

"Save your two cents." He glared and hurled a hunk of wall, like Ed did wrenches and sons. "Can't we have one decent thing in this dump?"

I didn't let myself shout back, "Can't we just have some peace in this dump?" Obviously, he didn't understand a thing I wanted.

He spent the afternoon throwing things and yelling about the stupid U.S. government that was too cheap to provide base housing for Airmen. I spent the afternoon placating him.

Once Jill said, "Steve's a great date but his family should throw up some red flags." I'd defended him. "Steve's not like his family." She'd said, "My mother never looks at the signs either," and dropped the subject.

Is this what Jill meant? I prayed to wake from the nightmare.

Eventually, Steve strutted window to window, surveying his makeshift curtain rods from all angles. "Now aren't those nice and straight?" His world was orderly, mine was crumbling.

"Not quite up to Charles McNeilly's standards, right?" He grinned. "But you won't see those holes when I get the drapes up."

Gaping white caverns sneered from pink walls.

My stiff body screamed at him. My Nana façade was slipping.

He chucked me under the chin. "Don't laugh now." He tickled my rigid ribcage. I wanted to throw up. My moon-shaped birthmark peeped out from under my shiny new wedding band, but its promise was shadowed by a doubt.... I closed my eyes.

Rap-pause-rap. Rod stepped into our silence and extended a stack of mail and an invitation. "Barb said *shish kebabs* sounds like the bomb. What do you say, man?"

Steve hesitated, pulling me close, or as close as you can hold a steel rod. "Cindy deserves something special after today, but ... Finance hasn't got my pay straightened out."

"Won't need to drop much bread." Rod explained. A couple of dollars a meal. A good exchange on money. No *araba* needed. The approved restaurant on the boulevard was an easy walk.

"Well," Steve hm-hawed, "we could throw on some spaghetti instead, right, Cindy? A little garlic sounds good."

I ignored him and tore open Jill's letter—summer classes, Merle's Jump School—then a note from her brother Julian, my first love, went through women like Kleenex. A profuse apology for missing our wedding. Grandpa would label it, "Blarney."

"So what's it to be, man?" Rod prodded Steve.

I ripped open a manila envelope—pictures from Tee, the traditional two sticks of Black Jack gum from Grandpa, the predictable July news (second-cutting hay, combining oats, snapping green beans). Then, the pot at the end of the rainbow. From our milk truck driver, "Missed your wedding. Wanted to send our congrats and a little something." A five-dollar bill.

"Manna from heaven." Waving Lincoln, I did a jig around the table. "It's a sign. We're meant to go." Dinners out were a rarity in PA. Dad said, "Nothing replaces good home cooking." But we all knew expense was the real issue.

"You can eat like the man on that fiver," Rod said. "Market paid me 8 for 5."

That's almost double base exchange, 4.50 lira for $5.00.

Steve's jaw tightened. "We should save it for an emergency but ..." He ran a hand through his curls. "Okay, we'll go. But I'm sticking to Base Exchange, even if it is a rip off." He glanced over at me. "Doesn't seem right to sell our currency. Guys are fighting in Nam for it."

He's a good moral man, I thought with a rush of relief. I'd harbored some doubts since his casual attitude toward Ray's black-market deal.

"Do it your way, man," Rod said. "I'll get Barb and we'll be back in a jiffy. Do a smell check and get suited up."

Steve closed the door behind Rod and twisted that curl. "You deserve a night out after the way I got so riled up. I just get frustrated, you know?"

Mama had warned me, "Expect a few lovers' spats. But learn to get over them fast." I snuggled close to my new husband.

On the boulevard, Steve whispered, "Stay in the middle. Don't want some Turk pinching that solid bottom of yours." He might've meant "solid" as a compliment, but he really needed lessons on flattery.

He spotted two soldiers/policemen marching toward us. "Americans can't take chances," he said and scooted us into an open-air market.

The overpowering scents of fruit, perfumes, and samovars of mint tea mingled with leather, wet wool, fresh bread, tobacco, and sweat. Craftsmen shaped copper with burin and hammer, molded brass, wove carpets, and stitched quilts. "Lira?" a toothless old man begged as his toothless old bear swayed on scrawny hind legs, displaying its scraggly tangled fur from all angles. *"Fuzzy Wuzzy was a bear. Fuzzy Wuzzy had no hair. Fuzzy Wuzzy wasn't very fuzzy, was he?"*

Rod and Barb stopped at a booth of Mersin pipes. I stopped for buttons. *Tee would love these.* Steve looked at the jewelry. "Pammy'd go wild over this gold, wouldn't she, Cindy?"

We made it to the restaurant. Surprisingly, a sit-down with cloth napkins and attentive waiters (as nice as where we celebrated graduation with Jill, Merle, and Denny). Using his unique Turkish-English-sign language blend, Steve ordered us both tomato-cucumber salads and Kasoose (a beverage like 7-Up). Then for me, *shish kebabs* (chunks of lamb). But for himself, Adana kebabs (ground meat). "Tastier, but sometimes they use spices to cover taint in old mutton. With you new in-country, I'm afraid if you tried Adana kebabs, you'd get the Turkish trots" (slang for diarrhea). I didn't protest.

The waiter brought out flatbread, loaves almost two feet long (cooling, it fell like puff pastry), and demonstrated filling it with meat and onions flooded with lemon, then wrapping it tight.

Steve said, "Oh, I forgot one thing. A Turkish delicacy for you, Cindy. A little expensive but you're worth it." He motioned, and a second waiter snapped over and extended his tray. "Goats' brains?" Steve offered, innocently—he's a pathetic actor.

"Madame?" the waiter waited for my answer.

I shriveled back. *"Yok, yok."* I couldn't cover my horror.

Steve grinned. Later, when the bill came, he grinned even broader. Only 3.75 lira.

On the boulevard, a vendor scooped mounds of ice cream into cones. It looked hand cranked. "We have money," I said. Steve set his jaw. "Local dairy products are off limits. T.B., undulant fever, you name it. I, for one, am not risking an Article 15 court martial for ice cream, no matter how good it tastes." A little further down the block, though, he bought three pounds of pistachios from a sidewalk brazier. "And we still have a dollar left over for the piggy bank," he said.

We strolled and munched. A white jet trail sliced across the sky. The half-moon under my wedding band tingled. It was the best of times.

But then came the worst of times—when Rod opened their door to ... reverberating shrieks!

Barb streaked off, hurdling piles. Steve, that pasty-white color you get right before you gag, clambered through the rubble to the balcony to escape the fetid ammonia blast. I stood riveted.

Barb reappeared, holding her thrashing son away from her white blouse. "It's okay. It's okay." His screams tore at my heart.

I waited for the babysitter to follow ... and waited ... and waited.... *We were gone almost three hours.*

My stomach churned. Slowly, I grasped the situation. *A four-month-old. Left alone.*

Timmy howled like Tee in a night terror. Tears streaked his velvety cheeks. *I never asked who was watching him. "Dee. Dee."*

Rod picked a newspaper off a tower of clutter. Barb squinted and said, "A bottle might help."

"I'll take him." I knocked over a pile of magazines, reaching for him. *"Dee. Dee."*

"But he won't quit screaming." Her blue-shadowed eyes darted aimlessly.

"It's okay, really. You get his bottle." *"Dee. Dee."*

She dropped her son into my arms and fled. Urine oozed out of his diaper. "Hush, little one," I whispered and cocooned around him. "You're safe now. It's okay."

Timmy squalled, comfortless. Rod glanced up from his newspaper, once.

I hummed, "Too-Ra-Loo-Ra-Loo-Ral," like Grandpa did to drive away the monsters that chased Tee in the night. "You're safe now, Angel." I crooned and swayed. *"Dee. Dee."*

Timmy shrieked. His torso as tight as if it were in a straitjacket. His legs trembling like that puppy having seizures in the haymow. His eyes red ... like Tee's.

"Hush, Timmy, hush, little one." *I never asked who was watching him. I never asked.* "Too-Ra-Loo...." *What if no one asks who's watching Tee?*

Steve slipped up behind. "It's okay, little guy. It's okay." He added an off-key bass to my alto.

Gradually, Timmy's rigid legs unclenched.... Howls settled into whimpers ... then deep panting ... his sweaty body melting against mine.

"I'm so sorry, little one. I'm so sorry," I whispered. *What if Pam and Jill get tired of spending nights with Tee? What if everyone gets as careless as me?*

Barb tiptoed back and handed me his bottle. "Would you? Don't want to get him stirred up again." She pushed clothes off an upholstered chair, kicked a space clear for my feet.

I pulled Timmy close, shook a few drops of milk onto my wrist. *Stone cold.* He latched on, slurped greedily. I rocked.

Rod shuffled cards. "Hey, man, ready to get your butt beat?"

Barb hummed a Johnny Mathis song and fingered a magazine. "I miss American Bandstand. By the time we get back to Ventura, the only new dance I'll know is that clomp-clomp Turkish thing."

I smiled, hummed, "Too-Ra-Loo...."

Barb picked up a bottle of lavender nail polish. I hummed.

Slowly, Timmy fell asleep. I picked my way through a precarious path to his crib, changed his diaper, fanned a muggy breeze over his porcelain back. He sniffled once in his sleep. *He looks like an angel.* "Too-Ra-Loo...." *"Dee. Dee."*

In the other room, cards slapped the tabletop, a chair slid. Steve said, "Spades next time. I'll get even."

I fingered Timmy's damp blond curl. I traced the little wrinkle on his brow. *How could they leave him alone?*

"Cindy? We better get going."

I ran my finger over Timmy's Cupid's bow.

"Cindy?"

I slowly turned toward Steve's voice. *"Dee. Dee."*

Neither of us spoke on the path. At the clank of our last bolt, Steve said, "I think that was normal for them, don't you?"

Counting the times we'd spent with Garzas without Timmy (card game, shopping), I'd reached that same conclusion.

"It was normal in our house, too. And nothing bad ever happened," he said. "Besides, Timmy's safer alone than with the wrong babysitter. Blond babies go for a premium on the black-market."

He's trying to convince himself. I climbed into bed without a word, but he knew what I was thinking.

"You promised to quit worrying about everyone else," he said. "You promised your mama to think about just us."

"Abandoning a baby so we could go out isn't what Mama meant," I finally said.

He stiffened. "What can we do about it? It's over. Don't you remember Nana's saying?" He was referring to the one that goes, "For every trouble under the sun/ There is a remedy or none./ If one, try and find it./If none, never mind it."

"Well, tomorrow's not over, and we have a remedy for it." I'd made a decision. "Promise we'll babysit every time they want to go out. Promise Timmy will never be left alone again if it's in our power. Pinky swear." I appealed to the Steve who did headstands for my Tee. My brown eyes held his blue ones.

Steve's not always known for his quick wit, but he could tell I wasn't backing down. "You're right," he said and pinky swore, "never alone if we can help it," then repeated, "He could be Pammy's boy with that coloring, couldn't he?"

I relaxed against him.... In no time at all, he was talking in his sleep. "Hush, Timmy. Don't cry, baby. Hush."

Just like the night before he had to leave me alone without an iron gate. I ran a finger over his curls. *He might act rough sometimes, but I married a good man.*

* * *

The old Cindy Alden, shadowed by Tee, would've agonized for weeks at being party to endangering Timmy, but the new Cindy Carmine repeated Nana's saying to "never mind" things without remedy, snuggled against her husband, and managed to forget ... almost.

Chapter 8

A Shadow of a Doubt

An old Jewish custom gave a man a year off work to get to know his bride. But it only took Steve and me a few days to learn way more than we wanted to know about each other, like that we all carry our families with us, no matter what we think. It was a roller-coaster ride, and my metaphor has nothing to do with that Turkish toilet scene—

It began with me hunched over the tub in a mist of Tide bubbles and steam, mumbling, "Thou shalt not covet thy nana's scrub board, nor thy neighbor's water heater, nor Sophie's wringer washer"—I'd refused Sophie's offer to use her washer. No way was my underwear sloshing around anywhere near where the pervert's had been.

Steve kissed one of my pruned fingers. "Wish I could afford a washer." He kissed another. "And a water heater." He kissed another. "And—"

I put my hand over his lips. "Our bathtub's just fine. Forget money. All we need is love." He grinned at my Beatles' imitation. "Now go get that pair of fatigues."

A moment later. A bellow like a Pamplona bull. A thump.

I sprinted to ... a murder scene.

Steve crouched by the closet, fatigue pants in his left hand, combat boot in his right. A paper-thin scorpion carcass on the floor. A second scorpion, a tiny baby, curled in futile defense. "What kind of dump are we paying for?" A smashed baby.

Him booting carcasses toward the door. "We pay twice what Turks do just 'cause we're American, and it's scorpion infested. This whole apartment was a stupid move. The price! The basement! So you could live next to Sophie? I should've known she'd be a dingbat if she married Fortier." He kicked a wall.

I retreated. Scrubbed a sweaty armpit of his shirt.

Grandpa never blew up, not even when the milking machine broke and he had to milk the whole herd by hand, not even when Bessie tangled her horns in the barbed wire and it took him hours to cut her free, not even when....

Steve stopped grumbling about our dump long enough to snatch up the basket of wet laundry. "I'll hang these." He threw the clothesline and key on top, slammed the door.

I gritted my teeth. Jill had told me not to forget to pack the wart remover. "Steve's family's not royalty, that's for sure. Don't expect a prince out of this frog, no matter how many times you kiss him." And I was stupid enough to think she was joking.

I stormed to the fridge, yanked out our purchases from the vegetable cart, decapitated carrots, chopped defenseless potatoes.

The door opened. "Back for the cards." I didn't answer him. "Now I know what they mean about being as boring as watching paint dry. In this case, it's clothes." He obviously expected me to laugh. I didn't. "It'll take a while for them to dry. The air's really still." He waited.

I almost screamed, *How can you act like nothing happened?* I assaulted a stalk of celery and lobbed it into the pot.

"I better get out there before the clothes get stolen," he said and fled outside.

Are we to pretend he didn't act like a jerk? I didn't know then that was the typical Carmine cycle. Get angry, explode, suck up.

I plopped a Promised Land-sized bunch of grapes (kilos still confused me at the vegetable cart) into Clorox water. Stirred up a pudding recipe I'd found to mask the taste of powdered milk.

I knew we should talk. The cold shoulder was outlawed in my family. So, eventually, I slammed the door, jiggled it to make sure it was secure, slouched upstairs.

At the picnic table, shuffling cards with the expertise of a Mississippi River gambler, Steve was talking to a shepherd in Turkish-English-sign language. "Chok. Hot." He wiped his dripping forehead, "baaed" a pathetic imitation of a lamb overcome by heat prostration, flopped limply to the ground. Any other time, I would have thought he was cute.

The shepherd's eyes laughed. He bowed his covered head yes. But when he spotted me, a female, he lowered his gaze and discreetly concentrated on his little flock pasturing on scrub brush.

Steve caught my eye and mouthed, "Love you, Cindy." He winked so contritely that I thought, *Everyone has little slips of temper. I should forgive him.* After all, as Grandpa said, the best part of a tiff is making up ... and I'd had a sample of the best part.

I smiled. Steve licked his lips, suggestively.

If I'd gone near him then, I would've offended all Muslim sensibilities, so I blew a kiss and flitted to the clothesline where the comfortable scent of Tide reminded me of Grandpa's blessing, "May you always have a clean shirt, a clean conscience, and a guinea in your pocket." And of stealing sheets off the line for ball gowns for Tee and me with our dandelions tiaras. And of ...

A wet towel fastballed over my head. "Missed. You're lucky today," Steve taunted.

I tore off to mete out retribution. Through the lines, down the lane, zigging back, around again. Our perspiration dripped.

"Truce, truce," he yelled. "It's too hot for this." He plopped down at the picnic table.

"I'll let you off this time." I patted sweat beads off his forehead. He kind of shivered, then dealt out a hand of double solitaire.

"These clothes are going to take a while to dry. Toss me the key. I'll get us some Kool Aid."

I rolled my eyes. "You and your stupid key jokes. Sometime it won't be funny."

"What do you mean? 'Sometime'?" He clenched his fists. "It's not funny now. Unless *you're* doing the joking."

"*You* have the key. I saw you pick it up. You laid it on top of the laundry basket."

I expected a "Gotcha!" ... I didn't get one.

His face reddened. "That was the first time I left. I came back for the cards, remember? I set the key on the buffet for you, remember?"

"No, I don't think so." My head tingled. "Check your pockets," I suggested with a prayer.

He yanked them inside out. His eyes flashed.

No key! I stiffened, cemented to the ground by the weight of my albatross since I arrived in Turkey. The motionless clothes seemingly stiffened, too.

"Now what, Miss Smarty Pants?" His words snarled like a tiger about to tear out its trainer's throat. I snapped the whip of humor. "Move to another apartment?"

Under my armpits, the trickle of nervous sweat gushed into a river.

"You're not in Kansas anymore, Dorothy. Grow up." His face transmuted into Ed's punch-out-the-wall-because-the-spaghetti-sauce-is-too-thin face. He swelled over me. "What were you thinking?"

Who did I marry?

Loudspeakers echoed across the city, "*Allah u Akbar. Allah u Akbar.*" The shepherd unrolled his prayer rug, faced the cotton field, bowed his forehead to the ground, and began his chant. Steve paused in respect, though his body language screamed obscenities in any language.

"*Lord, help us.*" I prayed as fervently as my Muslim neighbor. And by the time he rolled up his rug, God had given me an idea. "Maybe there's a passkey." And strength. I flew up two flights and tapped, deferentially.

The door opened to a little man, about 5'4", the type of man Grandpa would label a banty rooster, "not much good in a fight, except for the crowing." He bowed formally, as if to a courtly lady. "*Marahaba.*"

Eyes to the floor, I said, "Landlord?" These weren't the best circumstances to meet him.

He nodded.

"Us no key." I hoped he understood.

"Husband, key, yesterday day." With great dignity, he pantomimed handing over a key.

I pantomimed a key lying on the other side of a locked door. My performance wouldn't have won an Oscar, but he understood. "Madame, help necessary." He followed me downstairs.

"What about unscrewing hinges?" I asked the landlord in American Sign Language, pointing at the door.

"*Yok!*" He gestured. The screw heads were on the inside.

Steve hurled the deck of cards against the wall. The landlord's mustache twitched. I scurried about retrieving cards.

Ray unpadlocked their gate. "What's the pow wow about?"

"Brilliant here locked us out." Steve's tone made me feel like Tee would have if she understood her intellectual limitations. In the background Sophie chirped, "I told her. Put that key on elastic for her wrist. I told her be careful."

Steve heaved on the door handle. The landlord yelled, "*Yok!*"

"Just break the door in, Carmine. Better yet, let me do it." Ray waddled over, huffed like the Big Bad Wolf, and braced his shoulder against the door.

"*Yok!*" The landlord gestured to the step-up into our apartment.

"Impossible to break it in." Steve kicked the wall. "The step's bracing the door."

So why all the fuss about an iron gate? I almost snapped.

"Necessary." The landlord made a twisting motion and tapped on the three bars protecting the small square window. They unscrewed from the outside.

"Toolbox, broad," Ray growled, and Sophie skittered off.

Steve hunched in front of the door like a terrorist. The landlord attempted light conversation with me. "Soon wife, babies. Holiday, Istanbul. Meeting necessary. Soon day."

Sophie set down the toolbox. I swept up a screwdriver.

"Stick to cooking," Steve mumbled through clenched teeth, totally shocking me. *How dare you treat me like this?* I flipped him the flathead, along with a look that said, "Get a grip."

Steve unscrewed the first bar and heaved it—Grandpa's magical fingers crafted scrolled maple headboards, rocking horses, tree houses, but, *Stupid me. I married a Carmine who picks up a wrench and everyone runs for cover.*

"Might want to keep track of them screws," said Ray, the sidewalk supervisor, and Steve slid them into his back pocket.

It's pretty bad when that jerk has a clearer head than you.

Bang, kick, grumble, glare. Eventually, three bars leaned against the wall and Steve was digging putty from around the glass pane. *Please, Lord, don't let him break the glass. He'll really flip.*

The landlord must've read my mind. At the precisely right moment, he reached out and rescued it.

Steve rammed his arm through the hole, did several trampoline jumps trying to reach the lock inside. Ray smirked and linked his fingers in an awkward fireman's hold. "Need a boost?"

Steve balanced, unlatched the door, jerked it open—in the movies this was where a Vietnamese tunnel rat sprays us all with machine-gun fire—the key scoffed at us from the dresser/buffet.

"Now that wasn't so bad, was it?" Sophie chirped.

Steve glared at her.

I glared at him.

"Got the ole ball and chain ticked off, Carmine." *The observation of a rocket scientist.* "Wouldn't want to be in your shoes." He guffawed and slammed their gate.

The landlord stoically inspected each bar. "Monday day. Adana. Two keys necessary," he announced and strutted back upstairs, leaving me alone with a stranger.

Steve ran his hand through his hair and grinned. "It's tough being a farm girl in the big city, Cindy, right? Have to learn about all kinds of new things." He patted my head. "Like keys!"

"If I left all for thee, would you exchange and be all to me?" *What a joke.* I turned on my heel.

Mama's words haunted me. "I'll miss you. But go. You'll make me happy by making your man happy." *There's not a woman in the world who could make this ungrateful beast happy.* I'd scrubbed laundry in a bathtub, sewed curtains by hand, waxed tile so porous it swallowed up five coats of liquid wax, scabbed both of my knees in the process. *And he shows his appreciation by acting like Ed Carmine. I don't care if his shirts ever get ironed.*

My early twinges of doubt had given way to the call-the-lawyer-now type of doubt.

Steve swooped in with the laundry basket. "I'll fold these." He sounded almost contrite. The soup had simmered down and so had he. He ruffled through the laundry. "Uh, Cindy, aren't you missing a few things?" I saw what he meant. Every flimsy lacy item gone. "I told you, a minute unguarded is all it takes for a thief here."

My chin quivered. *I could wear Nana's full cotton pants for all I care.*

"Don't worry, Cindy." He winked, misunderstanding me. "Panties we can do without."

I shot daggers. *I'm stapling my underwear on. Flushing my birth control pills, too. You won't be touching me again.* I'd been a fool to leave Tee and Mama and Jill for him.

Steve twisted a curl. His brows furrowed. "Hey, you know I'm not mad anymore, right?"

My lips tightened. *That's big of you.* He didn't have a clue.

"Actually, I was never really mad. At least not exactly. I was just—" He played with his curl again.

I stormed to the kitchen and filled the kettle. *You'd get out of my space if you were smart.* But he wasn't. He tracked me.

He started slowly. "A house trailer on base got broken into. The Turkish guard shot a woman in the head." He stopped again. "And those scorpions. And I don't have a gate for you ... and no water heater ... and Finance hasn't figured out my pay for off base housing and DW [dependent wife] ... and...." He trailed off.

Pathetic excuses! I flounced to the bathtub and doused fatigues up and down in a frenzied green blur. *You'd never treat Pam like that. Or me, when we were friends.*

"Let me do that for you," he said.

With the ferocity of a killer tornado, I twisted a pant leg, wishing it were his neck.

Steve scrubbed a shirt. "You were right, you know." He grinned, shyly. "You don't need an iron gate to keep out assailants." He chucked my rigid chin. "Don't laugh now."

I didn't. *I should've stayed with Mama. She understands me—* when I wanted a pony, Dad said, "You can't milk one or eat it or make a sweater out of it. They're not practical unless you're Amish." But Mama said, "Princesses ride ponies, don't they?"

A bar of soap whizzed past my head. "Think fast!" Steve laughed.

I ducked ... and splatted face-first against sopping soapy coarse green cotton.

"Oops!" Steve's eyes bugged wide. "I didn't mean for you to fall in. Really. Let me help."

Hesitantly, I reached up. His touch triggered Mama's advice. *Get over spats fast.* I smiled innocently and heaved with all my tomboy strength. He sprawled face-first, too. "Oops," I mocked.

And the wet laundry fight began.

In all of her fantasies in the creek, Cindy Alden had never imagined the water play of Cindy Carmine....

At the end, olive walls shimmered wet, green fatigues swam in soapy puddles on the cement, Steve stretched in an empty tub with me on top of him. "Jill would title this picture, 'A Woman Victorious,'" I said.

"Mmm huh." He wrapped me tight, sighed. "I get so upset breaking my butt for nothing. You have to scrub clothes in a bathtub and risk incineration every time you use the oven. You boil water and soak veggies in Clorox, so we don't die from diarrhea. I break up the whole place, cobbling up something that passes for curtain rods. And I broke my promise to myself and flipped out—"

"None of that matters." I swallowed his kisses and the last traces of my anger.

He took a huge gulp. "And Pammy's letter." His blue eyes pierced me. "I didn't want you to read it. Ed broke Michael's leg."

Bruises, split lips, now this! "An accident?" I asked, knowing the answer.

"Not so lucky." He ran his hand through his hair. "Pammy said Michael was too slow loosening a brake drum, and Ed jerked him out of the way to do it himself. Cracked him with a wrench. Broke Michael's femur." He twisted a curl. "Pam said Ed finished the brakes, hooked up to his Stouffer's load, and left Michael there." His eyes glued to the floor. "My temper's like Ed's."

I held his face in protest. "No, you're nothing like your dad." The gentleness of his kiss almost convinced me I had told the truth.

He'll be fine when we get home. Grandpa and Merle will keep him in line. Until then ... I'd changed a bug-infested dungeon into a homey Sugar Shack. I could change a Carmine into a man as supportive as Grandpa, as romantic as Julian.

He lifted me from the tub, picked up a towel. "Let me." He tousled my hair dry, buffed my back and legs.

I felt like polished gold.

***

Grandpa was right. The best part of a fight is the making up.

Oh, and Nana's outdated marriage manual was right, too. "The wet human body *is* extremely sensual."

Chapter 9

A Damsel Distressed

That was our first big fight. Lots of practice since then. Professionals now, I'd say. But back then neither of us knew how to deal with even minor conflict.

Steve's idea of making up was buying something—

"I got the last two tickets for the bus trip. How lucky is that?"

He handed me a travel brochure, and I ooh'ed and aw'ed over each stop—the fishing village of Iskenderun, a ruins of a sultan's castle and bazaar and mosque, snowy beaches at Pyas, the breathtaking Daphne Falls, wall carvings in the secret first Christian church at Antioch, Titus' Cave, an ancient canal carved through the mountain for irrigation and small boats.

"It would be amazing." I kissed him.

Then reality barged in, as it sometimes does, and I stepped back. "But we still don't have my allotment check, and rent's almost due. We can't go now. We'll go next summer."

"No, I owe you now. Like Grandpa McNeilly says, bills will always be here. And think of the exotic stuff you'll have to write to your mama about." Steve knew when to throw his ace.

I've ridden a school bus over rough gravel roads on ice and snow and mud, but I've never had a ride, before or since, like that one—swerving around hairpin curves on a cow path with high crowns that leaned us precariously on 90-degree inclines toward thousand-foot drop-offs. And no guard rails.

"Wow, I can't see the edge of the mountain." Steve was standing with his face smashed sideways on the window, peering as far down as he could with one eye. "Can you see it?"

I made the mistake of looking. "Allah, Allah, Allah! Save us." I moaned, only half in jest. In Western PA, next to flat Ohio, our highest points were a few sled-riding hills.

"Relax!" He patted me. "The military wouldn't hire an untrained driver. We'll get there."

Steve was right. We actually weren't in any real danger. Well, not until the bus stopped, mostly in one piece, at Daphne Falls, named for the goddess of love. According to legend, Daphne pierced the rocks with her arrows, making six falls, tiered like a wedding cake.

Of course, we couldn't just stand around soaking in the beauty. Steve galloped off to explore. Normally, I would have been right on his heels, but that day my "modest" skirt handicapped me. I fell further and further behind to where he couldn't hear me.

"Steve, wait up.... Steve."

Unfortunately, someone else did hear me. Like in a bad dream, a Turk in English riding pants seized my hand. "*Gel [come], Madame.*"

I wrenched to get free, but it was as futile as a tug of war with Steve's ruthless brother Michael. Thrashing side to side, struggling to keep my knees covered, I was the decided underdog. I resorted to negotiation. "*Yawash!* [slowly]."

He continued yanking me over slimy rocks. I felt like a bathtub boat about to be dashed to bits.

And sure enough, my foot slipped off a stepping-stone. Twisted in the mud. Stuck.

"Steve!" My scream pierced through the roar of the falls. He whirled, saw my flailing free arm, waved back, took off again.

"*Gel, Madame.*" The order was tinged with disdain. The guide to the afterlife jerked. My foot wrenched loose from the mud pit. My sandal snapped. A single band clung to my foot.

My ankle throbbed. My knees clamped together and released in a kind of Funky Chicken attempt to keep my skirt down. "*Dur! Dur!* [Stop! Stop!]" I begged Mr. Riding Pants.

He didn't "*dur*" until he'd dumped me on the platform beside Steve. With a dramatic flourish toward the falls, he said, "*Chok gazelle,*" and extended his hand, palm up.

Steve handed over lira for a tip. Mr. Riding Pants streaked off to ferret out his next victim.

Money for hazarding my life? I collapsed into nervous giggles. Fiddling with my broken strap, though, quickly sobered me up. "How am I supposed to make it down off these rocks with this?" I unfastened the broken sandal and started, barefoot.

Steve grabbed me. "You want to slice your foot into shreds?" He sounded like a disgruntled parent. "Put it back on. You're a tough farm girl." Part of me had forgotten that.

"Then give me your handkerchief." I wiped off the mud and took a few steps. My sandal flapped like a snapping alligator.

"Let me try something." Steve ripped the slimy cloth into strips and bandaged my sandal to my foot. "What do you think? Not leather, but it'll get you to the bottom of this mountain to that market, right?"

Great. More money we don't have to spend.

He practically carried me to the base of the falls. "See? I told you we'd make it," he bragged. "No more problems."

But he was wrong.

I found the perfect pair of wooden sandals, "cheap." But when Steve reached in his back pocket to pay, his whole body twitched. Wide-eyed, he checked his front pockets, his shirt pocket, then, red-faced, demanded, "Do you have my wallet, Cindy?"

"Of course not. Where would I put it?" I didn't have a purse or a pocket.

"You have to have it. Or we're in big trouble. His wallet had our IDs, money, everything. He clenched his fists.

He's going to throw something! But since it was seemingly a projectile-free zone, he blasted gravel through an imaginary goal post instead.

Oh, God! Help us! "You tipped that guy. Did you have it then?"

"The guy in the riding pants?" Steve slapped his forehead. "I don't know. Did I give him a coin or a bill?" He kept spare change in his pockets and bills in his wallet.

Coins maybe, but I'd been fussing with my sandal. I was afraid to say for certain. "Not sure. Let's retrace our steps."

"Why? It's no use. That wallet is history by now." He turned Carmine cold.

A few booths over, two Turkish police paused, spun toward us. *Did Steve gesture with his left hand. Or maybe ...*

Steve whispered, "Vacate the premises. Now." I dropped the wooden sandals on the pile but couldn't make myself move. "Look down. Start walking."

With averted eyes, we started inching away. Hobbling along in my cobbled-up sandal, I probably looked like a terrified senior citizen being escorted by an impatient Boy Scout.

One policeman sneered. The other shrugged. They slunk toward us. Goosebumps stood at attention all over my arms. "If they ask for Visas, we're toast," Steve muttered.

Do Turkish prisons have double cells? Bug spray? Anything to eat but yogurt?

The iron-muscled Gestapo look-alikes stalked us down the street. *No Merle and Denny. No authoritative landlord. Just us ... alone.*

A small museum. Steve motioned. "Duck in here. It's free."

We sneaked past the attendant, snaked deep into the exhibits, crouched beside a case of Byzantine mosaics. Steve's heart thumped against my back as we poised for flight.

No voices. No clomp of boots. Waiting, waiting, listening.... Silence.

Steve nodded. We stretched cramped legs, crept to the exit. He peered out, eyes brightened. "Coast clear." I heard a plop of a drop of hope in his voice.

We scooted into a municipal park, shadowed two American couples. "Ask these officers for help," I suggested. "They were on the bus with us."

"Maybe tomorrow," Steve said, "if we get desperate."

I was feeling pretty desperate already.

He unlocked our hotel room and moaned. "What else can go wrong?" The tour company had booked single beds. He kicked the door shut, bounced on one. "Hard as those metal cots in Basic. How do they expect us to get any sleep?"

"Wasn't planning to sleep." I wrapped around him, a desperate ploy to cheer him.

He stood like a cemetery monument. "Give it up, Cindy. Do you think pretending will make our problems go away?" His jaw clenched. "Freddy the Freeloader has more money than we do. And no one's going to welcome two Yankees down in Cardboard City."

Silence crackled between us. I escaped out onto the balcony, into the comfortable noise from the bazaar and the aromas of fresh pita bread, roasting lamb, Turkish coffee. My stomach growled, the hotel's complimentary breakfast of hard rolls, *borke* [goat's cheese], and *chi* an eternity away.

"Close the door," Steve said. "Wouldn't take much of a cat burglar to climb up this far."

"We'll swelter if I do." August is Turkey's hottest month, this my hottest day to date.

"We'll get our throats cut if you don't."

I closed the balcony door. And the bathroom's, too, stuffing the crack in a futile attempt to contain stench. A squadron of mosquitoes strafed me.

I sandwiched against Steve on that cot and calculated the total volume of sewer gas—two floors above us multiplied by the number of hotel guests on each floor. Though my figures remained inconclusive, I confirmed one scientific fact: sewer gas doesn't work as anesthesia. I dove under the sheet.

Steve mumbled in his sleep. "Wallet," "money," "prison," "Cindy."

Oh, Lord, I know I've been neglecting you. But we really do need a miracle.

The next morning, we dragged exhausted bodies onto the bus just as the driver held up a wallet. "Lost?" he asked.

I launched into an orbit of joy. "Look!"

The brown leather wallet Nana and Grandpa gave Steve as a sendoff to Basic Training.

Steve seized it with the grip of a mountain climber grabbing a back-up rope. "Thank you! Thank you!" He flipped it open with a cheer. "Our ID's still here."

Then his brow puckered. He rifled through the wallet again ... then stiffened as if psyching himself for battle. "Money? No money."

The driver turned and nodded to an entering passenger, "Marahaba. Hello."

Steve persisted. "Money? Lira? Where's the lira?"

The driver shrugged vaguely.

"Lira?" Steve insisted, then changed approaches, "*Kimo*? Who gave it to you? Kimo?"

The driver shrugged again, motioned under the bus, then turned, waved over a passerby and began a grandiose monologue about who knows what.

I didn't understand Turkish, but I understood body language. The driver knew more than he was saying.

Steve knew that, too. His jaw clenched. I clutched his arm before his fist clenched. "Nana's prayers got us those IDs. We'll be okay."

Maybe Nana's name defused the Carmine gene. Slowly, his jaw relaxed. He threw up his hands in surrender. "Didn't I tell you Americans are targeted over here? Are you catching on that your husband's always right?" He slumped toward our seat.

My galloping heart slowed to a cantor.

Back in Adana, the Fortiers bickered across the hall. In the other half of my bed, Steve thrashed and moaned, "I'll pay. I'll pay." I escaped to dreams of second cutting hay, canning tomatoes with Mama and Nana, Tee and Pam grooming 4-H lambs ...

At the first call to prayer, Steve groaned, leapt from bed, and yanked starched fatigues off hangers for his K-9 demonstration for military dependents. "If I miss that 6:30 bus, my butt's in a sling!"

I jumped and grabbed a dress.

"Where do you think you're going?" he demanded.

"To see Lux, of course"—run the obstacle course, leap for the throat of the helmeted-and-padded "intruder," rip at the gloved arm until Steve called him, "Out!" And do his tricks. Remove Steve's hat, beg, walk on two legs, and "go to hell."

"No way," Steve snapped. "What if I get stuck on base? Are you crazy enough to think you could get back alone?"

I slipped on shoes. "Boy, you're irritable." In PA, the guilt card always worked.

Here, he buckled his belt and lectured, "You'd be irritable, too, if you took your head out of the sand. It's the 13th. Finance promised your allotment check in June, then July, and it's still not here. How do we buy groceries? Propane? Pay rent?"

"You sound like Dad," the man Steve accused of squeezing the buffalo off a nickel.

"Well, now I understand him. I have you depending on me."

He was getting way too serious. I flipped my hair like Cher and held out my arms for him to join in. "But I got you, Babe." I swayed.

He stood, rigid. "What are you thinking? Even Cher admits love won't pay the rent. We can't hold out any longer. Even your sister could understand this simple thing."

I winced. I'd never heard him make such a tacky reference to Tee's retardation.

He paced. "What do I have to do? Write it on the wall? We're broke. We can't wire home like Fortier. My folks don't care. Yours don't have it after the wedding"—Mama had said, "We can't skimp. Cindy's my only daughter who will ever be a bride." Of course, Grandpa couldn't say no, not even to that perfect gown from the Erie bridal shop, though Nana could've sewn one for less.

"But everything was beautiful," I said. "Wasn't it?"

He softened. "*You* were beautiful." He ran his finger down my cheek. "You still are."

"You're prejudiced." I still marveled that he could think of me as anything but plain.

"I don't like saying no, Cindy. I'd take you if I could. You understand, right?" His sadness melted me.

"It's okay. Just hurry home." I kissed him as a promise. He left with a skip in his step, obviously anticipating his return to a little "afternoon delight."

I plotted it all out. Our laughter would skim the air like skipping stones on the creek. He'd pin me beneath his lips. I'd....

But later, when I headed for costuming, that bridal gift that shocked Nana's friends, I threw open the closet door to— "afternoon disaster."

A scorpion, bigger than a fist, curved tail poised for strike.

It twitched!

"Lord, save me!" I hurdled onto the bed in a most amazing backwards broad jump.

It strutted several steps into the room.

"Calm yourself. Think rationally." I looked down (by then I'd accepted shoes as mandatory in-door attire), but my sling backs looked pathetically flimsy. *I need something heavier, wider.*

I spied the tip of a combat boot. *That'll work,* I told myself, even though it was only two feet from the scorpion's waving pinchers. I tiptoed off the bed and, leaning like a tree branch on a still summer day, reached for the boot.

The scorpion stood on tiptoe himself.

I sprang back. *How far can that granddaddy strike? Does its tail coil like a rattlesnake's? Can it jump? Which end is lethal?* All I knew is, *That thing has to be confined.*

But my feet balked.

A great gulp of air coerced my feet into action. A flick of a pillow out of its case, a hurdle into the dining room, a bang shut of the bedroom door. I stuffed the crack with the pillowcase, added a couple of dish towels for good measure, and my feet sprinted down the hall, setting Olympic records.

"Sophie, Ray, help me. Help!" I panted as if I'd run miles instead of just yards. "Ray, please." I hammered their door. "Ray, I know you're there, Ray."

The clock ticked ... and ticked ... "Ray!"

The door creaked open a crack. Sophie hissed, "Shhh, not a good time."

I'd lost my composure but not my brains. I got her hint. But I didn't leave. "Please, Sophie." I held their door open with my toe. "I need help."

Clasping her robe, black razor cut standing up like a scared Halloween cat's, she said, "You look sick. You should be in bed, *like my Raymond and me are.*"

I persisted. "I'm sorry, Sophie. B-b-but. It's a scorpion!"

At "scorpion," she twitched like in a startle seizure and buzzed off. A pleading drone began.

I prayed. An eternity passed ... then ... at paws scuffling my way, I collapsed against the cold damp wall, my fuzzy brain clearing.

Blam! The door crashed open to Ray in combat boots and those Bermuda shorts that hung under his jiggly Jell-O belly. "Better not be no false alarm."

Padlock snapped open. Iron bashed against cement. Ray lumbered out and down our hall. I scooted around him, unbarricaded the bedroom, pointed. "By the closet."

Sophie, craning around my shoulder, spotted the foe—curled, armed for poisonous attack. Her screech pierced all of Adana. "Kill it! Kill it!" Her fingernails dug into my biceps, drew blood.

Ray whirled, impaled her with an elbow. "You *!,- ! Move your fat *!- out of here!"

She looked like a windmill, arms and legs swirling but going nowhere. Eventually, building up enough steam, she swooped out our door. It crossed my mind to follow her.

Ray turned on the scorpion with less ferocity. A cursory overview. Raised wimpy hands. "Ain't no way. One miss and he's getting *me.*"

Part of me almost ordered, "Then step aside. Hand me the boot." But that part, the Cindy Alden part, had shrunk to miniscule proportions. I gripped his arm and pleaded like a woman on the way to the gallows. "Please, Ray. It could hide anywhere before Steve gets back."

He couldn't have left without a very undignified wrestling match, so he acquiesced, "You broads are a *!# pain." He snarled an order across the hall. "Lighter fluid, woman."

Sophie released her death grip on their gate, disappeared down their hall.

"Kitchen match," he growled to me, his other lackey. I almost clicked my heels before springing for the matchbox on the stove.

He continued bellowing, "I told you, broad, lighter fluid. *Now!*" Poor Sophie, gripping the can, had frozen with one foot suspended outside their gate. Temporarily at least, her fear of scorpions seemed to outweigh her fear of husbands.

"Move, broad. I tell you do something, you do it or you're on the plane home."

Bully later, kill the scorpion now, I wanted to scream but instead, I galloped over, pried the can from Sophie's fist, and ran back, extending it like a nurse attending a surgeon.

Fortunately for me, Ray, wife abuser, turned into Sgt. Fortier, professional U.S.A.F. killer. He squirted a trail of lighter fluid on the cement and drenched the scorpion. It seemed to attempt a backstroke.

Please let this work. Please. I struck the match. Ray snatched it. With a great flourish, tossed it. I held my breath.

Flames flickered down the lighter fluid trail.... Whoosh! Fire shot toward the ceiling.

Sophie screeched. Their door slapped shut. A shivering spasm propelled me into the dining room.

No, Lord, no, Not the curtains. Not the apartment! I sprinted to the sink, twisted the faucet on full force. "C'mon, c'mon." The water trickled. I prayed every prayer I could remember, including, "Now I lay me down to sleep." The pan filled. And sloshed.

A charcoaled skeleton whizzed past my feet. "Ain't got no fire. Got a corpse." Ray guffawed. "Dead enough for you?"

He leaned in. He'd grown an inch or two taller in the aftermath of victory.

I leaned away, choking on the smell of stale alcohol and cigarettes swimming in a gallon of aftershave. "Thank you," I managed, set the pan down, and trembled to the Turkish toilet for the broom and dustpan.

Ray waddled by, kicked the charred remains out the door like through goal posts.

But he didn't strut out to dispose of the corpse. Nor did he stride out to brag to his petrified wife. Instead, he swatted our door shut. And heaved forward, trapping me against the wall. My dustpan clattered to the floor.

"Need anything else a *real* man can do?"

Irrationally, I wondered why his face didn't touch mine when his Pillsbury Doughboy body swallowed up my whole body. The back of his hairy hand scraped my cheek. "Said yourself, don't know when Carmine'll be back."

My mind refused to understand. *He's comforting me*, it thought.

A paw slid past my chin, down my neck.

He's not—my mind halted in horror. My body, alert, lurched sideways.

A finger slimed the tip of my breast.

My nipple recoiled in shock. My arms flew up, protecting the body I'd promised to only Steve. "Sophie, get over here. Sophie, we killed it!"

Steel-toed eyes stomped all over me. "Make all the noise you want, Elly May. Broad ain't coming back after seeing that scorpion." Clumsy paws buffeted me away from the exterior door. "I groove on corn-fed dames like you." A purple vein pumped in his forehead.

I locked my elbows over my breasts and pushed back. "Help!"

His sneer poked me in the face. He shoved me *another* step away from the exterior.

My screaming mind plotted how to chop him into Kibble-sized bits, but my mouth reasoned like Nana. "You'll really hurt Sophie, if you don't leave right now."

He didn't deign to answer. "Guilt" wasn't in his vocabulary. He pushed again.

"Ray, quit being ridiculous!" I grabbed onto the jamb of the American bathroom. *The nightstick will back him off.* Steve had hung one beside the bathtub.

I grappled to get to it, but it was like wrestling with an octopus. I slipped out of one tentacle and got entwined by another.

My last finger slipping from the door jamb. The scuzz smirked, "You missed, Elly," clamped my arm, twisted it behind my back.

"You won't get away with this." Me sliding down the tile.

"What are you talking about?" A blast of booze. "U.S. Government trained to protect Americans." Sliding through the dining room. "Gotta inspect the bedroom. Real close."

"Not if I can help it." Kicking him in the shins.

Him roaring and bending over, just like Steve said an intruder would. But he didn't loosen his grip. "Thought farm girls was stronger, Elly. You gonna pay for that."

My last hope. The club on the refrigerator. Calculating the optimal escape point. Jerking with every ounce of my strength.

He jostled me past the kitchen.

Latching onto our bedroom door jamb. *"Oh, God, save me. Guide my feet aright."* I focused on his beady eyes. I'd get only one chance. I tensed to inflict the ultimate attack on a male....

Then, a baby's cries in our stairwell. Rap-pause-rap! "Cindy, are you there? Cin?" *Barb! My guardian angel.*

"Don't answer." His grip pinched tight. Hard eyes threatened.

I relaxed into the pose of the conquered. And the scuzz made that mistake I prayed for, glancing over his shoulder at the door, loosening his hold a bit. I twisted free and bolted. Weight put him at a decided disadvantage for running.

I snatched open the door, and Barb practically threw Timmy at me. "I'm going to flip out if he doesn't shut up. It's like that night after *shish kebabs.* And I thought you—"

She stopped mid-sentence. I probably looked like one of those bobbing dogs in a back car window. "You okay?"

The slime, still huffing, spoke for me. "Scorpion shook her up. Old man's gone." He elaborated on the scorpion peril, casting himself as hero, of course. In a grand finale, he swaggered out, pointing to his trophy.

If I could've made a sound, my screams would've rattled walls. If my brain could've formed words, I would've screeched, "Get out, you pervert! Crawl under a rock and die!"

I squeezed Timmy in a catatonic grip while Barb examined the carcass from a safe distance. "No wonder you're shook up." She shifted, awkwardly. "I'm sorry to be insensitive. You need to relax. I'll go, Cin." She reached for her inconsolable son.

The scuzz's triumphant smirk loosened my vocal cords. "No!" I clasped Timmy in front of me like a shield of innocence.

My shriek shocked Timmy into momentary silence, as it did the perpetrator.

Then another smirk. "Back to the ole ball and chain." He waddled out, the brands of his filthy fingerprints left behind. "Clank" of gate. "Slam" of door. My legs bent like pipe cleaners.

Barb steadied me to a chair and handed me Timmy's bottle. I curled around his sweet scent, rocked and rocked, crooned Grandpa's Irish lullaby. Barb accompanied me with the rasp of her nail file. Timmy settled into rhythmic slurping.

My breathing and heart rate slowed enough for me to speak my first thought. "Fortier's a douche"—Hartstown would've been shocked.

"That's not news." Barb filed her pinky.

The story tumbled out from the scorpion sighting to his manhandling me toward the bedroom. Barb commented at all the appropriate parts. "At least the dipshit didn't burn the place down and land you in debtors' prison."

I shivered. "I don't get it. He wasn't trashed. Steve's his supposed friend. Why would he put the moves on *me?*"

A matter-of-fact shake of Barb's hair. "You come from a different world, girl. The perv's escapades at the Pound should've given you a clue of what he's capable of."

I had that feeling you get when you arrive in the middle of a conversation. My face must have shown my confusion.

She set down her file. "You do know about *that*, don't you?" Her tone sounded like the one some people use with Tee.

"Of course I know. Legalized prostitution, a jail for women to work out their sentences."

"Or their husband's sentence or their father's or brother's. A man can send any woman to pay for his crime."

It was like something out of the Middle Ages. "Sophie didn't exaggerate?"

"No, believe every lurid detail." Barb twisted her hair and tucked her feet under her. "But she doesn't know, or at least pretends she doesn't know, the worst part. The part about her so-called husband being a Pound regular."

I gasped louder.

"If no one volunteers to escort Fortier, he leaves anyway. Someone always follows. A man's defenses drop with his pants, you know. And K-9 protects its own, right or wrong."

The code of thieves.

"The perv brags he keeps Sophie so busy she'd never suspect." Barb scrunched her nose. "Can you imagine the diseases he's given her?"

I couldn't. "It makes no sense," I said. "Sophie dotes on his every move. She's the cleanest person I know. And attractive. Why would he risk all that for a few minutes of action?"

As Timmy slurped, I lapsed into humming a slow "Frankie and Johnny Were Lovers." A dead cheater seemed an appropriate ending to this melodrama, too.

Barb interrupted my thoughts. "I've been trying to figure something out, Cin. You don't worry about an iron gate. You kill centipedes and laugh at mice. Why did you think you needed that jerk's help with a scorpion anyway?"

Bam! Her question clouted me upside the head.

Marriage has made me dependent and weak. My whole life I'd protected my Tee. Now, three months without her, I needed protected myself. *I must've left my strong part home with Tee.*

Chapter 10

The Black Night

The USA's Camelot crumbled in '63 with shots fired in Dallas.

My personal Camelot crumbled four years later with a choice made in a Turkish toilet, a choice that forced me to acknowledge that foreigners don't all live outside barred windows. Some sleep in the other side of your bed.... And some stare back at you in the bathroom mirror—

The clomp of boots sent Barb and me racing outside to the guys. We circled in the stairwell for a final viewing of the scorpion's remains, and I gave a blow-by-blow report, but when I got to the point of the carcass whizzing by my feet, Barb jabbed me to stop. (She'd warned me not to tell about the perv's attack. It'd cause problems at the kennels. I'd smiled, noncommittal. Of course, I'd tell Steve every detail. And he'd know how to handle the situation.)

With the clink of the last lock, I pounced. "What's this I hear about the creep going to the Pound and you guys protecting him? Is that true?"

Steve stared down both of my loaded barrels and didn't blink. "Yeah, it's true."

"Why didn't *you* tell *me*? I thought we didn't keep secrets." Mentally I cocked the gun.

He didn't retreat. "Because it's disgusting and there's nothing you can do about it."

"But if I'd known, I would've had a clue of what he was capable of. Rape, for instance."

"Rape?" Steve's eyebrows furrowed into question marks.

Building up steam, I reached to smack closed the slightly ajar Turkish toilet door, but the sight of two commissary bags stopped me. In all the confusion, I hadn't noticed the bags being set in there. "Rod left his stuff. If you run, you can still catch him."

Steve hung his head. "The bags aren't Rod's." He almost whispered.

I crunched him in a bear hug. "Our check came!" I rejoiced.

He stood as stiff and expressionless as a guard at the Tomb of the Unknown Soldier.

"The allotment check came, right?" I repeated. This time *my* eyebrows furrowed.

"No," he answered, flatly. "I put a $20 traveler's check back for an emergency." He scuffed his toe along a seam in the tile. "This was an emergency."

"Yummy! What did you get?" I peeked in, expecting to see groceries. And my heart plummeted, like in that nightmare when you fall over a cliff and keep falling and falling and waiting to go splat against the bottom.

I rubbed my eyes. Still no peanut butter or eggs or Saltines. Just Marlboro cigarettes. Two bags full of Marlboros.

I spun around to search for an old friend behind blue eyes, but his eyes stayed fixed on Tee's hooked rug. "I borrowed some ration cards," he muttered. "Some guys owed me."

"Why?" The question was rhetorical. The answer, incomprehensible.

He glanced up with a stranger's unresponsive eyes. Not scorpions nor sexual assaults nor tiffs over keys, nothing before this moment mattered.

I launched the offensive. "You said you don't agree with black-market. Was that a lie?" That got to him. He knew in my family lying is the unpardonable sin. His jaw jutted out.

"I'm no liar." His eyes narrowed. "I said I don't agree with black-market, and I don't. But you have to do what you have to do, don't you know?"

"Like steal?" He hated that word.

"I'm not Ed Carmine! You don't know what theft is." His face flushed. "I paid full price for these cigarettes. They're *mine*." He pointed his finger an inch from my nose. "I can smoke them, I can give them away, I can smash them into a thousand pieces, I can flush them down the toilet. And I can sell them. They're *mine.*"

I escaped from that face, stormed to the kitchen, yanked apples from the pygmy fridge.

He hounded me, invaded my space, prodded. "If Turks are stupid enough to pay outrageous prices and we make a profit, what's the problem?"

"The problem is it's against the law," I snapped.

He slouched away. Quashed, probably, by my daring to raise my voice to him.

I stripped peels off apples and formulated my argument. Breaking the law is immoral. Immoral choices destroy character. And according to Grandpa, "Character is a man's most valuable possession." Ergo, black-market destroys the most important part of a man.

I covered the bottom of the pan with water as Steve barged back in, waving a stack of bills. "Maybe we should just forget these?" Electricity, propane, rent, loan for plane tickets co-signed for by Grandpa. Steve had formulated his argument, too.

"Yes, we should. Until the checks come in." *My* family believed that right was right and wrong was wrong. Money was never more important than doing what was right. "You already told the landlord that our check is late."

"So you think he'll wait forever 'cause I tell him the U.S. Government screwed up? Or maybe you're waiting for a fairy godmother to wave her wand and, poof, hundreds of dollars."

I heard the distinct tinkle of shattering illusions. Nothing had prepared me for this moment.

Plopping the pan of apples on the burner (the last of the items from the vegetable cart), I inventoried our groceries: sugar, buggy flour, powdered milk, two cans of pork and beans, a half loaf of ekmek (cost, less than two pennies. Seared in the oven in hopes of killing bacteria), a box of macaroni (home to a colony of uninvited flour weevils). I washed bugs off the macaroni.

My little peasant friends, gold bracelets flashing in the afternoon sunlight, squatted and jabbered through the bars, "Hello, Hello." Beside them, two scrawny watery-eyed ash gray cats salivated against the screen.

At the airport, Steve had warned, "You can't feed all of Turkey. We'll be lucky to feed ourselves." He'd been right. Getting to the point of having to eat *ekmek* and meat from the market downtown should have been my clue.

Steve tickled the back of my neck. "You're trying to feed us out of Mother Hubbard's cupboard." For a moment I hoped, *He understands.*

Then the gas flame sputtered ... and died.

"See?" Steve sputtered, too. "I told you so. We can't wait." His voice cooled eerily. "Or maybe Miss Goody Two Shoes has a better idea?" (His dad had used that same stage whisper at our wedding when he said, "That moron shouldn't be allowed in the church, let alone in the wedding party." I'd never forgiven Ed Carmine for that cruel insult to my Tee. And I feared I'd never forgive Steve Carmine for this.)

I glared.

Steve glared. "I never sold a dime's worth on black-market before you came over. But it's different now. I have to feed you. And buy propane to give *you* safe water." Of course, somehow it was all my fault. "Can you blame me for trying to keep a roof over *your* head?"

I could feel the rafters crashing down. Grandpa had said, "You kids are young. You can live on love." And Nana had promised, "God will provide for you as He does the birds." For the first time, they'd both been wrong.

I ran to Sophie's to heat my beans-and-macaroni concoction while she fried four thick pork chops. The slime waddled in to gloat. "Too bad your ole man can't 'ford to feed you decent."

"Macaroni and beans is an old family recipe." I leapt to Steve's defense, out of habit, I guess. "If you're lucky, maybe he'll invite you over to try it sometime."

It was a waste of good breath. The scuzz was too stupid to get sarcasm. But he wasn't too stupid to read the threat my eyes shot him. He knew I could tell Sophie everything. He scuttled back to his beer and cigarettes.

Oblivious, Sophie chirped, "I'm pregnant. Gonna put my feet up when my Raymond goes."

"Good idea," I responded, automatically stirring to the rhythm of her clacking dentures. Then, dredging up a smile from a former life and a, "Thanks for your stove," I trudged back to my dungeon.

My fork swirled macaroni into lumpy mounds. The landlord's three children, back from Istanbul, squealed up the stairs.

Steve gulped down half a plateful. "Grandpa'd say it's better than the grass his ancestors ate during the Potato Famine," he joked. Then he tilted back his chair and mumbled, "Rod arranged things for tonight with his friend." He gestured toward the Turkish bathroom. A foul odor filtered down the hall. It took several minutes before I managed to translate his words.

"Friend? As in black-market agent?"

"Yeah, about 7:00." He sort of slurred his words from then on. "Rod had it all arranged for me. Then the roster came out. I'm scheduled to fire the M-16 and 38 before post. That means I have to take the 5:00 bus. Barb's never had a problem. She handles deals all the time."

In spite of my attempt not to, I understood his plan. Too late, I understood the "H-E-L-P" Merle and Denny printed on the bottom of his wedding shoes had been an omen, not a joke.

"The Turk is just trying to keep his family fed, like me," he insisted. "Don't make it such a big deal." He used his sad dog eyes. "Can't you see we're desperate?"

I wanted to scream, "What about all those rules because we don't have an iron gate? Now you tell me to open the door for a *bush bush*?" But my dry tongue couldn't argue.

"It's simple. You hand him the bags. He hands you the lira, enough to pay for everything except the loan." To my silence, he summarized, as if to a jury, "I promised your family I'd take care of you. There's no other way. If I don't show up for firing, I'm court-martialed. If the deal's not made, we don't eat. Blame the Finance Department of the U.S. Air Force, not me."

Slowly my tongue loosened. "Do you think our neighbors in the shanties would accept our *poverty* as a reason to break the law?" I whispered. "Or that toothless Syrian woman we saw throwing dough against the inside of that igloo-shaped oven to bake in the sun?" I got louder. "Or that old woman smashing branches with rocks so she could have a fire to cook?"

"And I suppose you've never done anything wrong before?" I could never outshout him. He boomed out a list of my dirt. I'd climbed onto the porch roof to sneak back in after toilet papering the preacher's house. (The stairs have squeaky boards. Only Tee heard me.) I'd bushwhacked for parkers by the lake, placed fox urine in a teacher's desk ala the Three Musketeers.

"This isn't the same," I argued. "This kind of thing gets jail time."

He lowered his voice. "So, what would your perfect family do?" He sounded defeated, not even sarcastic.

"You know," I said vaguely. To us, hard times meant hard work. Nana had baked and fried catfish on an old kerosene stove, picked wild berries, canned vegetables, even cold-packed rabbit. Grandpa had milked twenty Holsteins and one Jersey by hand. When the neighbors bought shiny blue Harvestore silos, Grandpa patiently re-nailed and repainted our old square wood one.

Steve heard my silent message. He shrugged and did that palms-to-the-ceiling gesture.

I stared straight ahead. *Merle would've said, "Think things through, man." Steve would've listened.*

Steve cleared his throat and turned back to me.

He's changing his mind. I knew he would. He'd never involve me in anything sordid.

He said, "Rod promised me this Turk's nothing like the gold-toothed dude, but ..." He twisted his curl for almost a minute without making eye contact, then said, "I know you can handle yourself, but I'd feel better if you let me bring Barb over to help you with this, okay?"

Like I'm supposed to worry about your feelings? I grew icy calm. And resolute. "No way! I'm not doing it. I won't answer the door."

He flipped those palms up again. "You never like my ideas." He sagged forward. "I never do anything right. Maybe I should've left you in PA with your family."

Those words, more deadly than a scorpion's tail, more cruel than a Carmine stage whisper.

He stomped out, slamming the door shut.

I folded onto the icy floor and shattered. A Titanic load of girlhood dreams slipped below the ocean's surface.

Chapter 11

Eve in the Garden

I wish I could say I didn't do it. But the fact is, while the Devil's Paintbrush bloomed in PA, the Devil stained my soul scarlet in Turkey, and I learned what I was capable of. Black-market turned out to be the smallest part of it—

The knock.

My hammering pulse chiseled a deepening canyon between Steve and me.

"*Bush bush.*" The muffled call hissed through the door like the serpent in the garden.

Motionless, I sensed Nana gently prodding, *"Flee from evil."* And Grandpa, "All we really own is our character." And Jill, "Stay true to yourself." And a sea of parishioners shaking their heads in disapproval, "Tsk, tsk, you know better than this."

My eyes burned from not blinking. *I'll find another way,* I promised myself. My ears rang.

"Bush bush."

Just inches apart. A door separating us. Conflicting value systems separating us.

"Bush bush."

"Shhh," I acknowledged him and the truth. *No, our values aren't different. Neither Carmines nor bush bush play by the rules.*

I set a Carmine jaw, grabbed the bags out of the Turkish toilet, and slid the bolt. A rooster crowed for the third time. The scene blurred surreal, like a Dali painting titled "Den of Iniquity."

I peeked out, prepared for a villain's leer. But no gold eyeteeth flashed. No suggestive smirk disrespected me. An unobtrusive little man averted his face.

I stepped back and motioned him in, hovering by the door as instructed by *my* evil master. Bowing in deference, he entered.

Alone! With a bush bush! An unescorted woman and a Turkish man, alone. The stench of corruption smothered my apple blossom cologne.

The scene played out like a low-budget remake of *Ali Baba and the 40 thieves*— the lira counted, the bags handed over, the nod, the door shut behind the mustached figure carrying two commissary bags. I chained our door behind him, tried to pretend I'd been a member of the audience. But I couldn't pretend away the reality. I'd played the lead in a crime plot.

Like Eve, standing naked in the garden of disobedience, too late I truly understood the difference between good and evil. The serpent's bite throbbed with its mark of shame.

I yanked off that mistake of a wedding band, ran to the kitchen, and scrubbed and scrubbed, trying to erase that mocking birthmark promise.

I should've known we'd come to this. Cynics had warned me that a marriage between a head-bashing Carmine and a *Leave-it-to-Beaver* Alden would never work. *I should've listened to Jill.* "Stay in school. The world needs educated women." *I should've listened to my own gut. Julian was the moon-beamed prince. I settled for a garlic-eating commoner.*

My raw ring finger oozed. The mocking birthmark still there.

A water bug scuttled across the floor, but not fast enough. I crunched it into juicy crumbs. *I'll obliterate this disastrous marriage. Get an annulment. Be Cindy Alden again.* All that it would take *was* a bus to base, a Red Cross wire to Grandpa, and a plane ticket.

But how could I ask? Grandpa had used the last penny of collateral in the farm for his "baby girl's" wedding? *How could I devastate him?* He said I was Mama's last hope for a child with a happy marriage. *How could I bear everyone's disappointed eyes?* Even Jill's mother's shortest marriage lasted over a year.

I was trapped by a foolish vow I'd made in a country church. "Love, honor and obey"—*Obey? Like Steve's grandma? Forbidden to go to her own grandson's wedding?* "Grandpa Vance says a woman's place is in the home," Steve explained. "She doesn't go anywhere without his permission."

Carmine men are all alike. I fumed. *Steve wants to keep me locked up until his next whim, like those women in the Pound.*

Music from the pavilion filtered in. It sounded a little like Dad's country song, "If I Had the Wings of an Angel," about flying over prison walls. *I'm breaking out of here.*

My unread Bible shook its finger at me from the dresser, warning me not to compound my sins.

I rammed it into the bottom drawer under Steve's boxers, grabbed my key, ran up the stairs, checked both directions, and sprinted down the dirt path. I never looked back.

Barb flung open the door at our signal. "What on earth are you doing here?"

"Felt adventurous," I lied, not airing my dirty laundry.

Barb smiled. "I'd like out myself. I …" She trailed off, not finishing her true thoughts either. She swept a chair clean. "Have a seat."

"No, please. Let me help with something. I like to keep busy."

"Well, there's obviously plenty to do around here."

I navigated the piles and swooped Timmy up off a small clearing in the floor, changed his diaper and rubber pants, played "this little piggy," fed him rice cereal and a bottle, sang Grandpa's Irish lullaby, rocked.

And time flew. Until I laid him in his crib and traced his damp blond hairline. His innocence jeered, "You're as slimy as Ray. Cindy's as slimy as Ray."

I fled to the balcony. Gulped for air in the stifling heat. Demons mocked me. *Miss Goody Two Shoes screwed up. What do you think people would say if they knew?*

The stars gazed down on me with raised eyebrows.

Barb wandered out with her makeup arsenal, opened it, sat listening to the music from the pavilion.

"Remember that ice cream the guys wouldn't let us have when we went for *shish kebabs*?" She blended blue eye shadow. "The pavilion's not far at all."

The exotic melody lured like a snake charmer's pipe. I swayed. "It does sound enticing." My old values gave me a kick. "But we shouldn't!"

"Well, I'm going." She paused. "But it'd be safer with both of us." She pushed. "We'll wear scarves. No one will notice us." She waited. "I have lira. Please come."

And leave Timmy alone? I'd never crossed the street without holding Tee's hand, never left the nieces unattended long enough to run to the mailbox at the end of the lane. Besides, Steve and I had pinky sworn.

"You go. I'll stay with Timmy."

"He's down for the night. Don't worry." She searched around and found her purse. "It'll be fun. Please come."

Fun, something I won't be having with Steve anymore. I rationalized. It took me a while but I came up with, *I'm not responsible for Timmy. Barb is. Timmy's perfectly safe in his crib, but an American woman walking alone isn't. It would be wrong to risk a sweet boy's mother when I have the power to help her.*

Defiantly, I kicked my values to the curb and closed my hooded eyes. "Well, okay, if we make it fast," I said.

Barb changed into a dark midi skirt (I couldn't believe she owned one that long), twisted a scarf over her head, handed me one, and said, "Let's go while it's still light."

Like heifers released into the pasture in spring, we bounded out.

On the street, men nudged one another and pointed.

Scarves don't help, I observed.

"Here comes a pack of pinchers and squeezers." Barb said. "Remember, no eye contact."

She clutched her purse against her chest. I slid against her back and shielded my thighs and buttocks. We slithered through the crowd, alternately walking side by side and then sandwiching together when men approached. "Yankee, go home," a Turk spat.

Strangely, I wasn't afraid. I felt liberated, in charge of my own destiny, almost confrontational. Until five mustached fellows fell into step behind us. I averted my eyes.

We passed Ataturk Park with its spotlighted Turkish flag. The crescent moon and star on a red background. "Understand, necessary," the landlord had said, explaining the design represented the moment when, after a famous battle, an Ottoman sultan saw the moon and a single star reflected in a puddle of his men's blood. I trembled.

Lord, please let there be no pools of our blood tonight.

Barb, glancing back at the five, whispered, "Stay close. We need to find out if these guys are trouble."

She zipped around three old men strolling along with arms linked.

The five tailed us, dropped back, then closed in again like a pack of jackals, stalking and yapping threats at our heels.

"Well, we found out," I mumbled. "They're serious."

"No sweat." Barb gestured with her white purse, but not in surrender. "I brought knives."

I wasn't comforted. She barely weighed a hundred pounds, and I gagged cutting up a frying chicken. Besides, according to Steve, "An American who fights a Turk is a fool."

Barb picked up speed, almost galloping.

The five shadowed us, effortlessly.

Lord, we need one of Your miracles! Nana had told me all of them—Daniel in the lions' den, baby Moses in the bulrushes, David and his five stones against the nine-foot Goliath, the loaves and the fishes, healing the blind and the deaf ...

"Look. We're saved." Barb motioned ahead at two Turkish policemen. My blood began circulating again. We tucked in behind the cops. "But not too close," Barb said.

Hopefully inconspicuously, we matched our steps to theirs.

Undaunted, the five jackals made themselves the third group in our parade down the boulevard—

Finally, we slipped through the wrought-iron entrance of the pavilion. The police marched on past. We cast furtive glances behind us. The five Turks smirked, like cats when the mouse is cornered. One pointed straight at me. *Please, Father, please.*

One Turk spit. One tossed gravel. One barked an order. I scanned desperately, futilely, for a second exit.

We're trapped. I'll never see Tee again. I'll never....

Unbelievably, the five strutted on down the sidewalk. Barb retied her scarf. "We can relax now." She sounded more confident than I felt. I leaned on a table and blinked spots out of my eyes.

Barb licked her chocolate cone. "Good as Dairy Queen, but nothing can compare to those hand-dipped ones from Tony's Beach Treats." She described their hangout back home.

How can she act like everything's okay? My cone shook. I felt wimpy and weak.

It took me a while to gather the strength to talk. "People would never believe I risked that block-and-a-half of no man's land. I'm known for living safe. I normally even order vanilla."

"Well, I've got a rep for catching the big wave," Barb said. "It's why I'm with Rod and—" She seemed about to continue. Then she asked, "Was Steve your first love?"

I almost choked at the word "love" but managed to say, "No, I had a thing for my friend's older brother, Julian."

"Romantic name." Barb took another icy bite.

"Romantic guy." I curled my tongue around my forbidden fruit, strawberry. "Traveling in Europe now." I took another lick and tried to relax into real girl chat.

Barb described Ventura, CA, north of LA, and its Surfer's Point. I described Hartstown, PA, and Pymatuning Lake. Neither of us mentioned the boulevard. Or our return trip.

Inevitably, though, we stood. And like in an Alfred Hitchcock story, several tables over, a group of men also stood. My stomach dropped into a crater. "I'd feel better if they left first."

Barb shrugged and we sat back down.

So did the Turks.

Darkness encroached. Barb said, "They're not paying any attention. Let's go."

We rose, as slowly as bread dough. Took a few mincing steps.

The predators stood, advanced. Mustached sneers bent toward us.

We plopped down. Launch attempt aborted. I reminded God of the chariot of fire that He'd whisked Elijah to Heaven in. Said we'd settle for a helicopter.... Silence.

I started converting the distance of city blocks into distances between farm fields. "I think we can outrun them," I said.

"No way!" Barb was emphatic. "Two American women racing down the street at dusk in Adana? It'd be like Negroes running in some neighborhoods of LA. We'd be dead meat." *Chum for sharks, carrion for vultures, carcasses for....*

A loud proclamation in Turkish. Raucous laughter. My mind steeled to icy clarity. No one to rescue us, and if worse came to worse, no one to identify our bodies. "Then an *araba* is our only chance."

She nodded.

Rigid, we strained to hear any approaching carriage. Heartbeats pounding my eardrums ticked off the seconds. Then, simultaneously, we turned to each other.

It was no mirage. Both of us heard it. Down the boulevard, the faint clip-clop of hooves.

"Thank you, God." I bowed in adoration at the approach of the *araba*, then slumped back. "It's full," I moaned. Two elegant couples faced one another in refined conversation.

Hope glided past us. The road fell deathly quiet.

"In His time, God always provides for His people," Nana had taught us, but I suspected God's promises didn't apply to disobedient people like me.

The predators erupted in a loud guffaw. I felt my spine shrinking. Barb and I leaned together, partners in a dance of death. The group advanced, like hyenas closing in for the kill.

Black dots obscured my vision. Barb unhooked her purse.

"Wait!" My hand stopped hers. "I thought I heard something." I did!

It wasn't a helicopter or a chariot of fire, but it was empty. It leaned precariously to the right and the bony nag wheezed. But it was a carriage and it was empty.

"Wait until it's right there." I indicated the palm bordering the entrance.

She nodded. We hunched, as if waiting for a starter's pistol.

The *araba* drew parallel to the palm.

In unison, we hurdled forward. "*Arabache! Arabache!*" We outran the horse. "*Dur, arabache! Dur, arabache!* [Stop, driver! Stop, driver!]"

The *arabache* scowled, pulled back on the reins.

We dove through the air like synchronized swimmers and thumped onto the *araba* bench. "*Git!* Quickly," we hollered.

But before he could click the reins, we were encircled. The tips of mustaches like fins of a shiver of sharks, ready for the kill.

I steeled into the Carmine intimidation stance and repeated the order to the driver. "*Git!* Quickly!"

The pack leader snarled a counter command.

The *arabache* sat like a tombstone.

110

Barb's hand reached into her purse. "It's time, girl."

"Please, God," I pleaded, my faith in a God of miracles waning.

Then, "*Yok*," a voice rang out. All eyes pivoted. Out stepped a gentleman as dignified as Ataturk himself. He issued a stern edict. And miraculously, like the Red Sea for the Israelites, the pack parted.

"*Git!*" the dignitary commanded, and the *arabache* clicked the reins. The horse shook its bridle. Amazingly, its creaky bones snapped into a fast trot, leaving the group half-circled in the street, the crescent moon of promise in its most gorgeous form to date.

Joined like legs in the stocks, Barb and I exhaled held breaths. *We're safe,* I believed.

But minutes later, the nag slowed. The *araba* rolled to a stop. At the mouth of an alley! Shadows flickering over a decrepit shack. Faint hiss of air escaping from our life raft. *The perfect setting for a dual murder.*

I signaled straight ahead down the boulevard. "*Yok, yok, git.*"

The *arabache* smirked. Decades passed.

"*Git!*" I stiffened with authority.

He shrugged, tapped the nag's rump. The *araba* creaked and dipped precipitously forward.

I whispered, "If a wheel falls off, run, and don't look back, or we'll be paying for it."

Almost there. Our side street. I motioned the *arabache* to the left. The carriage turned off the boulevard and creaked ahead. Barb's brightly lit building beckoned us. I risked hope.

At her walkway. I shouted, "Dur! [Stop.]"

The *arabache* swiveled with a lascivious sneer, slowed.

I stood. *We made it,* I thought.

The "crack" of the whip. The nag side-stepped forward.

No, Lord, please, no. I stood like a monument to fear.

But Barb tossed a fistful of lira at the driver and shot from the moving carriage. "Come on, Cin!"

Her "Cin!" chiseled my feet loose. I vaulted off behind her, sprinted to the foyer where she was flexing her muscles. "A California surfer and a Pennsylvania farmer proved their mettle tonight."

Snorting giggles, we raced up the stairs, threw open their door. Wails ... *Timmy!*

Laughter whirled away like an escaped balloon. *What have I become?* I reeled. *That viper Steve has totally corrupted me.*

Barb ran for her son. "Get the bottle, would you?"

I threw open the always-closed door. I've seen cleaner barns. On the counter, cockroaches scuttling over dried mounds and into half-empty baby food jars and cans. Spaghettios, Chef Boyardee, Campbell's soup. Flies in bowls of curdled milk. On the floor, mysterious piles, the consistency of rabbit pellets. My shoes stuck to the filth like wet sneakers in a gym. The fridge. Baby bottles clung precariously to islands of mold on long-defunct leftovers.

In the other room, Timmy's howls jackhammered my soul.

A slimy sink overflowing with dishes of petrified leftovers. I rifled through it. Found a pan (lined with paper-thin crusts, something like homemade paste). Wails behind me.

Barb grabbed the bottle out of my hand. "Don't bother heating it." She poked it at Timmy's clamped mouth. He looked like a writhing stick.

Trembling, she thrust Timmy at me. "Help, Cin. Help me."

Walking, swaying, cradling him close. *Why did I leave him alone?* I stroked his velvety back. "Hush, hush. Hush, Timmy." I hummed, "Too-Ra-Loo-Ra-Loo-Ral." Hush now, don't you cry." I kicked a chair clean and rocked and rocked and ...

Gradually, wails subsided into sniffles. I teased the nipple around his Cupid's bow. A shiver. He latched on, sucked desperately. Slowly, his muscles relaxed.

So did Barb's. She re-twisted her hair tie. "Guess tonight kind of shook us all up."

I nodded and rocked. *I can't believe any of this night happened.*

Lowering blue lids, Barb said, "I guess you think I'm a bad mom." She paused. "Really, I didn't leave him alone at first. But Rod wanted to go out 'but not with that kid.' I didn't have a choice. Rod's brother loved me. Rod never did. Understand? Rod only married me because he thought he had to. I have to be careful." Her sorrow echoed loudly. "Rod never loved me."

I wonder if anyone knows what love is. I wonder why I ever thought Steve loved me. I wonder how I could ever claim to love children after tonight. I played a silent "Itsy Bitsy Spider" on Timmy's little bare arm.

"Has Steve been talking to you about the Israeli peace talks?" she almost whispered.

I shook my head no. I didn't see the connection, but conversations always seemed to come back to the Arab-Israeli problems. The "Itsy Bitsy Spider" went down the waterspout.

"Rod says they hit a big roadblock. He says they're talking about evacuation of dependents again." Barb unfastened her hair, shook it upside down. "I'm scared Rod might prefer a single bed. Or the—" She didn't finish. "If I'm evacuated even a short time, it's kaput for us. He'll hit the road and be away forever."

Away from him forever. Barb's fear, my hope. A pardon from my life sentence. A ticket back home. *And no guilt. No one would suspect a thing.*

I held Timmy close and my thoughts closer. She'd never understand my anger at Steve. She dealt in black-market and left Timmy alone all the time. She'd long ago trashed any values she'd had. *Like I just did.*

Barb broke the silence. "I guess I shouldn't worry about evacuation 'til it happens, right? After all, things usually work out. Haven't you noticed that? Like tonight."

"I guess so," I agreed reluctantly. Maybe talking would help me quit thinking. "The doctors said Tee would never walk, talk, or feed herself. She'd be nothing but a burden. They told Mama not to bother nursing her, and Tee would just die in her crib. But Tee turned out good. Grandpa calls her God's angel baby, sent by God to teach us to love without expecting anything in return."

Barb nodded at Timmy in my arms. "Well, from what I've seen, it worked."

I winced. *I'm such a hypocrite. If I knew anything about love, I would never have left Timmy. Guess I deserved to marry a hypocrite, too.*

We fell into a zombie pace, absorbed in our own thoughts.

About 11:00, no longer able to procrastinate, I trekked through the mess, settled Timmy in his crib, and headed for the door. Barb stopped me.

"Wait for Rod. The *arabache* might've sold our address."

I wavered, then said, "I have to get home before Steve gets there or he'll lecture and 'I told you so' 'til the day I die."

Barb looked at my clenched hands. "Okay, then I won't mention anything to Rod either." With a nod we sealed the familiar pact of females. "But you're not leaving alone."

"No, I'm fine. Timmy—" I didn't finish my protest.

"Don't waste your breath. Just halfway. I'll be back in a flash, not like the pavilion."

My legs moved like cement columns. My tightly gripped key ran with sweat. Gravel scattered. We hunkered down beside the doorway. A bicycle passed.

Several minutes ... silence. "It looks deserted," I whispered.

Barb stood. "It's as good a time as any." We started. A casual amble. Increased to a march—shadows lurked between parked cars, blurred into sneering stalkers, *arabaches, bush bush.*

Why did I leave our apartment? Why did I leave PA? Why...?

I gave up all pretense and bolted for the dirt path, the midpoint. Waved at Barb, yards behind me. Sprinted on. "Thud, thud, thud." *Someone's chasing me.*

I raced down the path as if pursued by headhunters. "Thud, thud, thud." They sped up, too. *What if I can't outrun him? What if I can't get our door open? What if...?*

The footsteps pounded louder ... louder. I dug down for an inhuman burst of speed. They did, too. *What if they catch me? What if...?* I refused to answer my own questions.

A leap into the foyer. I rocked back on my heels to keep from falling on my face. Whirled to assess my foe—

And saw ... no one. Craning, I saw ... nothing.

I collapsed against the door jamb, I'd bravely outrun the echo of my own footsteps, again. *Just like when we outran the "Yankee go home" boys. Didn't I learn anything?*

On the balcony across the field, Barb signaled frantically.

I waved back and spun—smack into Ray's gold-toothed *bush bush.* He ran his tongue slowly over his gold tooth.

If he touches me, I'll never stop screaming.

He leaned forward, rubbed his fingertips together. I locked him in my old "You wouldn't dare" stare. But I'd lost my edge.

Leering, he raised his hand. *I'm dog meat.*

Then a car door slammed. I ducked under his shoulder and catapulted down the steps. A mocking guffaw echoed through the stairwell.

And an aberrant thought struck me. *Now I have to distinguish between Ray's bush bush and Cindy's bush bush.*

My chest tightened in a vise grip of guilt.

Chapter 12

The Stranger in My Bed

They say that Muslim men simply declare, "I divorce you," and the marriage is abolished. Unfortunately, it wasn't that easy for Christian women—

Rap-pause-rap. The stranger slouched in and thumbed through the lira on the table. "What'd you do to keep yourself busy tonight?" he asked, awkwardly.

I glared. *How stupid can you be?*

"After the deal, I mean," he said.

The deal you arranged, you mean? The deal that could've landed me in prison or the Pound or the morgue? That deal? I fumed, but said, "Not much." I was shocked at how easy it was to tell him a bold-faced lie.

He held out a stack of letters. I dove for a connection to home, an oasis in my desert, a ship on my horizon—news about canning and third-cutting hay and 4-H lambs at the fair and Merle and Denny's move to Ft. Bragg. Jill's advice, "There'll be repercussions from that supposed six-day war, Cin. Keep your eyes open and your head out of that white sand."

If you knew the half of it, my dear friend. Jill might believe I'd dealt in black-market out of desperation. She'd never believe I'd left Timmy alone in his crib.

I reached for the last envelope. He stopped me with a light touch. "Don't let Pammy's news upset you. Everything's okay."

His leg jittered as I read—Tee'd wandered out onto the road. Merle's Dawdi Hostetler saw her, took her back to Nana in his buggy.

My fists clenched. "Tee never left the yard before," I accused. "She could've been hit by a car, kidnapped, lost"—*"Dee. Dee."*

"Why are you making it such a big deal?" He squashed a bug. "She's safe, isn't she?"

Like you'd understand safe, I didn't say. I glared missiles. He didn't even duck.

"Don't look so glum." He tickled my ribs. "Don't laugh now."

"I'm not your baby sister."

I jerked away, grabbed a stick of Grandpa's Black Jack gum. Its sweet licorice seemed to release Nana's gentle wisdom, "Forgive and forget, yourself and others."

I was so confused. *My kingdom for a phone. Jill could help me make sense of this.*

Her logic would probably go something like, "Steve was just trying to feed you. The past is the past. Go on from here." She'd probably quote Edna St. Vincent Millay, "Love is not all: It is not meat nor drink."

Maybe Steve and I can figure this out together. Maybe ...

Like a willow, I swayed toward him ... until he pulled that government envelope from his back pocket.

"I don't know if you'll think *this* is good or bad news." An allotment check, two months' pay in one, scoffed at me.

I stiffened back into oak rigidity. "I sold those cigarettes for you for nothing." My voice lowered several decibels.

I sold my soul to the Devil for you for nothing. I sold my soul to the Devil for you for nothing. The sentence pummeled my brain.

"For *us,* not me." He fired and retreated. "We did what we thought we had to do."

"You did what *you* thought." I glared.

"Do you really think that's a fair statement?" He stomped to the bathroom.

What would you know about fair? I stomped to the sofa.

Nana'd warned, "Bad company corrupts morals." But stupid me hooked up with the first toad who hopped over from the wrong side of the tracks, warts deep in his character. And Nana was right. He corrupted me. *He scarred Pam's lip with his fastball. Now he's scarred my soul.*

"Can't you understand, Cindy?" He'd returned, haunting me like a bad nightmare.

I hurled a wild pitch of my own. "Just so you know. You might've changed my name to Carmine, but next time I'll starve like an Alden before I do what you tell me to."

My voice dropped into bass register. "And another thing. I'll wipe myself with toilet paper *I buy*, not with what *you steal* from the barracks, or I'll drip dry." My fury hammered the cement blocks.

For the first time since I'd met him, he didn't have a comeback.

I paced the hall, around the dining room, back down the hall.

Jo was right. When I opened her shower gift, a scarlet-red garter belt and black lace nylons, she said, kind of sadly, "Be ready for a big disappointment." I thought she was taking a shot at our wedding night, and she was wrong. Now I understood the sort of disappointment she meant, and she was right.

"If I left all for thee" ... *"Dee. Dee."*

In her own way, Jill warned me, too. "Don't get married now. Finish college. You need to know you can take care of yourself if you need to." *"Two roads diverged in a yellow wood," and I took the one with him on it. What a mistake!*

I should've stayed with brooding philosophers in tweed. Men who quote Tennyson and Byron. I should've majored in Guys 101 before the neighborhood Jekyll turned into a black-market Hyde.

I desperately needed to talk to Jill.

I picked up stationery, told her how we got locked out and had to take the door apart. How Steve lost his temper and booked a bus trip out of guilt. How his wallet got stolen. How we came home to the scorpion and Ray's rape attempt. And I stopped.

Jill's my alter memory. If she knew about black-market and my leaving Timmy, I'd never be able to forget it. Maybe if I didn't tell her, it'd be like it didn't happen. It was all just a bad nightmare. *"Dee. Dee."*

If I don't sleep, I'll go crazy.

I crawled into bed, clung to my edge. Eventually, I dozed. I dreamed. The rescuing hero looked a lot like Julian.

"Morning, sleepyhead." My eyes slit open to reality, my villain rooting under my arm for a kiss. I jerked away. His lips smacked a cool cheek. My mind sang "Cathy's Clown." I didn't want his love anymore and surely not *his* kisses.

"I got propane. The water's boiling." He must've sneaked out to the market while I slept.

I brewed tea. Nana says, "There's nothing so bad that a cup of tea won't make better." I sipped. Nothing got better. The fragile white roots of our marriage lay shriveling in the August Middle Eastern heat. *"Dee. Dee."*

"What's wrong?" he asked stupidly.

Really? Do you want the list? I thought, but said, "Nothing."

Stupidly, he accepted that answer. The man who was supposed to fulfill my every need didn't understand the simplest things.

I traced the rim of my teacup. *If he hadn't involved me in his black-market deal, I would never have left Timmy alone in night terrors.* I had never done anything that terrible before—*"Dee. Dee"*—I was going stark raving mad.

I snatched up Raggedy Ann and a paper bag. *I'll make a visible promise.* I created a pattern, slashed a strip off our top satin sheet, cut silky ears the length of Raggedy Ann's legs and paws the size of her feet. I cut my chenille pillow sham into pieces for her body. *This will be Timmy's security, like Raggedy Ann is for Tee.*

"What're you making?" he asked.

I basted a seam. Every stitch an act of penance. *Timmy, I'm so sorry....* *"Dee. Dee."*

"Looks like a rabbit to me," he said. "Is it for Timmy?"

I turned pieces right side out. I chose those black lace panty hose for stuffing. *They're useless to me now.* But black showed through the white chenille. I switched to my flesh-colored hose.

"Bet Timmy will carry that bunny like Tee does Raggedy Ann, Cindy," he said.

I stitched. Every stitch a promise. *I will be there for you, Timmy, as long as we're here.*

"You could use buttons for eyes, right?" he said.

I almost sniped, *Timmy could choke on them if I did.* But, as stony as Mount Ararat, I stuck to the cold shoulder.

"Must be an Amish rabbit." Amish don't put faces on dolls or have photos taken, something about "graven images."

He ran a hand through his curls. Like in Simon and Garfunkel's song, silence like a cancer grew. *"Dee. Dee."*

"Does he have a name yet?" He switched on that grin of his.

I almost slipped and answered. My behavior was feeling a little ridiculous, even to me. I clipped off the last stitch.

He leapt up. "Let's take it to Timmy right now. Can't wait to see his reaction."

He probably wanted to escape. But no more than I did—

Barb "ooh"ed and "ah"ed over my creation. Rod tapped off an ash and proclaimed, "We christen thee Mr. Fluffy," then went back to his game of solitaire.

Steve hopped over piles on the floor, tickled Timmy with Mr. Fluffy. "He's gonna get you." Two sweaty blonds bowed together. *Looking so perfect. What a phony.*

Rod said, "Fortiers are running to base for some stuff." *Probably code for a black-market run.* "You two want to go or stay?"

Barb and I stayed. Barb wanted to talk about evacuation fears. I wanted to hold Timmy. *How could I have left him? Nobody better leave Tee.*

The guys' trip to base had been a setup.

The minute they returned from base, he practically dragged me back to our apartment, straight into the bathroom, of all places, and gave a triumphal, "Ta da!"

There hung the water heater we'd ogled at the AFEX, the one we couldn't afford. *Typical, Mr. Viper. Buy something.*

"Thought a nice hot bath might sound good." Grinning that grin of his. "I wonder how Turks stand ice cold water. Well, by the smell, most don't stand it very often." He shuffled a few times. "It was a great price," he bragged to my silence. "Still a little money left over, even after bills." He touched my arm. I shuddered. "Oh, Cindy," he mumbled, "don't you know you deserve it?"

Never, I silently vowed. *I'll never use that besmirched water heater.* I elbowed him aside.

He followed, doing his little-boy-pout thing. "You know I love you, Cindy, right?"

I used to believe that. My heart was as wooden as Pinocchio's. My nose would've grown if I'd said, "Love you, too."

He ran his hand through his hair, set his jaw.

I calculated days until September, 1968, my release date from this nightmare. I came up with 396 days. Each one 24 hours, 1440 minutes, 86,400 eternal seconds long. *"Dee. Dee."*

He tried again, the very next night. The guys helped him lug in a kerosene stove.

"Too bad Elly May ain't hot enough to keep you warm, Carmine." *Always the double entendre.* So certain I wouldn't break the code and tell Sophie everything.

The scuzz smirked and waddled out.

Rod blew a smoke ring. "Way I see it, man, this job will be that much easier without Fortier in our way." They measured a pipe, scraped the metal base across my waxed tiles.

Steve gloated. "Got it from a guy rotating Stateside. Cheap. Only $35." I noticed he didn't call it a "steal" like usual. "Won every cent playing pinochle."

Gambling money's so much better than black-market. He was so clueless. Fuming, I beat batter and flipped pancakes.

Typical men, they grunted and argued until, finally, Steve announced, "Finished!"

And I agreed, *Just like us.* Our marriage had curdled like the milk on the edges of the cats' bowl.

With a "Later" and a plate of pancakes, Rod left me alone with the stranger who was strutting around what looked like a metal barrel. "Really lucked out to find this." *What an eyesore.*

I had to know. "Why'd you store that nice shield in the Turkish bathroom instead of installing it?"

At the sound of my voice, he practically gushed. "To maximize heat. It doesn't snow here, but winters drop into the 40s and no central heating, you know?"

If I knew anything, I wouldn't have married him.

"But watch Timmy when he starts crawling. If he gets too close, he could get burned."

Same goes for you. Stay back if you know what's good for you.

The big man lectured. "It's easy. Turn the switch, let the fuel flow in, make a paper wick, light it, and throw. See? You'll be toasty in no time." He grinned, waited.

It's complicated and dangerous. I'll never use it, no matter how cold I get. I tramped to the kitchen.

He bounded up to follow and, "whap," hit his forehead on the pipe they'd run into the chimney. Rubbing a growing red spot, he added, sheepishly, "Oh, and make sure you duck."

Make sure you get a concussion, I stopped myself from saying, but my disdain must've shown.

He sighed. "I can't do anything right. Maybe I should've left you with your family."

I didn't disagree. Grandpa said, "Be careful. You only get one chance to do it right." Steve had had his chance.

My tongue felt like I'd been licking the salt block, porous from cows' tongues. Unlike McNeilly cows, I was not contented.

After several weeks, he confronted me. "Can't you let it go, Cindy?" He'd seen way too many sitcoms. Lucy and Ricky always resolved issues in a half hour minus commercials.

He pushed. "Can't you forgive me? Can't you?" His piercing blue eyes drilled through to my teaching, forgive 70 X 7.

No, I thought, *no.*

Nana's Bible verses hammered at my skull. "Let not the sun go down on your anger." "Turn the other cheek." "Go the second mile." "Forgive us our trespasses as we forgive those who trespass against us."

I slumped under the barrage. *I can't forgive this. I'd never put him in the position he did me. I'd never drive him to the point that he'd do something as bad as leaving Timmy alone.*

He touched my ring finger. "Please forgive me, Cindy. I'm sorry."

I flinched. I'd never heard him say "I'm sorry" before. Pam said I'd never hear him say those words. Carmines weren't allowed to say, "I'm sorry."

Nana whispered, *"You know what's right, dear. You can do it."* I lifted my eyes. *"That's right, dear. You can do it."*

His blue eyes begged me. "Please?"

"You're your mama's last hope for a child with a happy marriage." Grandpa reminded me.

And before I knew it, "I'll try" popped out of my mouth.

He jumped and held out his hand. "Pinky swear?"

I shrunk back.

"You heard what you said, dear. You said you'd try."... *"You're your mama's last hope."*

122

I know. I know. I have to try.
I forced my little finger to loop his.
He suffocated me in a sweaty bear hug.

Grandpa had warned, "Don't depend on your mama's happily-ever-afters, Baby Girl. Catholic fighting Protestant, Protestant fighting Catholic. All that fighting drove the fairies and leprechauns plumb off the Emerald Isle. If there's no magic left in sweet Eire, there's surely none in Turkey. Get ready to put on your work boots and make your own happiness."

So for three months, I got up, put on my work boots, and tried.

First, I tried Mama's method, play. She'd puff away a dandelion's white fluffy head and say, "Blow away your troubles," then flop back and play "make believe" about clouds. So, I taught four-year-old Zu-Zu that staid Dancing Bear number and played Korebe. I was always "ebe" [it]. I sang Tee's "Jesus Loves the Little Children" to the peasant children over tea parties of cake and Kool-Aid. (They bowed as if I'd served scones and clotted cream.)

I tried Jill's method, learn. I browsed magazines at the base library (*Newsweek* articles on race riots and burning cities from Boston to LA, the *Times'* analyses of Vietnam and the Middle East, even an old *Look* series on the crumbling of Camelot in '63). Checked out stacks of books I'd always meant to read. Visited the landlady, puffing on Marlboros like a high school girl in a bathroom stall, and she taught me about the Whirling Dervish, the Spoon Dance, the Evil Eye, Turkish cuisine (my favorites, a stew made with a ground lamb stew and Turkish Delight), and politics. (Interestingly, she said the Turks believed JFK's assassination was masterminded by LBJ because he didn't declare a long-enough period of national mourning.)

I even tried Grandpa's and Dad's method, work hard. I slaved over that green linen tablecloth and babysat Timmy (though I knew I could never make up for *that night*). Scrubbed until I'd memorized every speckled tile, every crumbled hole on the walls of my prison. Sifted weevils and baked. Fried up pale ground meat for casseroles. Bought cheap yarn to knit 29-inch-long scarves and wool socks for Christmas gifts. (I wished I could buy a meerschaum pipe for Grandpa, copper etchings for Mama and Nana, Kurdish dolls for Tee and Pam, suede for Jill).

That stranger I lived with watched me busy and quiet, trying hard, and assumed black-market was in the past. At the Carmines' if they weren't screaming or punching walls, all was well.

He didn't question why I wrote daily tomes to Jill but never shared one simple thought with him. (Trying to explain feelings to him would've been like trying to explain color to a blind man.) Or why I traded my flimsy nightie for his T-shirt, swapped out satin sheets for cotton ones, submitted to his advances like a woman at the Pound, smiled when I popped birth control pills.

"Can't wait to get rid of those and keep my promise to Pammy," he said. (I was thanking my lucky stars I hadn't grown up Irish Catholic with its prohibition on contraceptives. I never wanted to pollute this earth with another Carmine gene.)

"What happened to our wedding picture?" he finally noticed. (I'd covered it with a photo of Tee sorting her buttons on the farmhouse stairs.) "Needed the frame," I said, using my new skill, telling him bold-faced lies. He never questioned.

But inside it kept festering. Like when one of those long thorns from a crabapple tree gets in your heel and you dig it out with tweezers, but a piece breaks off and the skin grows over it and every step you take drives a sharp pain into your foot, and eventually it breaks open.

That's what happened one October day when the Nova rumbled away, and Sophie called, "Yoo hoo," breaking the scuzz's obvious prohibition on seeing me alone for fear I'd squeal on him.

Curious what had made Sophie so bold, I grabbed my tablecloth, half cross-stitched by then, and a plate of cookies. Like before, she sprayed my path in, picked up a tumbler of rum and Coke, and rambled into a monologue.

"I'm scared. The Arabs might start up again. They'll send us home." Her fear of evacuation, her latest incomprehensible phobia. "I can't be separated from my Raymond. I need him."

As much as I need head lice. Like before, my internal monologue of snarky comments began.

"He ain't never happy. I try and try, but—" *Tell me about trying!* She gulped her drink. Unconsciously, rubbed her arm. And I saw what had changed.

A fist-shaped bruise. *A bad one!*

My horror must have shown. She rushed to the scum's defense. "He didn't mean to do it. I was backing away and I'm such a klutz. My Raymond grabbed me to keep me from falling. By accident, he kind of hit me. It was a mistake."

I nodded noncommittally, suppressing my desire to shout, *You know that's a crock. It wasn't a bump and a grab to stabilize. It was abuse.* But even acknowledging the bruise was a first for Sophie.

"Booze sometimes gets him a little rough." She took another gulp of rum. "My Raymond sobbed and begged me to forgive him. He said he didn't mean to hurt me. Said I was his everything."

That sounds like one of Julian's lines.

"My Raymond said he wants a kid so bad it made him get crazy drunk. If I told him he had to give up booze, he'd do it. For me. So he wouldn't get crazy again." Another gulp of rum. "It hurts me to see my Raymond upset. I can't stay mad." Her dentures clacked rhythmically. "I held him and told him how sorry I was for upsetting him."

You apologized to him?

"He promised me a dozen times he'd never slip and do that again. Not even if I deserve it." She pondered that a moment.

I stabbed an X in green linen, wishing it was Fortier's manipulating face.

Bruises for now. What next?

Forgiving 70 x 7 made sense around the great oak table, but here it was masochism, insanity, like using perfume to cover B.O.

How stupid can she be? Sophie needed to face truth. *It's time to tell her that manipulating abuser of hers put the moves on me.* Maybe she'd smarten up and leave him.

I opened my mouth to tell her. But then I saw myself— holding bags of cigarettes, upset and running to the pavilion with Barb, leaving Timmy screaming alone. Because of my manipulator.

If people knew, would they wonder why I stayed, too? Would they say forgiving a Carmine makes me no smarter than Sophie?

Silent, I gouged X's in green linen, pretending it was Carmine's treacherous face. My abscess of anger throbbed dangerously.

Then, the final straw. He clomped in with a letter from Jill.

She opened with a delightful tale about going to a job fair at Wisconsin U. to protest Dow Chemical Company's manufacture of napalm. Then she got to her real point: "Your family won't risk upsetting you, Cin. But I don't want you blindsided. So here it goes."

Short and to the point, the news building in intensity—

1. Jo was job hunting. "She says next fall when Hayley's in kindergarten, Sean will be free to spend the rest of his life with his mistress, the bottle. She won't let the girls visit your farm anymore. Doesn't want them so attached to your family when she splits from Sean." *It was just a matter of time.*

2. Pam was hanging out with Michael's friend. "That guy's bad news, but don't worry. Your grandpa and nana are talking sense to her. She'll listen." *Pam better listen.*

3. Tee had a grand mal seizure. *I can't believe it!* "She's okay. Just bumped her head a little on the door frame. Dr. Franley prescribed Dilantin, but it takes a while to regulate. You know how those things go." *If I hadn't left her alone, Tee's seizures wouldn't have escalated from petit mals. "Dee. Dee."*

4. Then. "Now don't freak. Your mama found a lump." *No! Not again!* "Dr. Sherman says it's a cyst. Nothing to worry about. I'd tell you if it was, you know that." *Nothing to worry about? "It" was supposed to be in the past.... Mama.*

I crumpled that obscenity of a letter. *What am I doing over here when everyone I love needs me at home?*

That's the day my abscess of repressed resentments erupted and I quit trying.

I can't fake it 300 more days. I have to get back home. Now.

Miraculously, within the month the perfect escape route opened up.

Chapter 13

"Be Ye Thankful"

It wasn't the Arab-Israeli problem that was my hope after all. (The Middle Eastern issue dragged on and on.) It was a fresh political tension that erupted between Turkey and Greece over the Greek Cypriot National Guard killing of 27 Turkish Cypriot villagers in Cyprus, an island less than fifty miles from the Turkish mainland. Sudden and volatile—

The landlady and I were enjoying baklava and tea when her husband barged in. "Soon—war! Fighting necessary." He strutted around the apartment, ranting on about the Greeks. I could barely contain myself.

This has to be it. Evacuation at last.

When he lapsed into total Turkish, I excused myself and dashed down to flick on Armed Forces Radio, hoping for the scoop, though I suspected it was probably a waste of time. AFR hadn't even reported on the Arab-Israeli War in June. They broadcasted nothing that might jeopardize our welcome in Turkey, strategic to the USA for a staging base to the Middle East and to the USSR—the Bosporus Straits by Istanbul were Russia's only way out from their Black Sea Ports.

Typically, not a word on the radio about Cyprus. I had to wait impatiently for that stranger I lived with to deliver the news.

"The Turks are moving huge convoys of men and supplies. Lining the taxiways with F-84s and F-86s. They're really serious about this thing."

Yes! I knew it. Evacuation! My hopes did a cartwheel.

Stupidly, the stranger misinterpreted my expression. "Don't worry. Everyone says we're pretty safe this far east."

"I don't see the logic." I managed to hide my scorn. "Adana's the closest city to Cyprus."

"No, I think Mersin's closer." He twisted a curl. "No, maybe Adana is." He shrugged. "Either way you have to admit there's nothing in Adana worth blowing up, right?"

"What about the base?" *And he wants me to believe he's always right?*

He gave that stupid look of his. "Well, whatever. Anyway, it's the Turks' war, not ours."

I could've said, "Vietnam isn't our war either, but that's not keeping Americans from returning home in body bags." But arguing with him wasn't worth my energy anymore.

"The commander distributed these." My mistake-of-a-husband handed me a bulletin from the U.S. ambassador, written in Doublespeak. It jelled down to, "We're about to be bombed off the planet, but maintain courage."

"He ordered us to have our families pack essentials in readiness. They're evacuating dependents at any hint of local danger."

Finally. A free ticket home. I rejoiced. Though not even a hint of a smile betrayed me.

He ruffled my hair. "I married quite the trooper."

He hadn't understood me for months. Maybe never.

"Bet Garza and Fortier don't have it so easy telling their wives. Bet Barb and Sophie freak."

I bounced to the Turkish toilet for a suitcase. *I'm coming home, Tee, Mama. Back to "yesterday," to tie dye and bell bottoms and party lines. Back to where school begins with the Pledge of Allegiance and the Lord's Prayer, and ...*

Thanksgiving Eve, Incirlik AFB on high alert, Adana in a mandated blackout—all windows completely covered, only low-voltage table lamps, foil-shaded to reflect light straight down. Everyone was holding their breath. Out of the entire population of 290,000, I was probably the only one praying *for* war, not fearing it. My packed bags squirmed excitedly in the dark hallway.

Wind whipped off the mountains and whistled through the cracks. Dank cold permeated walls and bones. Holding fast to my vow to never use that vile kerosene heater, I huddled by the warm oven, folding paper napkins for a pre-evacuation Thanksgiving dinner for us wives.

"Dear Father." I stopped. How do you beg a God of peace to start a war for your own personal agenda? How do you pray for deliverance from a husband you've promised to love 'til death?

I fell back on the rote list. "Father, let Mama's lump be just a cyst. Bless Tee, Nana, Grandpa, Jill ..."

My words bounced off the ceiling, back onto my shoulders. "Thud, thud, thud, thud." I startled. Yellow napkins scattered across speckled tile. *Those thuds are outside!*

Marching. Heavy rhythmic in-step marching. *Soldiers? Police?* Synonymous in this oppressive land. My heart thudded in double time.

Then ... my worst nightmare.

The footsteps clicked to a halt. Outside our kitchen window. *No! Not here!*

My shallow breath puffed softly. The black silence shouted threats. Several eternities passed as I concocted explanations—smoking, resting, urinating, checking the path.

I'd almost convinced myself their stopping had nothing to do with me when—

A stern bass voice exploded out of the tomb-like darkness. "*Yok!* Ampul. *Yok!*"

My mind grappled with the slippery words. *Yok.* That meant "no." *Ampul* meant "light" or "electricity," I couldn't remember which. But "No, light, no*,*" didn't make sense. I had one tiny foil-shaded bulb in the dining room. Not possibly visible from outside.

He's talking to someone else, I argued with myself. Then, "Clang, clang, clang" on *our* kitchen-window bars.

I twitched once, then paralysis.

Rap! A single bar, like a conductor signaling his orchestra. A cacophonous bass voice, "Police! *Ampul!*"

I could say terror gripped me, but that's an understatement. I could say my heart leapt into my throat, but that's trite. So, let me just say my complete memory bank emptied, except for one file, "Horrors of the Turkish Prison by the River." That one fused my motor nerves.

My feet sprang onto the counter. Apple and pumpkin pies teetered on the window ledge. I groped along the side of the tacked curtain. *This is it!* A slight gap. *That space, the oven door open, the gas flame exposed.*

Fumbling with pins, jumping down, twisting lead-heavy vise grips, whacking oven door closed. "Sorry," I croaked to the darkness, attempting to sound "cooperative," "demure."

A deathly hush ...

"Okay?" I pleaded. Every Turk knows the word, okay.

Silence ... Flashback to the TUSLOG bus. The two policemen clubbing the peasant man.

"Gule, gule." I choked out my "good-bye." Hoping to be labeled "useless," "subservient," "pathetic," too unappealing for the Pound. (Though, according to Sophie's sources, imperfections didn't deter government-forced prostitution.)

A muted shuffle. A guttural growl. Exchanged mumbles ...

Please, God!

Shuffling boots. Purposeful clicking down the sidewalk ...

Please, God, please make them go away. Black dots threatening my consciousness ... *Please, God.*

The clicking slowing. Near the foyer.

No, keep going.

It stopped.

Not downstairs. Don't come downstairs, I begged Heaven.

Silence ... A distinct whine.

A fighter jet. The Greeks bombing Adana. They honed in on my light. I've aided and abetted the enemy.

I flexed to run ... but to where?

No due process. I'll rot in prison. My packed bags will mildew in the hall.

I calculated sentences. In ten years, Tee'd be thirty-three. Twenty years, Mama'd be on Social Security. Thirty years, Nana and Grandpa'd be buried.

The jet droned louder.

I won't unbolt the door. I'll wait for the American Consulate. No one can break in without unscrewing the bars. I grabbed a billy club. *Failure to cooperate? How much will that tack onto the sentence of a hated Yankee?*

Thump, thump. A boot kicked the step-up to the foyer. I fell flat on cold marble tile.

Oh, God, can You hear me in this strange land?
Stone silence. A century passed. The tile swimming with clammy sweat ...
Thump, thump ...
Oh, God, I know I've messed up. But please. For Tee, Mama, Nana. Save me!
Shuffling ...
Lord! I stiffened in the first stages of rigor mortis. *Please!*
Click of heels ...
I'll be yours forever.
Cadence of marching ... marching ... marching ... ?
Lord?
Marching away? Not down?
Lord?
I strained ... *Yes*, softer ... less distinct ... fading ... A hush?
No boots ... no planes ... the city not even breathing. A trickle of blood braved my veins. Marble under me, warming.
Maybe I just freaked over the police. Maybe it wasn't a plane engine. Maybe it was my ears ringing. Maybe—
"Maybe it was an answer to prayer, dear." A vision of Nana shaking her head in disappointment caught me with my lack of faith showing.
Repentant, I blurted out, "Thank you, God." I collapsed against the warm oven, gobbled half the cinnamon twirls I'd made for Timmy from leftover piecrust.
I shook.

Dawn. The muezzin's musical chant calling the faithful to prayer interrupted the fitful dozing of one very unfaithful one.
I inched out of the igloo of coats roofed with Nana's crocheted bedspread, untacked the curtains. *No cops.* Just an old peasant, surrounded by his scrawny goats, bowing toward Mecca, the sacred city to the east.
My heart turned toward Hartstown, PA, my sacred town to the west, and to another old man surrounded by his sheep and cows.
Surely after last night, they'll fly us home. I'll be home in time for the first piece of candy—on Thanksgiving and every Sunday until Christmas, in a type of Advent ceremony, Grandpa let us choose one piece from a six-pound box of Brach's Assorted Chocolates. I helped Tee pick the creams. *"Dee. Dee."*

That so-called husband of mine said we couldn't afford even the tiniest box of chocolates at the AFEX.

I relit the oven, mixed and kneaded dough. In the picture on the wall, Nana smiled through a cloud of flour dust. Wispy gray strands escaped her hairnet-covered braids. *I'll tuck in between Tee and Sean,* my place at the great round oak table.

Just as I set the rolls to rise, the clomp of familiar boots and, "Pop! Whoosh," the puncturing of all my hopes.

No, it can't be! I unchained the door.

"They canceled tonight's blackout exercises." He beamed.

No! I slumped over from the stab wound to my heart. *I was coming, Tee. Honest. I was coming home to you.*

I bled out while the guys hung in the stairwell, bs'ing. "Turks don't put up with crap. Even Greeks know that. Probably why they backed down, don't you think?"

"Ain't worrying 'bout why. They all grease balls."

"Dumb Turk almost had the Captain delivering condolences to our widows, man."

"Can't believe that pilot panicked like that. His head hit that canopy so hard I expected to see eyeballs rolling down the runway."

They all had a good laugh over that.

"Well, man, bad day for the Turk, but good one for us. Sounds like new peace talks stopped all that evacuation talk."

No, I can't stay trapped in this rat hole with these people.

"Got room for three more, Cin?" Rod looked like a salivating alley cat. So did the scuzz. "Slop at chow hall ain't fit for a hog."

"Everyone's welcome. Right, Cindy?"

I almost puked. He always assumed he knew what I thought.

"Cindy could feed half of Adana with our leftovers."

As the guys left for their places, my heart wept, mourning the loss of the governor's pardon I'd been so sure of.

He tramped in, invading my space. "What a stinking night." He might have expected me to ask questions, but it'd been months since I'd cared what kind of night he'd had. He told me anyway.

"A Turkish fighter plane crashed-landed on the north taxi-way. Just missed us." He pulled off "Eskimo" parka, muddy fatigues, two pairs of long johns, filled the bathtub with steaming water from that illicit heater of his. "The transport driver saw those landing lights and freaked." He acted out the driver spotting the ball of flames in the rearview mirror and swerving. "Can't believe the metro didn't roll when we hit the grass."

I didn't respond.

"It's a wonder anyone has any eardrums left, between the yelling and those afterburners."

I managed an "Uh-huh" and thought of my Tee.

"How'd the blackout go?"

I shrugged. It'd been months since I'd shared my night, even with police involved.

Peace talks worked? No evacuation? It has to be a lie.

He escaped to a nap, soon spewing out incoherent ramblings. "Move it! Move it! Duck!"

I shaped dough into cloverleaves, peeled more potatoes. *Nana could stretch any meal with potatoes*—mashed, boiled, scalloped, fried, soup, patties. I carved orange rind baskets for the fruit salad. The lump in my throat strangled me. *"Dee. Dee."*

The couples arrived.

"Smells heavenly in here," Barb said. Timmy squealed and reached for me. "Ma, ma, ma, me." *His absolute trust in me.* I pushed back the guilt. *"Dee. Dee."* Rod lit a cigarette.

Fortier clutched a bottle of whiskey in one hand and shoved Sophie in with the other. "Cops last night got me scared," she chirped. "Slid the bed 'gainst the door and hid."

The scuzz shoved her down our hall. "If you knew how to chill, broad, you'd be knocked up by now. Learn to loosen up." He deposited his wife and his whiskey bottle at the table and swayed to a stop in front of Barb.

"Bet those jugs keep you floating in the Pacific." He ogled Barb's breasts and belched.

Barb shot him poisoned darts, spun on her heels. Rod searched for Timmy's blocks in the diaper bag and pretended not to hear.

The perv staggered over to me. "Mmm! Hot buns." He sized up my hips. "Gonna share, Carmine?"

I braced for the explosion.

"You better be talking about those rolls you smell, Fortier, or you'll be gumming bologna across the hall." Carmine stiffened, inches taller, and the scum simpered, "Don't need no threats."

Nana's wrong. A full table doesn't always make a happy holiday. I rushed to carry out chicken, stuffing, mashed potatoes, corn, Jell-o salads, sticky buns. I had to duck each time under that pipe to the chimney. But then squat thrusts are good for the thunder thighs. *Let's get this over with.*

"Come eat, everyone," I called like Nana. *Grandpa would've added, "Soup's on."*

That Carmine-mistake-of-mine sat at the head of the table and sniffed. "Hey, you know what I don't smell? Sauce."

What an ingrate. Grandpa would never complain. Even if a biscuit was as hard as a hockey puck, Grandpa would say, "Better than snowballs," or "My ancestors fed their babies grass during the Potato Famine." Carmine dodged the daggers I shot him.

"Forget I said anything. Our traditions are just different, right? For us it's a big pot of pasta and a big fight."

I would've gladly accommodated him in the big fight tradition. I reached for solace. "Let me hold Timmy, Barb. You eat."

"You have to be tired from all that cooking," she objected as she handed him over.

I hummed, "Too-Ra-Loo-Ra-Loo-Ral," spooned him mashed potatoes, and moved morsels around on my plate like pieces on a checkerboard. The guys rehashed the crash, "A ball of flames!" Sophie and Barb chattered on about the blackout, "Cops on the stairs." "Expected to get axed."

I drifted back home—Grandpa and me fishing over the iron bridge: "Tell me about the war," I begged. "Tell me about the Battle of the Marne."

His bobber sank, he jerked, and the bluegill eluded his hook. He eluded mine. "I'd rather talk about those bobwhites scooting across the road."

Tipping my straw hat to watch the birds, backs straight, heads proudly erect, I didn't give up. "They look like tin soldiers."

"You're right, Baby Girl. Soldiers. Right here in PA. Plenty enough excitement right here in Amish country to last a lifetime." Prickly stubble on my cheek. "Plenty enough love, too." As usual, Grandpa had been right.

I have to get home. Fast!

The perv pawed a third sticky bun. "Uncle Sam's stingy with the dough. Without a good *bush bush,* no Christmas. How about you, Carmine? What're you getting Elly May?"

All I wanted was a one-way ticket home.

"Looks to me like your old lady's needing a little bit of entertainment to put a smile on that face, Carmine."

My "mistake" leaned forward, tensed his jaw.

Perv dropped back. "What's wrong with you? Talking about a good price on tape players at the AFEX. Music entertainment."

Rod jumped to the rescue. "Hey, Fortier. A Turk at the market's selling turquoise and silver real cheap. Good stuff, too. I'll hook you up."

I bolted to the kitchen, cut pies ... *Grandpa's mincemeat pie topped with freshly churned vanilla ice cream, an extra sliver for Laddie. "Come here, me wee colleens." Tee and the nieces scurry onto his lap. Grandpa's spoons. Mama's fiddle. "Geese in the Bog" and "Blarney Pilgrim." Sean shouts, "'Whiskey in the Jug.'" Mama slides into "I will never play the wild rover no more"* ...

Fortunately, Fortier believed in the old "eat and run." Or in this case, "eat and stumble." "Time for some real action." Our door slammed shut behind them.

I set Timmy on the floor. He took off like an Army man pulling himself through an obstacle course, feet fishtailing behind him. *Nieces ... Tee.* I handed Timmy down a cookie, started cleaning the table off.

Rod launched into a story about Fortier tying his dog, Rex, to the Concertina wire and walking away to deal with a *bush bush* over the fence—Turks refused to deal anywhere near dogs.

Rod can really tell a good story. Barb and I laughed as hard as the guys. Rod ended with, "Rex got so tangled in his leash, he almost hung himself before the fool got back."

"His wallet always rules his common sense." That mistake-of-mine acted so astute. "How would he have explained a dead dog?"

"A bottle of Jack Daniels would be enough explanation for Sarge," Rod said. "The guys with the brains would be the problem."

"Then Fortier would be okay. Anyone with brains isn't in the Air Force." *Typical Carmine statement.* He tweaked Timmy's cheek. "Kind of cool down there, little buddy?"

He walked over and flipped the switch on the heater, rolled up paper, lit it, dropped it into the kerosene streaming into the firepot. *Maple logs crackling and settling in the Franklin stove.* "It'll be warm in a minute, buddy."

He picked Timmy from the floor and tossed him into the air, then scrunched that nose of his. "Someone here needs a change."

Barb searched her diaper bag. "Forgot the diapers and, you're right, I can smell him from here. Guess we better head home."

I panicked. "Oh, no, stay for cards." *Jill and Pam and the guys stopping after oyster stew at Dawdi Hostetler's. Monopoly, Chinese checkers, Clue.* "I have an extra dishcloth to use for a diaper." No sacrifice too great to avoid being alone with him.

"Groovy solution," Rod said, "but I need a nap after that spread. Best I've ever had." He sounded sincere, but he'd never had Nana's rolls. Or her pies, crust flaky from lard, four-inch-high meringue.

"I'd wear two sizes bigger if I ate like that often." Barb wiggled Timmy into his sweater.

Rod sucked in a plume of smoke. "Still can't believe all that pilot needed was an aspirin for a severe headache, man. Guess fact *is* stranger than fiction." He blew another smoke ring. *Sneakers crunching over unraked leaves.*

The guys squabbled over how much the crashed F-86 cost. Rod concluded, "Not sure, man, but less than the cost of that whole squadron"—Rod was referring to the base legend about the U.S. gifting Turkey a squadron of old F-100s. In the "if Allah wills it, there's nothing you can do about it" view of safety, the Turks took off without training in the "much faster than they were used to" jets and flew in perfect formation, "bam, bam, bam," into the side of a mountain.

Barb zipped Timmy's jacket and fastened his hood. *Tee's pink snowsuit.*

Rod snuffed out his smoke. "Better get booking. Kid'll be sweating, all bundled up like this." Rod got a puzzled look on his face and stretched his fingers over the heater. "It's not even warm, Carmine. Something's wrong."

Something wrong?

That mistake-of-mine peered into the heater, then slapped his forehead. "Fuel didn't catch." A pond covered the firepot.

He switched off the fuel and twisted a napkin. "Toss me a lighter, Garza."

"Don't know, man. That's a lot of kerosene."

"Wait!" I cried. "I'll get a rag." I fled to the Turkish bathroom.

"You worry too much. We don't have all night." He flicked off the fuel supply, lit the napkin just as I ran back, shouting, "Steve, don't!"

Too late. He already "did." The napkin wick landed in the kerosene and whooshed up into a lake of fire.

"It's your life." Rod shook his head in disbelief. "One thing's for sure, man. You won't be cold much longer." He bustled Barb to the door.

"Thanks," Barb called over her shoulder. "It was real special. I'll always remember my first Thanksgiving away from home."

So would I.

Timmy waved Mr. Fluffy in an empathetic good-bye. The door slammed—

He flashed that smile of his. "Not too bad for your first holiday meal, I'd say."

"Not bad?" I pressed.

"You know what I mean. It was good." He lowered his eyes, perhaps sensing he could do or say nothing right. He tried another approach. "Want me to help you clean up this mess?"

"I have all night." I eyed the heater. "Besides, I'm used to cleaning up messes."

He looked quizzical, as if not quite sure if I'd alluded to black-market or not. He let the topic drop, tried another. "If the guys had been here, they could've cooked rabbit today."

I knew what he meant. Rabbit hunting Thanksgiving morning was one thing Carmines did together, other than fight, of course. And in survival training, Merle and Denny learned to roast meat under a number-ten can with a flash fire and pine needles. But I didn't comment. His efforts were too little, too late.

"Remember how Zeke ends up running the rabbit backwards?" He mimicked the beagle getting the scent and taking off, the rabbit taking a sharp turn, Old Zeke going straight, then running straight back to them because he missed the trail again.

I was thinking, *I'm no brighter than Old Zeke. Can't sniff out the path that leads straight home,* when—"BOOM!" Like someone upstairs dropped a piece of heavy furniture or something.

He lunged, threw me down the hall toward the door. "Run!"

I stood like that woman strapped to the tracks—*A roar? A rumble?* The locomotive puffing relentlessly closer.

"Go!" A second shove cut those straps loose.

"If it blows, hightail it to base," he yelled. "Fortier's car. Stop for no one. No one. Go!"

From there, the scene gets fuzzy. I know I landed in the foyer at the same time as the top-floor neighbors—babbling, shaking fists. The landlord, like a general in battle, crowed orders. The iron gate whacked against the blocks. Sophie swooped out, screeching like Chicken Little. "The Greeks are bombing! The Greeks are bombing!" Behind her, the perv's belly swayed side to side.

I know the landlady bustled the children past me. "Hello, hello, hello." And my mouth answered, "Hello, *marahaba*, hello, *marahaba*, hello, *marahaba*." And my brain hammered Heaven with fuzzy prayers. "Save us. Save us from it." Though I had no idea what "it" was.

The wheezing below sounded like a flaming dragon.

The perv heaved Sophie at the Nova. "Get moving, broad. Might need outta here." The landlord shouted instructions down the stairs, all in Turkish, so kind of useless to the arsonist. Then, "Git," ordered me away from the building.

And a trembling arm hauled my dead weight back. "If that thing goes, won't be a pretty sight." Rod propped me against the fence. "Where's Carmine?" A little shake. "Where's Steve?"

I pointed down. The dragon wheezed and puffed my answer.

"All heart and no brains!" Rod bolted to the stairwell. "Hey, Carmine, get out now. Remember that explosion last winter, man?"

No answer.

"Please, God. Please, God." My fuzzy mind refused to finish thoughts.

"Don't be crazy, man," Rod yelled to the silence. "You planning to make Cin a widow?"

No answer.

"Please, God, please," I clung to the story of the Hebrew men in the fiery furnace.

Rod dumped me at the picnic table. Beside me, the Fortiers huddled in the Nova for a fast getaway. The perv ranted about Carmine's stupidity. "Fool got that heater of yours too hot. Got a vacuum in the chimney. Happened on base. Blew the place to smithereens."

The jerk might actually know what he's talking about. That thought pierced my brain like an ice pick.

"Oh, Father, save my husband," I begged. My sincere fervor must have shocked God. "Please. This wasn't the way I planned to get rid of him. Please."

On and on, the kerosene heater wheezed. On and on, I prayed, wishing for Nana's direct line to heaven.

The afternoon passed. Dusk fell. Evening prayers rose. The fiend wheezed but ...

Is it tapering off? Maybe. *Is it slowing?*

Afraid to hope, I hoped.

Turks milled back down the lane. *I'm not imagining it.*

Time between gasps definitely lengthening. Slower. Slower. It seemed to sigh.

"Looks like you guys are out of the woods," Rod said, "You'll be okay now, kid." He patted my back, headed across the cotton field.

Time turtled by. Not a sigh. Not a whisper. Nothing.

The landlord strutted down the stairs to our apartment, then up to the other floors, then out to make his pronouncement. Our neighbors and their kids filtered back in. I knelt for hugs. The parents towed their kids past me, even Zu-Zu, her mom's heels clicking tersely by.

Then, he surfaced, damp curls tight against his head. He looked as drained as Grandpa after a day's baling straw in 90-degree heat. He rushed to me. "Are you all right, Cindy?"

The landlord followed him, shouting, "*Chok fina! Chok fina!* [Very bad!]" Fortunately, I didn't understand the rest of the words. The banty rooster looked about to strike out with his spurs. An angry rooster is a frightening thing.

"Sorry." Those sad blue eyes. "*Pardon.*"

The landlord glared and strutted off.

Fortiers skulked past. "Won't be using no padlock with Carmine across the hall. Might need to make a fast break out," the jerk mocked, but slammed the gate and snapped the padlock anyway.

I don't know how long we slumped beside the barbed wire. I know he'd aged in a sad way, like in photos of Vietnamese children from a village razed by the VC (or the Americans). I know it was already dark, and he worked a mid that night. I know some things we said.

"It's strange, isn't it?" he said. "Just when you think you know where the danger is, it sneaks up from behind. We worry about another Arab-Israeli war. Instead, the close one is Turks and Greeks. Who would've thought?" He ran his hand through his hair. "I freak out over a flaming fighter plane and almost get blown up in my own apartment."

I remember he held me by the elbow, and we descended the steps with the vigor of geriatric patients. I remember repeating, *I can do this.* Most of all, I remember tripping on our step-up and falling, straight into a pair of green bulging eyes, as startled as my own. It croaked. I started giggling and didn't stop.

"Cindy, c'mon." He flipped the frog outside. "You've seen a frog before. Settle down."

I couldn't settle. I was thinking of Michael blowing frogs out of pipes with firecrackers. Frog guts spewed over everything. *The cops could've been collecting our guts in buckets.* I couldn't stop giggling.

"Stop it," he pleaded. "Please stop it." He helped me up. "Everything's fine now. See?" He escorted me down the hall like a prisoner to the noose and gently forced my hand onto the pipe. "See? Barely warm. What are you worried about?"

I remember the heater, exhausted, meek. Like him. Like me. Like Daniel after his night in the lions' den. But mostly I remember what happened next.

He tossed starched fatigues on the bed. "Time to be thinking about getting to base. The security of the world doesn't take holidays."

He dropped his jeans, turning away quickly. But not quickly enough. I gasped at the sight.

Two nasty cuts on his inner thigh, a couple inches apart and about four inches long. Solid black bruising from his knee to his groin. "What happened?"

He shrugged. "Kind of jooked when I should've jogged."

"Huh? What's that mean?" He wasn't getting out of it that easily.

He shifted side to side. "Do you really want to know?"

I nodded yes, and he crashed through the crack in months of my icy coldness. "Well, it's like this. Sarge came out to agitate dogs before post. Trashed as usual. So I put Lux on short leash. You never know what Sarge will do drunk. Or Lux anytime."

Instead of clamping onto the protective sleeve, Lux whirled. "Wasn't expecting that move. Had him pulled in too tight. I yanked his choke chain to get his attention, but he still got me a little." He grimaced. "Good thing he has those broken canines, right? Just kind of skimmed my leg."

"Some powerful *skim*."

Tracing the railroad-track scabs on his leg, it hit me. These legs, in perfect-pike position, had entertained Tee for hours. Over and over, she'd tap him, "Stee. Stee," and point to the floor. Over and over, he'd flip into a headstand. She'd snort. *That's how he won my heart.*

Or maybe it wasn't the headstands. Maybe it was the day he took "the Alden sisters" on a "date," a matinee of *Parent Trap*. Tee kept snorting and pointing at the screen. I think she understood the concept of twin sisters. The man behind us grumbled, "Quiet the retard or get her out." And Steve gave the man that look of his, folded Tee in his arms, and deliberately planted a loud smooch on her cheek to make her snort even louder. The man stormed out.

His legs stayed in the theater seat. No other guy, not even Julian, ever accepted me just as I am, the younger sister of one people refer to as a "retard."

Affection, like maple sap in spring, trickled back into my dormant heart. I touched his cheek. "Why didn't you tell me Lux mangled you?"

Long eyelashes covered blue eyes. "I didn't think you'd care."

I didn't say he'd been right. I simply asked, "Why'd you tell me to get to base?"

He rubbed his head. "Don't you know?"

I waited.

"U.S. custody was your only chance. Downtown you'd be under Turkish law. What kind of man would I be to let my wife go to a Turkish prison?"

I'd been asking what kind of man he was since the black-market deal. Now I questioned the conclusions I'd drawn.

"What I mean is, why didn't you run to base with me?"

"I couldn't." He clenched and unclenched his jaw, then blurted out, "Ed says I'll never amount to anything. If I saved myself and someone else got hurt, he'd be right." He shifted away. "When I was little, I couldn't protect Mom, you know?" He faced me. "I thought it'd be different with you, but it isn't. I'm not taking very good care of Grandpa's baby girl, am I?"

I felt anger melting into pity for an old friend. For the first time in months, I answered him as a friend. "Taking care of someone else is a lot to ask." Tee and Mama had taught me that. "Besides, I'm not Grandpa's baby girl anymore. I'm your wife." I smiled.

Steve bowed into my smile. "God seems to have a thing about protecting the Alden girls. Nothing stops an explosion when a heater gets that hot. Do you think maybe we saw a miracle?"

We stood, quiet. Then I said, "We haven't darkened a church door since our wedding day. Can we start going to chapel?" I didn't have to explain the connection.

Steve thought a moment. "Shift work. And bus schedules. It'll be tricky." His blue eyes held mine. "But I'll figure it out, Cindy. I can do things if I understand." He ruffled my hair, "So it's a date. This Sunday." He reached for his fatigues.

I reached for him. "What's your hurry? You have over an hour ... to rest ... before you go."

"Are you sure?" Steve sounded almost shy. "It's been a while since you cared if we ... rested."

"Come here, big boy." I jerked on his arm.

"Hey! You want to give me whiplash?"

And the tug-of-war game began. A creak, a groan, and the bed came tumbling down. I squealed like Tee. Our noses pressed against the frame.

"Looks like where we could've been—behind prison bars," Steve said, seriously.

I smiled. He kissed my smile.

Again, the Turkish flag's red background symbolized Valentine romance. Again, my heart raced at his touch and the moon-promise under my ring pulsed. And like the Turks and Greeks, the Carmines began peace negotiations after months of hostility.

***

Everyone on base said it was a miracle the heater didn't blow and burn everything to the ground, including life as we knew it. It took that near explosion to save our marriage. Maybe we wouldn't have divorced, but I don't think I'd ever have forgiven him for black-market if something hadn't shaken me up and made me really look at him—at us.

Chapter 14

Faith the Conqueror

Sunday morning after Thanksgiving while Muslims all over the city bowed toward Mecca as they'd been taught from birth, I pondered, *Do I believe in Jesus just because that's what I was taught from birth?*

Merle's dad had walked away from Amish pacifism to fight in World War II at about my age. Like him, I knew it was time for me to decide if my childhood teaching applied only to the farm ... or to a lifetime—

When Barb heard we were going to chapel, she said, "I have some serious praying to do myself. Maybe we'll go, too"—her Catholic service preceded our Protestant one. The military provides services for all faiths. And for those of us wrestling to find our faith.

We all arrived soaked after our dash from the bus stop. The priest had already started his liturgy. "We pray to the Lord."

The guys, Timmy in Rod's rigid arms, plopped into a pew. The congregation responded, "Lord, hear our prayer."

Barb made the sign of the cross and knelt, red beads swinging gracefully against her damp white princess-style dress. I perched on the kneeler beside her.

Chalice, trays, vestments, candles. Grandpa's Irish Catholic tradition. For the first time I understood Ed Carmine's reaction at our wedding. When Rev. Minnow stepped to the altar in a suit, Ed stood and announced, "I'm outta here! No priest, no wedding."

Everyone held their breaths. Steve's mother cajoled, "You want to see Mikey and Pammy all dressed up, don't you?" She didn't bother to mention Steve, the groom, the son he referred to as Oops. "Protestants!" Ed cursed and thumped back down. Everyone exhaled…. Grandpa explained the Catholic-Protestant divide this way: "We talk about a God of love and kill each other over where we put candles in the house of prayer."

Barb, eyes fixed on the crucifix, prayed fervently. The congregation chanted, "Lord, hear our prayer." I struggled in vain to join them. Bitter rain pinged against the windowless metal chapel.

Timmy stretched his arms toward me and whimpered. *My out,* I thought. But Rod escaped with his son before I could.

The priest chanted another petition. The congregation repeated, "Lord, hear our prayer."

This time I managed, "Lord, please hear my prayer, too."

And over me came that strange awkwardness I get meeting an acquaintance after a long absence. Since May, I'd nodded to God like to a neighbor on a porch as I scurried by. Except for crises, that is. Then I'd rubbed the magic lamp of prayer and made demands, expecting Him to say, "Your wish is my command," and vanish in a puff of smoke, with no further interference. I fidgeted.

The priest offered communion. Barb, hands folded, head bowed, glided to the altar.

I stared at the crucifix, desperate to say something to Him, coming up with, "Lord, please bless the missionaries in Vietnam." (Every night since the '62 VC capture of Dr. Ardel Vietti, Dan Gerber, and Archie Mitchell, Nana had stopped by our bedroom. "Don't forget to pray for the missionaries, girls.")

Now, though no bare maples waved through autumn-frosted windows, no curved oak pews creaked, no lead bell gonged, strangely, that familiar prayer linked me to the little church nestled on the PA-Ohio line.

The last Sunday of the month. The cherub choir will sing— three dark-eyed nieces in pink frills, black hair gleaming as brightly as their patent leather shoes. Beside them, Tee, moon-face shining, intoning a song of her own creation. God watching over them, smiling.

More boldly, I lifted my soul to *that* God. "I'm worried that Dr. Sherman is wrong about Mama's lump being a cyst. They maimed her last time. Please don't let it be malignant. And—" I stopped, unsure how to go on.

I'm listening, child, God coaxed.

I started again. "I feel raw without Tee, Father. I'm useless over here." I battled to hold back the sobs that'd threatened me since Jill wrote that Tee's seizures had escalated. "I'm afraid Tee will bang her head or choke, and no will be there for her."

Cindy, you're forgetting. I love Charity, too. I sensed a solemn pause. *I never leave Charity alone.* A fragrance more comforting than vanilla or cherry tobacco encircled me.

And I offered Him a cup of tea at the table of my heart. I poured out my truth. My disappointment in Steve. My disappointment in myself. My shame for leaving Timmy. I suspect God already knew about the elephants-in-the-room I'd been tiptoeing around.

He listened, whispering encouragement as all good friends do.

The priest interrupted us with the sign of the cross. "The Lord be with you and with your spirit." The congregation responded, "And also with you." *And with me,* I whispered.

"May Almighty God bless you, the Father, and the Son, and the Holy Spirit. Amen." *Yes, bless me once again.*

"Go in the peace of Christ." After months, I sensed a possibility of that peace.

I joined the congregation saying, "Thanks be to God." *Thanks for not deserting me when I deserted You.*

Love showered down on my dry spirit.

The priest processed out. Barb genuflected. Bach echoed off the metal rafters. Altar boys removed sacred cloths. Barb slid out to check on Timmy and Rod. Steve followed.

I flipped through the missal, stopping at the prayer of St. Francis: "Make me an instrument of your peace. Where there is hatred, let me bring love. Where there is injury, your pardon."

I'm not there yet, but I'm trying. Help me to try.

I settled back as Incirlik's Protestant congregation trickled in. Crisp officers paraded wives down the aisle, inspecting us as they passed, and by their haughty expressions, finding us lacking.

I tucked my rumpled navy skirt under my solid thighs.

They posted themselves in the front pews, soon singing solemn duets like Stuart Pendleton I and II back home. Steve had dubbed them the "penguins" because of their penchant for black suits and white shirts.

The familiar songs and prayers brought me solace. But the sermon—back home, Rev. Minnow, old and gentle, peered through reading glasses at a worn King James' Bible and comforted us with 52 varieties of "Love the Lord thy God first and thy neighbor as thyself."

Here, where early Christians chose to be torn apart by lions rather than deny Christ, a sophisticated professor-type chaplain adjusted his notes and jarred me out of the pew: "Each person must reason through his own moral choices." He stared a hole through my forehead.

I squirmed. The truth was, I'd always let others think for me. *First, all-wise adults. And now, it seems, Steve.* Worse yet, my decisions weren't even reasoned, just blind reactions to rules. Cindy Alden could quote them all: Attend church. Pray. Get baptized. Work hard. Cindy Carmine struggled. *Who am I without Tee at my side? Without family and teachers dictating my life?*

The chaplain said, "Consider Sapphira"—the wife who lied for her husband and dropped dead in God's presence. I dug at my cuticles. When Steve proposed black-market, I sold the cigarettes and, like a Nazi guard, blamed him. "I was ordered to." Then I abandoned a baby for ice cream and plotted to desert my marriage vows. Like Flip Wilson's Geraldine, I whined, "That devil husband of mine drove me to it."

"Don't judge others or use others to justify your failings. Each person is responsible for his own choices," the chaplain repeated.

I shifted. *Coming to chapel was a rotten idea.*

I fastidiously straightened my skirt. *Being Protestant stinks. My North-Irish cousins confess to a priest and he hands out simple absolution. We Protestants face Jesus alone, our guilt on our own hands.* I slumped.

Nana's gentle teachings slipped in. "God wants us to turn to Him in honesty." *The truth is I've lied to God and to myself.* "Jesus came to free us from guilt, dear."

So, I summoned all my courage and lifted my head. "Father, I guess it's time to talk honestly with You."

Truth answered immediately. "Child, I've wanted that."

"Can you love me again? After all I've done?" *Black-market, child neglect and endangerment, scapegoating, lying, accessory to attempted arson ...*

"Shhh, child, I never stopped loving you."

Even in my disobedience, God had delivered an araba and saved a building and... Rev. Minnow always said, "God's family isn't perfect. They simply choose to accept His love."

So, I chose. I dropped my fig leaves of anger and blame.

"Thank You for loving me, Father." *Love your neighbor as God loves you.* "And Father," I hesitated, "about Steve—" My anger had blown us so far apart it'd be impossible to put the pieces back alone. "Can You ever make me love Steve like I used to?"

"Shhh, child, don't fret. Believe. I am All Love, remember?"

I nodded, warmed and clothed.

Steve's calloused hands opened the hymnal to the closing hymn, "Great Is Thy Faithfulness." His taut shoulder brushed mine. I glanced over. He winked.

Grandpa would say, "Think how long it takes a seed to grow. But we expect love to grow overnight? Shouldn't we be more patient with people than seeds?"

I felt a glimmer of the hope I'd felt when Mrs. Minnow banged out those first notes of Mendelssohn's "Wedding March."

At the final "Amen," Steve said, "I'll see you on the bus," and sprinted off with a mischievous wave. At the next stop, soaked from cold rain and out of breath, he vaulted on and extended a Whitman sampler. "It's not Brach's five-pound box, but it's just you and me now."

"It'll do just fine," I said, quietly.

"It seems like a good Christmas tradition to keep going," he said.

Rod butted in. "Hey, man, you two wouldn't be sharing Christmas traditions this year or ever if that heater had blown the other night."

"Thanks for the reminder, guy." Steve landed a playful punch. "The candy was supposed to help my wife forget my stupid move."

While the guys harassed each other, Barb said out of the corner of her mouth, "Rod keeps talking about your perfect meal on Thanksgiving, and—"

"Even with the after-dinner pyrotechnics?" I asked.

"Quit joking. You're so lucky someone taught you things. I don't clean or cook much." She acted as if she'd revealed a great secret. "Do you think you could teach me?"

We'll start with a shovel for the dirt and Jell-o for supper, I thought, but said, "Sure."

We both had some hard work to do.

On the soggy dirt path home, I clasped Steve's arm. "Good service."

"Sure was," he said. "No bathroom trips for Tee or the nieces."

"Interruptions have their advantages in a sermon like that." It'd been hard facing God. It wasn't any easier facing my husband. "Steve, you know how Barb leaves Timmy alone and says it's for Rod? Well, I sold those cigarettes and said it was for you."

He waited, without expression.

"I shouldn't have left you to solve all our problems." I summarized my view.

He almost shook his head off saying no. "I'm supposed to take care of you." Guess he'd read the fairy tales, too. The man protects and provides. Silent, strong, explosive, that's a man.

"Let me try again." I fidgeted. "Remember how Grandpa says marriage is like two people in a rowboat? Well, I've been sitting on my oars taunting you while you fought to stay afloat. I was so mad I wanted you to sink. I forgot I'd drown, too. I'm sorry."

Steve's brows furrowed. Then he said, "All I understood of that is the 'I'm sorry.'"

I smiled. "That's probably enough, darling."

"I understood the 'darling,' too." He kissed me, and I melted against him, then stiffened. "We're on the street." He grinned sheepishly and stole another peck.

"You're so bad." I stood rigid. We'd offended enough Muslim neighbors in the last week. "But I've always liked bad boys."

"I'm glad you're back, Cindy." He shifted. "You know how your grandpa says, 'As long as I live, there'll be a potato on the table for a friend or a stranger in need'? I just wanted to feed you. I never realized dealing would hurt you." He turned away. "I thought hitting was the only way to hurt a woman."

And I always thought cheating was the only way to hurt a man. I felt so bad.

"Merle and Grandpa always told me what to do for you. I don't know anything about women and—"

I put a finger on his lips. "That's not true. You're amazing with Sophie and Mrs. Cole."

He pulled away. "But they're different. They have problems like Mom and Pammy." He halted. "But you? You take care of yourself. You jump on centipedes and don't even scream. You don't need an iron gate. You never need anything."

How could he believe that? I wondered, but said, "No, I need a lot. I'm just learning that myself."

Time to lighten the mood. "And about Grandpa always knowing what to do? He didn't. Like with my pony. He just got it because he wasn't good at telling me no."

I pondered that example.

"Actually, you were right. Grandpa does always know what to do." I paused for effect. "Never tell me no. Always give me what I want."

Steve didn't miss a beat. "Did that once. The bus trip before Finance got our checks straight. Big mistake."

He can be such a smart alec. I punched him and zipped down the stairs for the opening of "the games," like in the days before black-market.

Afterwards, I prayed shyly. "Ah, Father, I was thinking. Maybe it's time for us to give Mama that grandbaby she's always talking about. Could you help?"

I heard Him answer, *Trust me. I'll give you what is best.*

Did His eyes twinkle?

***

Sometimes the biggest crises in life result in the greatest renewals—forest fires in the Grand Canyon, Mississippi floods depositing silt, and the Thanksgiving of '67s near explosion that made two newlyweds believe again.

Chapter 15

Two Holy Seasons. Two Advents

I'd reconciled with Steve and God. Turkey and Greece had made peace in Cyprus. North and South Vietnam were close to peace talks. But after we almost blew up the apartment building with our heater, peace with our Turkish neighbors didn't look so promising.

I baked sticky buns to apologize for "yesterday night" (upon reflection, perhaps not the most sensitive approach during Ramadan). The landlord glared and left me standing on the landing. The landlady accepted the warm platter, then slammed the door as if I were part of an American terrorist cell. I retreated to the less disturbing chill downstairs.

Steve nuzzled me. "Relax. They'll either get over it or they won't." Another brilliant Carmine family motto. "Don't worry about things you can't change."

Well, I couldn't change the heater incident (nor the black-market deal nor leaving Timmy). So I focused on what I could do. Change Barb into a cook and her filth into shine—

The next morning, Steve escorted me across the cotton field.

Barb threw open the door. "How long do you think this'll take?" She bounced as she waited for my answer.

Wanting to be both kind and honest, I came up with, "Don't know for sure, but it'll go faster with two of us. Let's redd up first."

Barb cracked up. "You and your Pennsylvania Dutch expressions."

I laced one bucket with Pine-Sol, another with Clorox, and we began the first of days of scraping and scrubbing.

Barb made the first great discovery in the kitchen. "This counter's gray. I'd forgotten." Then, a stovetop under layers of grease, glass refrigerator shelves under a carpet of mossy mold, and a shiny white porcelain sink under slime. We scoured dried food and grease off walls and doused them with spray. Cockroaches stampeded like hippies fleeing a rock concert fire.

The next afternoon, we emptied the bathtub of rancid laundry soaking in what felt like icy pond scum—my biology prof could've made some interesting slides out of that stuff—and transformed a three-dimensional sculpture of toothpaste mounds and hair into a glistening washbowl. Timmy ran Mr. Fluffy over the fresh grout lines on the tile floor.

The next, we erased layers of film from the ceiling-high windows in the living area and master bedroom—I had to remind myself, "Thou shalt not covet thy neighbor's gorgeous view"—and draped them with sheet-curtains. The day we finished cleaning the main area and arranging the furniture into conversation areas, Rod opened the door and jumped back. "R-r-r-rad! I dig it. Looks like a spread in *Good Housekeeping.*" I snickered, recalling my earlier analogy.

By the afternoon we got to Timmy's room, we were giddy. I slid the crib away from the window. "These Venetian blind blades are sharp."

Barb came back with, "They were perfectly protected by dirt before you got your hands on them."

Wrapping the cord safely over the rod, I did a Sophie imitation. "I shouldn't reach like this. Might be pregnant, you know." Our running joke.

But hilarity had ended. Barb plopped down on the soapy floor and burst into tears.

"What's wrong? What's wrong?" I asked and asked until, finally, she sniffled it out. "I'm ... I'm ... pregnant."

I whooped. Threw my arms around her. Hugged her to the point of strangulation. "Two beautiful babies!" Steve and I hadn't succeeded in making one.

I tickled Timmy under the chin with bunny ears. "You're going to be a big brother." He squealed and bounced.

She blubbered. "You don't understand. Rod said right up front that Timmy better be an only child, and I agreed. I used foam and a diaphragm, too. I know there's the pill." She answered a criticism I hadn't made. "But I was afraid it'd make me fat. Rod hates fat women." She clenched red chapped hands. "Now he's going to hate me."

I grappled for something positive to say and came up with, "Maybe you're not really pregnant. You haven't been to a doctor, right? Look how many false alarms Sophie has had."

"No, I'm sure." Barb pointed to Timmy. "He was the first period I ever missed." She pointed down to her abdomen. "I'm late for my third one now." Her hair shrouded her face.

Timmy chewed on a red block. "But look what a blessing he is." I sounded like Nana.

Barb twisted her hair into a knot. "You know the saying about the straw breaking the camel's back? I'm afraid this baby's the straw."

The hand cupping her belly trembled as she repeated their story—her dating Rod's brother but having a secret crush on Rod. Rod asking her out before reporting to Incirlik. Her knowing she shouldn't cheat on his brother. Her knowing Rod would forget her the minute his plane took off. "But I said yes, every day for two weeks. That last night I made up my mind ... just one time. I didn't know a virgin can get pregnant."

She sobbed and sobbed. "His brother would've married me, but that would've been wrong." So she wrote Rod, said she knew she'd just been a fling. If he agreed to a proxy marriage to give the baby a name, she'd divorce him and never bother him again.

But he surprised her. He asked the chaplain to patch through a call and told Barb, "It's copacetic, Babe." He got an emergency leave and a military hop to Travis [AFB] and found a Justice of the Peace to marry them. After her six weeks' checkup, he flew Barb and Timmy over to Turkey to "be a real family."

Barb got up from the floor. "I thought maybe if this place didn't smell like pee, maybe he'd want to come home, even with two kids here. But I'm just fooling myself." She covered her face. "Rod's brother sent me that Johnny Mathias' record, the one about chasing 'the bright, elusive butterfly of love.' I don't think he meant I'm his elusive butterfly. I think he meant Rod's mine."

I could think of no appropriate words.

I'd only seen have-to marriage from the man's point of view. Sean had to go to the steel mill instead of college because Jo got pregnant. Too young for such responsibility, he drank. Jo turned shrewish. (Grandpa joked about her Seneca Indian heritage. "Don't get her riled, son, or she'll scalp you.) Mama cried for her boy-turned-man-too-soon. But Barb's pain showed me there truly are two ends to every rope.

She moaned. "I don't know how to tell Rod."

I urged her, "Just tell him. Straight out. Nana says most of the things we worry about never happen."

"Help me set the mood. You know how to do everything."

It was comical. In spite of my big hips and mousy hair, she sounded like she envied me.

"Okay. A good meal makes a perfect setting." I whipped up scalloped potatoes and meatloaf, set out placemats and candles, and repeatedly interjected, "Don't put it off. Tell him tonight."

Rod froze mid-step through the door. "Far out, man! Is that something in the oven?" He twirled Barb across a clutter-free floor. Gleaming like a surfer who'd ridden the largest wave of the day she made the okay sign over his shoulder and mouthed, "Thanks."

He lit the candles with his cigarette, then they took off to inspect Timmy's clean room. I heard him say, "Just one thing kind of bums me out. In your laundry frenzy this week, you girls seem to have lost all my underwear. Any clues?"

And Barb's laughter. "Did you check your underwear drawer, silly?"

A pause. "What a novel idea. Now where is this supposed underwear drawer of mine?"

A giggle. "In our bedroom, of course." Another moment's silence, then another giggle. "Rod, stop it!" It had the familiar sound of our games.

"Time to go," I whispered. Steve grabbed our basket of meatloaf and potatoes. We let ourselves out. "I haven't had this much fun in months," I said, obliquely.

"Not even with me?" His full lips pouted.

"You know what I mean, smart alec." I punched him. "Like Nana says, people need to be needed. It's been lots more fun helping Barb than sitting around waiting for you to wake up."

He nodded. "Barb has turned into quite the June Cleaver. But she's a little peaked. Think housework is too much for her?"

"No," I said, keeping my promise not to tell about her pregnancy. After all, she'd kept my secret about pavilion night. But I couldn't resist adding, "Bet Rod's lots happier now."

"Why? If he wanted clean and peaceful, he could've stayed in the barracks with a Turkish houseboy pampering him for peanuts."

I smiled, chafing to know how Rod was taking the pregnancy news.

But Barb didn't break the news that night after the meatloaf. Nor the next day, after a scrumptious shepherd pie. Nor when we babysat Timmy so she could serve Rod a romantic candlelit Swiss steak dinner with chocolate cake topped with chopped pistachios for dessert.

"I get myself all psyched to tell him, then can't make myself spoil the moment," Barb apologized. "Besides, maybe you're right. Maybe I'm not pregnant. Maybe I've got a serious medical condition. Like uterine cancer." She sounded almost hopeful.

Chapter 16

The Greatest of These is Love

In the Middle East, birthplace of three major religions springing from Abraham—Judaism, the sons of Isaac. Islam, the sons of Ishmael. Christianity, the sons of Christ through the line of David—the answer to "Is Christ a prophet or the Son of God?" made all the difference.

To Muslims in 1967, December meant the fasting and spiritual reflection of Ramadan. To me that year, it meant the excitement of waiting for Barb to tell Rod their pregnancy news and for Steve's reaction to the bomb of a Christmas gift I came up with for him—

Rod lugged home the biggest tree on base, so big it almost dented in the Nova's roof and finished off that broken spring.

"Remember how Grandpa always chopped down a tree that filled the living room?" I hinted.

"Remember how our tree always ended up shattered all over the floor after an Ed tirade?" Steve retorted. "There's nothing jolly about a Carmine Christmas. Plus, do you have any idea what Garza shelled out for that tree? We can't afford even a Charlie Brown one." Turkey's great forests were centuries gone.

But when Grandpa sent a surprise five-dollar bill, Steve bought us a little silver tree from the AFEX. "It's one of those things that's important to you, right?" He shifted back and forth.

"Yes," I answered simply, slightly sad. Proper decoration of a tree requires laughing children, but since that Thanksgiving heater fiasco, our apartment had been declared Off Limits, Potentially

Hazardous, Flammable. (Logically, good parents the world over protect children from pyromaniacs.)

Fortunately, though, the Missionary Circle sent us boxes of scarce commissary items—a pantry shower of coconut, walnuts, butterscotch chips, bug-free flour, bags and bags of Nestlé's chocolate chips. (Jill said I'd eat dog food if it had chocolate chips in it. Of course, that came from a health food fanatic who believed carob chips and dried fruit were staples.)

I baked up a double batch of Toll House cookies and ran upstairs. One whiff brought the landlady's kids running to the door.

I held out the plate. "For you. *Chok gazelle*." Black eyes begged their mother. She hesitated, shrugged yes, motioned me in.

To remind themselves of how the poor and unfortunate feel every day, Muslims don't eat or drink or smoke during daylight hours of the month of Ramadan. But children are exempt.

The kids gobbled contentedly on warm gooey chocolate.

The landlady, a faithful fasting adult, continued mixing up a traditional cornmeal bread made without salt for Iftar. (Their after-sunset meal was high-protein, low-salt, and low-spice to make the next day's fasting easier. It appeared Ramadan didn't affect how much you ate, just when you ate it.).

Out of respect, I should abstain, too, I thought, but only for a moment. My appetite, lost during black-market depression, had returned, doubled. My pear shape had replumped.

Munching, I grew courageous, pointed downstairs, and asked, "Zu-Zu? Boys? *Gel?* No fire. *Gel?*"

The landlady slid the cornbread into the oven, valiantly marched her children downstairs, and placed her hand on the criminal heater, cold with Steve on base. Losing a few extremities to frostbite seemed less serious to me than having the fire-breathing monster spew my body fragments across the Middle East.

"Okay," she said and tripped back upstairs, leaving her children in my care.

Yes! I did a silent fist pump.

The kids rearranged that little silver tree on our "buffet" ten times before agreeing on the exactly right spot. We decked it out with popcorn, paper candy canes, a paper star, and laughter. Then we snow-stenciled the windows and cut out a green construction paper mistletoe. *An island of Christmas in the middle of an ocean of Ramadan,* I giggled to myself.

From then on, every day they ran down and pushed chocolate kisses onto the tops of peanut butter cookies, pressed out gingerbread men and green-and-red spritzes, frosted dozens of sugar cut-out cookies and swilled eggnog (substandard because it was made with powdered milk, no matter how I doctored it).

When they skipped back upstairs, I made Christmas gifts. For the kids, Raggedy Ann and Andy dolls and drums from oatmeal boxes. (I'd saved a plethora. Oatmeal seemed the only bug-free staple at the commissary.) For their parents, peanut brittle, college fudge, and divinity. And for Steve?

Steve's present is a whole story unto itself.

We'd agreed. No gifts. "Nothing bought or made" (because he wasn't crafty). It was hard to come up with something that didn't break those rules. But I did.

My first idea was a baby. Well, actually, everyone's idea. Mama had written, "My loneliness for you is bearable, Princess, only because I know you're making Steve a father." Pam wrote, "So when's the big news? Girl or boy, doesn't matter as long as it has Steve's curls." And Grandpa, "A wee lad or lassie'd be good medicine for your mama." I had stopped taking birth control pills and was practically standing on my head to capture every sperm, but it'd take three months to confirm success and, technically, a baby is "homemade."

So, I resorted to Plan B, a real lulu.

"What do you know about belly dancing?" I asked Barb, heat rising in my face like it did the first time I had to take a group shower after gym class.

Tea sprayed out her nose. "Is this a joke?"

"Well, you do a mean Watusi. Thought you might've tried a belly dance or two." I crawled under the kitchen counter and pulled out a paper bag full of books from the base library. Hidden on the bottom, *The Ancient Art of Seduction* and *Belly Dancing Simplified.*

Timmy and Mr. Fluffy about landed on the floor. "You're serious, Cin. Who would've guessed farm girls have a wild side?"

I whipped a pamphlet at her head. I wasn't always old and stodgy, you know.

After hours of reading diagrams and swiveling—great exercise, great laughter, but a dismal dance failure—I ran to the landlady's in desperation, even included a few newly acquired moves in my explanation to her. Now that was a conversation to watch.

"*Yok, yok*, me good Turkish girl." The landlady made no attempt to hide her dismay. Apparently, *respectable* Turkish women don't do belly dances, though obviously *respectable* men watch them. Her husband's evening trips to the "coffee shop," a pseudonym for belly dancing shows, had given me the idea in the first place.

"*Allaha ismarladik.*" I bowed in disappointment. I was back to winging it.

But while I'd been gone, Barb had been thinking. "I've got it. There's a teenager in our building who struts her stuff pretty good for a Muslim girl. You know the one. Every time we meet her in the hall, she breaks into, 'I dig rock 'n roll music.'"

I knew who she meant.

Barb's instincts were right on. The teen wasn't a "good Turkish girl." Yes, she did the belly dance. Yes, she'd give lessons. Negotiations began.

"Lira?" we asked.

She shook her head no and clasped her hands together, rocking and repeating "medicine" and rocking until it clicked—baby medicine ... *Birth control pills.*

"*Yok*, doctor necessary," Barb explained.

The teen settled for two pair of blue jeans—though where she'd ever wear them, we couldn't imagine—and I had my belly dance instructor.

Steve escorted me to class without suspicion. "Cleaning with Barb," the perfect cover.

Barb and I waited for the furtive taps on her door and let her in. Our tutor checked all the window coverings, flipped the dial to find a station, clicked her fingers, and shook out her black silky hair. "I show you," she said and began to shimmy. Now that was intimidating.

Barb (the Azure Princess) accompanied every move with grace. I (the Country Clod) stumbled along, feeling just plain silly. Well, eager and silly, like when I danced with Mama's scarf in front of the hall mirror. Nervous giggles are excellent toning exercises for the abdomen, by the way.

Strangely, our instructor praised me, the klutz, for the smallest successes like we did Tee. "Gazelle, gazelle." Her frequent gestures to my rounded belly and elephantine hips made me suspect why. I'd read that belly dancers can't reach star status until they weigh 300 pounds. I feared she saw in me the potential for training a new star. *It's diet time,* I vowed for the millionth time.

Hour after hour, I practiced my swivel and hummed my Eastern rendition of "I'll be home for Christmas, if only in my dreams." *Sleighs of teenagers caroling through the neighborhood, hot chocolate and Christmas cookies, bell ringers beside Salvation Army barrels outside holly-decked Woolworth's department stores. Saucer sleds, snow forts, roasted chestnuts, fruit cake, eggnog ...*

But, of course, things got messed up. Sarge scheduled Flight B of Incirlik's K-9 unit to work a swing shift on Christmas Day.

At 2:30, with a clank of the iron gate, Sophie and I walked our husbands, slouches in their clomps, to the Nova. Steve pecked my cheek. "Hate to leave, Cindy. But Santa heard you've been an exceptionally good girl this year. Be ready for a surprise."

I protested. "We promised. No wasting money we don't have. Did you cave?" Our Turkish toilet had been a department store of gifts—for Barb, a fabulous wine-colored leather skirt with matching purse and the ultimate wringer washer. For Sophie, bundles of suede, Turkish rugs, towels, gold chains, turquoise. Fortier had flaunted every gift he stashed.

"Of course not. Do you think Santa would lie?" He tweaked my nose. "Next month after promotion, I'll have an extra $40 to buy you something. But, no, Santa didn't spend a penny. Want to guess what it is?" He grinned. "Maybe it's a nice fire for a cookout like on Thanksgiving? Wouldn't that be nice?"

"Not funny." I whacked him. Better at keeping secrets, I gave no indication he was getting something to unwrap, too.

A crack of thunder sent Sophie and me scurrying. *Grandpa would've said, "Pshaw! That's no blarney," and watched it pour.*

I slammed our door, barely made it to the kitchen when "rap-pause-rap."

"Steve?" I sprinted back down the hall. "What did you forget?"

A little snicker. "Have makeup, will travel."

"Barb! Are you crazy? Pregnant. Out in a storm. And—"

I rattled off chains, flung open the door, sighed in relief to see Timmy. "You'd better be here to tell me how Rod took the news."

We'd certainly created "the right time"—a Christmas dinner of stuffed Cornish hens, sticky buns, pumpkin pie—but I knew her answer before she shook her head no and said, "Thought you might need a little help with your beautification program."

An astute conclusion. In spite of all her lessons on applying eye makeup and lipstick for a glow-in-the-candlelight look, my smeared attempts always ended up in the raccoon-in-the-spotlight look and me arguing, "I tried," like a student who got an F on an exam.

Barb handed over Timmy, said, "Hair first," and transformed my boring flip into soft curls—she had Jill's touch. Sometimes Jill let her hair hang free like a chestnut filly's mane. Other times she coiled it up like a stunning pretzel.

"Now for your face. All great artists use paint." She opened her cosmetic bag. Squinted. Sighed. Evidently, this great artist found my canvas challenging.

But upon final inspection, she gloated. "Fab. You could dance on any stage looking like this."

"Yeah, as long as all the lights are turned off." Right then Adana's electricity blinked off. "See? God agrees with me," I said.

Barb huffed. "That's just plain sacrilege. Now show me what you got from home."

She pulled a flashlight from the diaper bag to see more clearly—a hooked potholder. "Tee worked really hard on it," I said proudly. Matching blue sweaters from Mama and Dad. "Mama thinks dressing alike is romantic." A patchwork quilt from Nana and Grandpa. "Every fabric is from an outfit she made me. I'll sit and tell you the story of each some night."

Barb's eyes riveted on the framed photos from Jill. "So this is your farm"—Nana unpinning a sheet billowing on the line. In the background, Tee on the tree house porch, sorting buttons with Pam.

"And your gang"— crammed into a self-photo booth. Jill (ironed-straight mane and tie-dye), Merle and Denny (buzz cuts and Army green), holding up black construction paper silhouettes (Steve and me). Photo labeled, "Incomplete."

"And these bedroom eyes have to be the famous Julian"—he and his new girlfriend. In Myrtle Beach after he broke off his previous engagement the week before. (Julian was like their mother, in Nassau with *her* new beau. Jill, the opposite, said she wanted a man who'd be there the next morning, the next year, and ten years from now. In other words, Merle.)

"So where's the stuff Steve's folks sent?"

"Not even a postcard." My sarcasm showed. "Steve says I should be smart enough to catch on. His folks and Michael don't care if he lives or dies. Just Pammy does."

I unfolded the T-shirts from Pymatuning Lake that Pam sent to make us laugh and explained her "Muppier" jokes (a word Pam made up imitating tourists saying, "I'm up here from Pittsburgh).

Intercepting Timmy in his little Army-man crawl, I played "Itsy Bitsy Spider," the spider going down the waterspout over and over until the storm outside settled into a steady rain.

"I better get home before dark." Barb said. I jumped up to escort her halfway, but she stopped me. "In this weather? And undo my great work?"

I didn't want to seem unappreciative. "Well, move fast and signal when you get there. Anything over two minutes, and I'm coming after you." A young American woman and a blond baby boy, prime black-market merchandise.

I lingered in the foyer, my thighs tensed to race to their rescue. Then, Barb's balcony door slid open, and she sidled out. Arms above head. Twirling her hips. *Doing a belly dance, the nut.*

Giggling, I scooted down to my dressing room and, accompanied by the "Thump, thump" on our ceiling, our neighbors dancing after Iftar, donned the first layer of my costume, a filmy black nightie cached away for a special occasion.

A spin for the mirror. A bend forward. A press of arms against sides to enhance cleavage. A futile search for swan-likeness. A review of the script. (A modification of "the wet human body is extremely sensual" attempt. You remember it, don't you?)

The setting different—dining room table, black tapers, green cross-stitched tablecloth. The goal the same—passion.

Finger traces her spine. Kisses skim her throat, hollow of neck ... her naval ... Remember now?

Finally, rap-pause-rap. The audience arriving. A shiver of stage fright. *Break a leg.* The curtain rose.

Steve stumbled over the step-up into our hall. "Electricity out again? This hole's getting on my nerves."

Irritation—not exactly the intended emotion for the evening.

I ran my tongue over my teeth, gave an enigmatic smile. "No, a little candlelight to set the mood for our luncheon"—mini quiches, sticky buns, Ovaltine.

"Did you forget that lunchbox you packed? I'm still stuffed."

Work with me here.

"Maybe just a little nibble?" I purred in that raspy sex-kitten voice I'd been practicing.

"Catching a cold? That nightie's a little skimpy for this weather."

His protective side? Well, that's a start.

I wrapped myself against his back. He bristled away.

"Want to get filthy? Lux was a total mud ball after post. Had to hose him down."

We're getting off track here.

He stripped out of his parka, stripped off his shirt, stomped to the bathroom.

Kill that set!

As undaunted as the Coyote in the *Roadrunner*, I mentally crossed out, "Dining room" and wrote, "Bathroom."

I slipped to the bedroom and grabbed the veils I'd designed out of black lace curtains from the AFEX's bargain table. Adjusted them for the "I Dream of Jeannie" look and—

Action!

Shimmying in stage right. (Or was it stage left? I never got those straight.) Singing the "Da, da, da, da, da" version of snake charmer's tune, clacking tutor's castanets, swirling sturdy hips, peeking provocatively out one side of lace-curtain veil, then the other. (Bare feet vulnerable to centipedes and scorpions, prancing high steps of a trotter. Well, maybe of a grape stomper.)

Steve gaped, soap bubbles dripping from his curls. Hooted and howled. "You're goofy. I take you off the farm and you go crazy."

I lurched to a stop, mid-swivel. "Now what kind of reaction is that?" He was supposed to be "enthralled?" ... "aroused?" ... "mystified?' I couldn't decide what word fit, but I knew "cracked up" wasn't it.

Indignant, I refired the humming clacking love machine, and he almost drowned himself laughing.

"You look like a hen pecking for corn."

My swivel deteriorated into writhing. "Hrumped" to a halt. I mentally tore up the script.

"Aw, c'mon. Why're you stopping?" He ducked under for a quick rinse, scrambled from the tub. "I got it now. I got what you look like. Pammy that time the bee flew up under her skirt."

"Brat!" I whacked his wet shoulder. "GIs pay good money for a show like this."

"I'm sure this show's one in a million. You're one in a million." He smacked my butt, "Great weapon in that tail. More sting than a scorpion's."

He danced me down the hall, his "da, da, da ... da ... da," slightly out of tune. "Now what're *you* hiding under there?"

He twirled me dizzy by the bed.

I stood naked, except for my black veil and the red garter belt holding up black-seamed nylons.

He chuckled. "Aha, Mrs. Adana. The where-East-meets-West version of the dance of the veils."

I settled into his kiss.

This is why Mama sent me away. This is why I deserted Tee.

The curtain dropped.

When black seamed stockings lay balled on the floor beside white BVDs, Steve jerked back, smacked himself on the forehead. "How could I get so distracted?"

Duh! I kissed him.

He leaned back. "Did you spot anything outside?"

I shook my head no and kissed him again.

He wiggled away. "How about on the living room windowsill? Something furry?"

"Couldn't see without electricity," I said. "Wouldn't have noticed it anyway, unless it had wire snips for teeth."

He sighed. "Wonder what held Santa up? Guess he'll have to fly back in the morning." He wrapped me tight—

The muezzin's call.

Icicles on uncovered legs. The blanket zapping out of my fingers left brush burns. "C'mon, sleepyhead. Ready for a walk?"

"Later." I snuggled into my nest. "It's freezing."

"A little wind off the mountains, Cindy. What's wrong with you? Your bedroom was colder than this." He had a point there. The farmhouse had no ductwork to the second floor. Once I convinced Grandpa to buy me a goldfish. Set it on the bedstand by Tee. Woke in the morning to find the bowl iced over and a suffocated pet. *But it was a magnificent flushing, accompanied by a pipe-and-strings duet of "Danny Boy."*

"Light the oven. I'll brave it when it's warm." Steve popped the loaf pan into the oven and crawled back in to pester me, but I got him. "Did you set it for 350 degrees?"

"Funny!" We still didn't have an oven regulator, of course.

At the aroma of warm cinnamon, I stretched like a barn cat nudged out of its sunny spot on a hay bale and shuffled out.

Steve bolted down hunks of coffee cake, chased them with great gulps of Ovaltine. "Relax, you're barely tasting it," I said.

"All that gyrating last night got me charged up." He mussed my hair. "Let's get going."

Deliberately, I cut another slab, savored the warm crusty edge. "It's too early."

"Early? Can't you hear? The kids are already outside playing. C'mon. Be a sport."

I ignored him.

He resorted to orders. "You think I'm joking? One minute, Cindy, and I drag you out."

"Aye, aye, Airman Carmine." I mocked but knew he'd do it.

I layered—thermal underwear, slacks, two sweaters, my coat—and with the grace of a sumo wrestler, galumphed up with the leftover cake.

The landlord's children and their cousins scarfed their pieces. The shanty children bowed, sniffed, licked up every errant crumb, mined for specks of strudel under fingernails. Then one said, "*Gel* [come]*, Madame,*" and a gaggle of children echoed, *"Gel,"* and tugged/pushed me down the dirt path.

"So my surprise is at Garzas'?" *Finally, a baby announcement.*

Steve flashed those blue eyes and shrugged. "Wait and see."

But we passed Garzas' building. And a lean-to grocery. And a vendor selling baskets. Almost to the boulevard, the kids stopped at a construction site, pirouetted like a Broadway troupe, and pointed, black eyes gleaming. Steve's grin almost swallowed his face.

"I've seen cement blocks before," I said. "Unless Turkish ones are different."

"Aw, Cindy, c'mon. Give it a chance. Don't you think you should check this out?"

The children bounced and clapped. I tiptoed forward. "What am I supposed to see?"

"Look harder." Steve nudged a grubby pile. It compressed like a furry porcupine. "Aren't you curious? Aren't you going to pick it up?"

"I don't think so. Not 'til I know what it is."

He grinned. "Ooo! Need some protection?"

That provoked me as he knew it would. "No," I snapped and swooped up the gritty pelt of—

Not one, but two, shivering muddy puppies, all scrunched together. Their new-puppy smell melted my heart. "A-a-a-w." They burrowed between my coat and my first layer.

"Merry Christmas!" Steve's eyes danced. "I named them Mutt and Jeff. Is that okay?"

I nodded. *Grandpa said the humane society would fight for a mongrel in a woodpile, but our so-called doctors would've starved our Angel baby.* "Tee would love them."

Steve smothered me in one strong arm and enfolded as many kids as he could reach with the other. "I put my buddies here on the hunt, but the storm messed up our plan, right guys? They were supposed to put the pups on the windowsill for you to find."

"Thank you. Thank you." I hugged each child. Steve played "got your nose," the old thumb-between-the-fingers trick, with a shanty boy. The joke didn't seem to translate well into Turkish, but the attention was internationally appealing. It was an amazing party of laughter ... until I panicked.

"What if the landlord won't let us keep them?" The landlord despised dogs. *"Keupek chok fina* [very bad]." And us, too, for that matter since the heater incident.

"No problem. A tough sale, but I lined up his kids with those sad eyes, and he threw in the towel. 'Okay, dogs necessary.'" Steve did a perfect imitation of the scene.

Again, I repeated, "Thank you. Thank you." The kids squirmed and romped away.

"And thank you, Steve." I leaned against him. "Let's show Timmy."

Rod rustled up Johnson's Baby Shampoo, and Steve and Timmy dunked the fur balls in the bathroom sink and found that under the mud, Mutt, the roly-poly one, had black raccoon markings on his face and paws. Jeff, the tall-skinny one, had a few brown spots on his tan.

Barb watched it all with a Mona Lisa smile.

At our place, I guided the pups' noses into a mixture of powdered and condensed milk. They dipped and slurped and waddled off with bellies weighed down like hammocks, probably fuller than the shanty kids had ever been. I felt like the Prioress in *The Canterbury Tales* who fed dogs refined white bread and roasted meat while the peasants starved.

Later, in a basket with a warm water bottle and an alarm clock, Grandpa's method of comforting a pup taken from its mother, the pups clung together, quivering.

Steve patted my butt and said, "You're a natural mother."

I tingled, hoping I'd soon have the chance to find out if that were true.

***

With all the money we've spent on Christmas these last decades, we've never topped those gifts of '67 that were free.

Chapter 17

Caged by ... Love?

Ramadan ends with the Sugar Festival (Seker Bayrami). Children dressed in new clothes prance from house to house for doting adults to hand out sweets and coins. "It's like Halloween," Steve said. To me, it was like Grandpa's stories of first communion in Ireland.

Zu-Zu and brothers arrived. Steve flipped into a handstand. Change fell from his pockets, rolled under the table and buffet, down the hall. (He'd won the money in a Pinochle tournament. I hadn't even criticized.) The pups joined in the chase. The landlord ordered, *"Gel."* Each child grabbed a bag stuffed with Toll House cookies, kissed our hands, held them to their foreheads, and *"Gule, gule,"* off to the next elder.

Steve smiled. "Fun way to start '68, isn't it, Cindy? It's going to be a good year. Eight months and, 'Good riddance, Uncle Sam.' We'll get our houses built to fill with babies."

Grandpa was hauling gravel for our driveway in the corner of the sheep meadow. Dawdi Hostetler had deeded Merle land next to ours. Merle's cousins were on standby to "raise" both houses. Jill planned: "Wrap-around porches. Shaker style to fit the setting. Split-rail fences ..."

We just didn't know—

Mid-afternoon, another knock. I grabbed goody bags. But, sadly, Turkish traditions had ended. "Head 'em up, cowpokes.

Doggies branded. Whiskey's out!" Steve moaned. My promised encore belly dance had been replaced by a break party.

What seemed bizarre in May had become the norm by January—rancid odors, blaring music, drinking games, me in Jill's hand-me-down lime green dress, Mrs. Cole all decked out in Christmas gifts—pastel blue suede, gold bracelets and chains. By then I could look her eye-to-eye when I said, "Lovely outfit."

Rod stumbled around, clutching his boda bag until the Beach Boys played, then, "Hey, man, need my Barbie doll." She set down her ginger ale and Saltines and handed me Timmy—one tiny fist grabbed Steve's glasses.

Barb's sea-green complexion complemented her sand-blond hair. (She said she got evening sickness with Timmy, too.) In her fifth month, she wasn't as thick as I was. But empire lines without waists were in fashion, and my clothes, two sizes bigger than hers, fit her fine. No one suspected her secret.

A burly guy yelled, "Ace, panty waist," and a scrawny guy threw his cards. Fortier burst back in from the street and shoved his fist against Sophie's jaw. "See this? Know whose fault? Yours, broad." She was doing the boogie in the corner with a phantom partner. "GIs gawk at you, you stinking barfly."

He shook her like a throw rug. Her turquoise pendant bounced on its silver chain in sync with her head. "Can't ... ever have ... fun at no ... party 'cause . . .gotta ... check corners ... for you.... Look at me, tramp"—two drunks watched with the concern of Ozzy Osbourne's audience when Ozzy bit the head off a live bat.

"Hey, Fortier!" Steve trickled Black Velvet into a tumbler, and the rat fink dropped Sophie like a used Kleenex. "Must be messed up. Nobody'd be wanting you. Bigger than a knocked up elephant." The crud chugged the drink. Steve poured him another.

Sophie cowered against the baseboard. "I didn't mean no trouble." I didn't know what she'd supposedly done, and I was sure she didn't either.

"It's all right, it's all right," I said, wiping her brow, though I knew I was lying. I buffeted the scum's empty skull with dirty looks.

"Ooo, Elly May ain't happy?"

I wanted to punch a hole through that smirk for every woman he'd ever disrespected. Maybe I'd find out if it's true that knocking out a jerk's teeth will keep his mouth shut.

At last, Mrs. Cole swept us all out to sober up in our own abodes.

The tilted Nova jolted to a stop. Timmy perched on her hip, Barb prodded Rod down the path. Every few yards he'd snicker, "Shh, shh, quiet now," like a tipsy teen sneaking into the house.

Sophie wailed, "If I tell, they won't send you no more money."

"Shut your face, broad, or I'll shut it for you!"

Steve cinched the crud's belt and balanced him downstairs. I almost carried Sophie. Steve clanged the iron gate shut, snapped the padlock, and strode into our place. He didn't look back.

The puppies covered our ankles with wet welcome-home kisses while I hummed the snake charmer's tune and flaunted a seductive belly roll. Steve ruffled my hair. "You're goofy."

Across the hall. A chirp, a snarl, "You stupid broad."

Silence ...

Steve stopped, mid-kiss.

A chirp, a growl ...

Steve relaxed. "Fortier must've ˏbeen holding on"—our running joke. Once Sean got so smashed he fell over a rut in the yard and lay clutching the sod for hours, afraid he'd fall over the edge of the earth—"Thought Fortier would've passed out by now."

He stole a kiss and stalked me like the Pink Panther. The puppies yipped behind, in hot pursuit. I leapt onto the bed and braced. A second later he landed.

A slam of Fortiers' outside door. Another screech ...

Ominous silence ...

A roar. "Broad, you've been warned."

A chirp ...

I rolled away from Steve. "Things are getting out of control." I'd gotten good at rating Fortier fights. This registered high on the Richter scale. "Sophie needs help. She needs us."

A bellow, a growl. A scream, a cheep. The crescendo and decrescendo of the melodramatic score.

Steve mumbled, "We can't help Sophie 'til she's ready, Cindy. I learned that young." He ran his fingers through my hair. "Now where were we?"

And I put Fortiers out of my mind ... until the next afternoon.

The padlock scraped. "Move your @!*, Carmine." Boots clomped up stone steps.

The pups and I trailed Steve to the door. The thump of a trunk lid. Steve stepped out. A case of Air Force toilet paper hit him in the chest. "Make yourself useful, Carmine."

Fortier followed with an armload of cigarette cartons. "Move it, broad."

Sophie scrambled to open the Turkish toilet. The Neanderthal knocked her aside.

And I saw it. Thumbprint bruises on Sophie's neck and wrists, finger-like stripes forming on her arms and biceps.

How could he? I couldn't formulate thoughts.

Methodically, the slime-ball secured their door, then the gate, then snapped the padlock, dangled the key from its elastic, and dropped it into his parka.

No, he can't be!

Steve's jaw tensed. "Hey, Fortier, isn't that Sophie's key you've got there?"

The crud leaned forward, confidingly. "Caught her making goo-goo eyes at Sarge, right in front of me. Tramp's got no sense."

This is crazy!

"What about fire, Fortier?" Steve's voice deepened. "How would she get out?"

"Should've thought of that before she slutted around."

Behind the door, Sophie whimpered, "Didn't mean no trouble. Didn't mean no trouble."

"Then the broad made me beat up my own pal."

I'd seen the crud stumble and slop whiskey all over a guy, but that was all. He, apparently, had a magnified sense of his fighting prowess.

"Broad made me outta fool."

Steve stiffened taller. "Think it'd be a good idea to give Cindy the key? In case of an emergency?"

Silence hung between them as thick as cobwebs in a dungeon.

The creep blinked first. "Broads are all the s-s-same." His "s" hissed. He shot javelins at me. "Can't trust any of them."

"I trust *Cindy*." Steve emphasized my name, then hit the punchline. "Think a dead wife might look bad for you, Fortier? Think your folks might not be so generous if something happened?" Steve gritted his teeth. "Thinking about it, Fortier?"

Steve took one step forward.

The crud cringed back, said, "Just for fire," and tossed the key. "Now getta move on, Carmine." He stomped up the stairs.

The slime's dark eyes and white teeth snapped. Every shiny black hair lay perfectly. His spit-shined boots gleamed like glass, thanks to Sophie. It amazed me that such a monster wasn't hunched and covered with warts.

Steve slid me the key. "Take care of the poor kid, okay?"

I burrowed against him.

The rumble of the Nova blended in with street sounds. I rapped on Sophie's door.

No response.

"Sophie ... Sophie, it's me. I've got your key. You can come over. Or—"

I didn't know what to say. In my world a "lock-in" meant a youth overnighter in the church basement, not a sadistic husband's torture method.

An unfortunate water bug made an escape attempt toward the stairs. I squished it into a mass of black juices and crunched particles, wishing it were that slime trying to pass for human.

Finally, a whisper. "I'm resting now. Go away." Her voice quivered.

I bolted our door, ripped a set of dampened fatigues from the refrigerator, set up the ironing board. Pretending it was Fortier's foul face, I smashed the iron against the shirt until it scorched.

I should be home with people who understand love—helping adjust the dosage of Dilantin to control Tee's seizures without over-sedation. Talking straight to Mama's surgeon. Visiting the Allegheny Airlines' stewardess school with Pam.

Adana's electricity flickered off. The call from the mosque. I picked up the flashlight and the Victoria Holt mystery Pam had sent. The heroine, flames snapping at her feet, screamed and fisted the barred door.... Time moved like a slug on the wall.

"Cindy!" Sophie's screech pierced the dusk. "Cin!" I dashed toward the rattling gate, the pups yipping at my heels. "Cindy!" Sobs. "I'm scared in here." I threw open our door.

"Cindy?" The landlady's voice echoed in the stairwell. "Cindy? Problem?"

"*Yok.* No problem, Madame. Thank you, Madame."

"Yankees!" The landlady's sister's voice. Doors thudded shut.

"I'm scared in here." I'd never heard Sophie's register drop so low.

I broad jumped the hall, extended the key dangling from its elastic band. "Here. You can unlock the gate. You can get out."

Sophie shriveled up. "He'll know I touched it." She crouched, gripping the bars.

Through those bars, I wiped her cheeks and nose with my shirt. "It'll be all right, dear." I reassured her. "I'll open it for you."

The key dove into the lock. Sophie fled so fast she forgot her bug annihilation arsenal. She collapsed on our sofa.

I brewed tea, munched Snickerdoodles, jabbered. She stared listlessly into her cup, not responding until I said, "The landlord's kids helped make these. I think they ate more dough than we baked."

She mumbled, "I wouldn't want kids like that," then lapsed back into numbness.

I wanted to say, *Like what? Intelligent? Energetic? Curious? Obedient? With the genes you're working with, you'll never have to worry about kids like that.* But this wasn't the time.

I refilled tea, wrestled with the pups, picked up my novel, read two chapters.

Eventually, she reached for a cookie, then two, then four, rubbed the marks on her wrists, cupped her neck ... and began clacking out a sad monologue:

"I try to party like my Raymond. But he says I make a fool of myself."

And you trust the opinion of a stumbling perverted wife batterer?

"I drink to keep him company. I wish I could drink enough to forget."

No, you need to remember it all and protect yourself.

"I say he drinks too much. He says his drinking's none of my business. I say I can't live like this. He says I better learn if I know what's good for me. So, I don't say no more."

Then a truth slipped out. "Sometimes he hurts me." She recovered quickly. "Nothing bad. Just my arms and legs."

Just? What do you mean, just?

Sophie rushed on. "My poor Raymond feels so sorry when we fight. He lays his head on my lap like a little boy." She repeated his usual excuse. "My Raymond says thinking about a baby sometimes makes him go a little crazy. He says if I got pregnant, he'd quit drinking."

Grandpa taught us to work to understand people. "We've all got our own row to hoe," he'd say. *But understanding and tolerance don't apply to abuse.*

"I'm not good enough for my Raymond. He says I never will be." Sophie shriveled, folding in on herself. "I disappoint him every time I get my period."

How can she possibly think any of this is her fault? That crud sucks the energy out of every room he enters. He's incapable of creating life.

"This time I got scared. I screwed up. Told him I was leaving. I know better." She snatched another cookie. Pondered.

"He grabbed my neck. To stop me, I think. That's why he locked me in, too."

Grandpa wouldn't cage Laddie like that.

She repeated, "I know better than to threaten him. It scares him. He says he can't live without me."

Part of me couldn't believe her excuses for him. Part of me understood concocting stories to make sense of life, especially the insane times.

She kept talking but never admitted the obvious. The creep grabbed her, choked her, hit her.

"By the time he gets back home, my Raymond will be real sorry. It's just the booze." She paused. "But it can't happen again. This time he has to promise not to drink anymore. Not at all. Not even a little."

Like Sean promises? My brother had taught me the one thing drunks are good at is making promises they don't keep.

Adana's electricity glared back on. But Sophie saw no more clearly. She fidgeted. "I better go. We'll both be in *big* trouble if my Raymond knows you let me out."

Four years older and five times smarter than that twit, yet you let him bully you. Why?

I heaped my tea with sugar and popped another cookie but couldn't get rid of the bitter taste.

Steve snuggled against me and asked, almost timidly, "Sophie okay? And ... you?"

Dammed-up words surged out. "That slime. I had no idea. I thought your dad was bad." I ranted on and on but couldn't articulate my horror. Or my rage.

Steve waited for my words to trickle dry, then said, "You're not used to things like this. I wish *I* wasn't." His curls tickled my shoulder blades. "All I could think of tonight was Sophie locked in, waiting."

His voice grew husky. "In first grade, I ran in from the school bus. Pammy was in her playpen, crying. Mom was in a kitchen chair. Tied up."

For the thousandth time I asked myself why Steve's mother hadn't left Ed.

"I couldn't untie the knots, so I got a paring knife and started cutting. Michael said I'd get my butt kicked if Ed found out. Then he ran out and rode bike."

I waited for him to continue.

"I cut the clothesline one strand at a time because I was afraid I'd slice her skin. All the time, I kept jumping, thinking I heard Ed's semi downshift. I knew he'd kill us both if he caught me getting her loose. I was so scared." He paused. "But he was probably already in Michigan by the time I cut through."

I kissed him, wishing I could kiss away the scars left from growing up in a house of horrors.

"I told Mom we could run away. I'd take care of her. And she gave me a real kiss. First time she wasn't pulling away at the same time, you know?"

His mother held Steve responsible by his very conception for every injustice she'd suffered at Ed's hands. No wonder Steve ran to the sheltering arms of the McNeilly Farm maples. No wonder Jill said, "Give the guy a break. He's Ed Carmine's son, for goodness sake."

"But it got worse," Steve said.

I couldn't imagine.

"Every night I laid awake waiting for her to pack our things ... but she never did. That weekend Ed came home, and no one said a word about it. I had to remind myself I really saw the cords."

He paused a long time. "When I asked her why Ed tied her up she said, 'Shut up! Never mention *that* again!' I thought *I* did something bad!"

I could think of nothing to say.

"See why I never know about getting involved?" Avoiding my eyes, he brushed my flip off my shoulder. "I never know if Sophie, or anyone, will let me help."

The next afternoon, the Fortiers opened their gate, and Sophie kissed the crud with the suction of a barnacle clinging to the bottom of a ship. "Hurry back, Teddy Bear," she twittered.

"I can't believe it," I muttered as Steve brushed my cheek.

"Unfortunately, I can," he said and stomped off to work.

Chapter 18

The Code of Thieves

In January of 1968, the whole world was unraveling, not just the Fortier household. North Korea captured the USS Pueblo. At Tet, the "Year of the Monkey," fireworks and feasts, a holiday truce, and the VC concealed explosives in truckloads of rice and tomatoes and simultaneously attacked hundreds of towns in the South (murdering six Protestant missionaries and capturing two others plus a US AID advisor).

And on Incirlik, Lux raised hackles to warn of jackals outside of the post perimeters but, sadly, he had no way to warn Steve about the jackals wearing fatigues on the inside—

Rap-pause-rap. "Hey, Cin, Steve got held up. He'll catch the bus." Rod offered no details.

Steve stomped in several hours later, eyes to the floor, his only explanation, "Had a couple things to take care of." Holes gaped in his mud-caked fatigues. Knees and palms oozed.

"What happened?" I ran for the First Aid kit.

"Let's just say, for Turks, the end of Ramadan means a new year and a clean soul. For me, it's just a new year and a new problem." He ignored the pups scampering around for attention.

"I don't get the riddle."

"Want it straight?" His question sounded like a dare. "Security breach. I'll probably get court-martialed. Any more questions?"

"Actually, yes. What on earth are you talking about?"

He shrugged, poured peroxide on his hand, inhaled a sandwich and crawled into bed, rolled into a cocoon and fell into fitful sleep—thrashing about, poking his index finger in the air, cursing, "I'm sick of this *#@!"

The puppies whimpered in sympathy. Like Mama taught me, I told myself there was no use worrying when I didn't know what to worry about. But I didn't succeed. Stewing is one of my great talents.

The next morning, mute and wooden, Steve hunched over a hand of solitaire. The pups, strangely still, curled at his feet. An impenetrable silence fogged up our cramped apartment.

Lord, let him talk to me. I poured cups of tea.

He dropped sugar cubes, one by one, watching each sink, stirring until not a granule remained.

My needle and thread pieced together the knees of his fatigues but not his untold story.

The pups raced down the hall. Steve followed, threw open the door to let them out.

"Hey, man, how's it hangin'?" The Garzas.

Steve shrugged.

Rod grabbed an ashtray, crashed at the table. Steve dealt out a rummy hand. Barb curled feet under her on the sofa. Timmy, in cute little denim jeans and a red handkerchief bandana, wiggled onto the floor, started to walk, then dropped down and fish-tail-crawled to the kitchen and ferreted behind pink cotton for the cookie can.

"Oatmeal today," I said.

Timmy, tolerating puppy slobber, crammed a cookie into his mouth with both hands, then scooted, pups at his heels, and threw cookies into their basket. At some point he'd decided their basket was their dining area.

Rod blew a smoke ring. "That whole scene was a real bummer, man."

"Yeah." Steve tapped the cards on the table.

I washed doggy saliva off Timmy's fingers, scolded pups, "This one's for Timmy." Mutt and Jeff trampolined beside me, begging for a crumb. I flipped pages of *Go, Dog, Go,* mumbled to Barb, "What's going on?"

"Chill," she whispered, "It's all going to come out in the open."

I blurted out, "You're finally going to tell him!" I thought she meant her pregnancy news.

The guys looked over.

Barb hushed me, "Shh, not about me," then covered my slip by saying louder, "Yeah, about the chase."

"Oh," I played along, though I had no idea what the "chase" was.

"Cin's gonna find out eventually, man, so fill us in." Rod tapped off a long ash. "All I know's some Turk gave the APs quite a run for their money. Ripped off a barracks and a house trailer, then booked. A real slippery one. Can't believe Lux didn't nail his butt."

"Me either," Steve muttered. "Out walking post, minding my own business and Lux alerted."

I strained for his every word.

"This Turk came running at me." K-9 guarded the perimeters of the base, the final apprehension point. "I yelled, 'Halt. Dur!' three times like we're supposed to. Had Lux's leash hanging right at the tip of my fingers."

"So? That black menace of yours should've dropped him in his tracks."

"Yeah, he would've, except I pulled him back in."

"No way! You crazy, man?"

Steve explained, rapid fire. "Big-shot tech sergeant, that's why. In hot pursuit. A Barney Fife. Can't have a brain. Penetrated my post, waving and yelling, 'Release that dog, Airman.' Course Lux swirled and alerted on *him*. *He* was making all the noise."

Steve smacked his fist. "What would you've done, Garza? If I'd released Lux, he would've shredded the idiot." Steve said he shouted for the tech sergeant to vacate the area. "If he'd backed off and let us work, I think I could've got Lux's attention back on the Turk." Instead, the tech shot at the intruder, right past Steve's head. "Release that dog. That's an order, Airman," then fired a second round. "Lux almost broke my arm, trying to nail that tech. I had to pull him in, right?"

"I see where you're coming from, man." Rod leaned back.

"It was all stand down after that. Lux and I pursued on foot, but the Turk had too much of a head start." Steve shuffled several minutes, sorting the cards and the event.

Rod pointed at Steve's palms and knees. "Pretty torn up there, man. You left that part out."

Steve scratched Jeff's ear.

Rod insisted. "We're waiting, man. The Turk. What'd he do?"

Steve shrugged and petted Mutt. "Turk didn't do anything."

Rod's eyebrows twitched in impatience.

Steve went on, sheepishly. "Lux and I were motoring across that field. Pitch black. And splat! Flat on the ground. Didn't see the ditch."

Visualizing that scene, I was overcome by the giggles. After all, it's me, the klutz, who falls over a blade of grass. Not Steve, the athlete. How ironic.

Steve scowled. "You wouldn't be laughing, Cindy, if Lux tore up that tech. Lux goes for the throat, you know."

I sobered up fast.

"Lucky for us, I'd slipped the loop of the leash around my wrist, or I'd have lost him. It would've been the brig for me."

"Well, man, doesn't sound as bad as the buzz at the kennels made it out."

"I ignored a direct order. Isn't that bad enough?" Steve twisted a curl. "The tech sergeant said he'd see my butt in a sling for disobeying a direct order. I meet with the squadron commander tomorrow."

"Don't sweat it, man. The tech's all talk." Rod blew a great cloud of smoke. "Besides, hearings are routine when a man leaves his assigned post, or a weapon is discharged."

"Not so simple. There's another factor." Steve patted Mutt's nose. "I was filing my incident report, and the clerk let it slip. That idiot tech's Cole's NCO buddy. Great luck, right?"

I cuddled Timmy. Of all the things that Sarge's parties had taught me, one of the main lessons was that drinking buddies stick together, no matter what.

Rod tapped out a cigarette. "For what it's worth, I got in Fortier's face. Said, 'You heard it all. Speak up!'" Rod lit a match. "That gutless wonder got all defensive and said, 'Don't need no trouble for no rat fink.'"

Steve pounded his fist.

Rod took several drags. "You meddled, Carmine. This is Fortier's revenge."

Steve sighed agreement. "Bad timing, to say the least."

Barb's brow puckered. "I haven't heard this part. What're you two talking about?"

We waited. Timmy slid poor Mutt across the tile by the tail. Steve intervened, plopped Timmy on his knee. "Ride 'em, horsey." Jeff scratched for attention.

Finally, Rod filled in the blanks. "Before post, Steve confronted Fortier for a little chat." He turned back to Steve. "You gonna tell the girls what about?"

Steve set Timmy down, "Don't torment our little buddies now." He looked up. "Okay, it's like this. I told Fortier he'd better listen up while he could. Told him locking Sophie in was the last straw. Told him he'd better pick on someone his own size, or we'd covered the last time."

"Covered." We all knew what that meant, but Rod said it out loud. "The Pound's a sore spot. Fortier's folks want grandkids. That takes a happy wife. His folk's dough rides on Sophie. Course threats about telling her about the Pound don't go down good with him."

"It wasn't a threat," Steve said, softly.

"Fortier knows that. That's the problem," Rod said. "He'll get even."

"Right now I'm more worried about Sarge's tech buddy getting even," Steve said.

Like Nana, I hit my knees and prayed straight through four calls from the mosque.

Steve clomped back in after the hearing, subdued and confused. "I don't get what just happened," he said. "The Commander called me in and asked, 'Why didn't you release your dog as ordered, Airman?' And I said, 'Because I didn't think you'd want one dead tech sergeant.'"

I imagined Steve's defiant tone and moaned. Why couldn't he ever just play the game?

"That was it. One question, verification of a couple of details in my report, and dismissed. I about crapped bullets." Steve saves great phrases like that for only special occasions. "Later the Commander called me back in. You know why?" Steve shook his head. "Not to chew me out. To commend me on my restraint. But the scuttlebutt is the Commander gave the tech a verbal reprimand for discharging his gun when not shooting to kill."

Great news! I planted a resounding smack on his lips, "It's the power of prayer," then punched him. "Next time don't torture me with scary details. Get straight to the happy ending."

"Well, to be honest, I haven't decided if the ending was happy or not. Got one mean hate glare from the tech sergeant. The barracks says I should've padded my statement a little. You know, like the Turk had a gun and shot first, or something like that. Think they're right?"

I didn't understand the question. "Why? You told the truth, right?"

"Truth isn't enough around here, Cindy. Gets you labeled a snitch." Steve's pause was ominous. "They say I'll have hell to pay for getting Cole's drinking buddy chewed out."

And "they" were right. Hell began. That very night.

Rod knocked. "Hey, Cin, Steve's gonna be late." Sarge had ordered Steve to wash the transport van after post. The next night, an extra CQ duty. Next, Steve's transfer to C Flight. "So it's the bus to base from now on. And no three-day breaks with Garzas. What else can happen?"

That answer came quickly, too.

Promotions came down. Fortier and Garza earned a stripe, a $40-a-month pay raise. Carmine didn't.

"We needed that money, Cindy." His mood darkened. "Good thing you had your period. We can't afford a baby."

"There must be some mistake, man," Rod insisted. "You work harder for those dogs than anyone in K-9. Check your AFP [Air Force Performance] file. Find out the reason."

Steve set his jaw. "Wouldn't do any good. We both know why. I wouldn't lick Sarge's boots ... or his buddy's."

It seemed the policemen of the world needed policing themselves.

Help my husband, God. Save his career. Nothing could be worse than this.

Chapter 19

The Walls Come Tumbling Down

Steve's telling the truth about the tech sergeant added us to the upturned world. Then, Barb's telling the truth about her second pregnancy added the Garzas.

Barb abandoned her "clean house and good meal" plan to prepare Rod for the news and switched to the "knit a baby blanket and pin the news on a note" plan. She was clearly nuts from hormones or something.

Watching her untangle a clump of yellow and green yarn, I couldn't help teasing, "You'd better come up with something different. Your baby will be out of college before you finish this." We were close enough by then I could get away with cracks like that.

Anyway, it's still unbelievable to me how Rod found—

Frantic pounding. Steve loped for the door.

Rod fell in, thrust Timmy at me, and caught Barb before she hit the floor. Babbling gibberish about Turks and knives, Rod propped Barb on the couch.

Her head collapsed on the back of the sofa, her hair folded back from her face like the flap on a tent, and Steve and I gasped.

Blood dripped from her mouth and onto her neck.

"Who?" Steve doubled up his fists.

"Why?" I ran for ice. Timmy bounced on my hip.

Barb and Rod slouched together as limp as Raggedy Ann and Andy,

"What a bummer. Totally blindsided." We waited for Rod to continue. "Took the long way over." The street instead of the path. "Horsing around with Timmy. Throwing him up in the air like a baseball. He was giggling like crazy." He paused. "Then ... right out in public—" Rod rested his forehead on Barb's, as if transferring healing messages.

Steve's hands twitched for action. He closed the pups in their room, reached out for Timmy. But I clutched my solace tight. Steve mouthed, "Please." And I slowly relinquished Timmy.

Eventually, Rod said, "Two guys. Respectable-looking types. Followed us into your lane."

Ours? Even the Yankee-go-home boys had stopped at the mouth of that lane.

"Out of the blue, one dude goes ape and—" His jaw locked, imprisoning the words. His dark head nestled her fair one.

I repositioned ice.

Barb whispered the end of the sentence. "He ... bit me."

"Bit?" I gripped her shoulder.

Rod's voice quaked. "Yeah, man, clamped on like a snapping turtle. On her mouth. Couldn't get him off. And couldn't put the kid down. Might've been a diversion to kidnap him." Rod wiped his forehead. His hand quivered.

"I'm pounding and pounding on that *!#@, and the kid's laughing like it's some kind of game." Rod demonstrated holding Timmy in a death-grip football hold, buffeting the attacker with the other hand. "Finally landed a punch flat on that #!@%'s ear. Hope I broke his !@* eardrum."

Rod acted out the Turk shaking his head clear and whirling ... with a knife. "I yelled, 'get booking,' and tossed the kid. He splatted on the ground." *Timmy on the ground?* "But the kid didn't make a peep. His diaper must've padded him."

Barb mumbled, "I saw that knife flash and froze. Like a pile of ice up at Lake Tahoe."

Rod rubbed her shoulder. "We would've been goners without that other Turk."

The second man pushed in front of the attacker, coaxing him to put down the knife, giving Barb time to snatch Timmy off the ground. The Turks, arguing, widening the ring around Garzas, moving closer to the street. Neither party turning a back until Garzas reached our foyer and made a dash for it.

Barb sniffled through the story. "Watch out for gypsies, everyone says. A poor Turk will slice your throat for a nickel, everyone says." She shifted, mournfully. "No one warns you about wealthy businessmen." Rod patted her. Steve bounced Timmy.

I iced Barb's mouth (already swelling at the corners) and murmured. "We should take you to the dispensary. You can't be too careful in your condition."

"I'm fine." Barb shushed me with a look.

Now, remember. For months Rod had been oblivious to hundreds of our slip-ups. But, crazily, in the middle of this chaos, he twirled around and asked, "What condition?" His tone made the question rhetorical.

He would choose this time to listen.

Barb lowered blue lids, shifted on the sofa.

Just tell him. Get it over with.

Blond hair, again a shroud. Shifting restlessly on sofa. A heaved-out sigh (or sob) and "I'm pregnant," she confessed.

I held my breath.

Rod stiffened away.

Steve sprang over and slapped Rod on the back. "Congratulations, you lucky son-of-a- gun." He do-si-doed Timmy around the table, so fast that Mr. Fluffy's ears looked like a helicopter prop warming up. "And you, little buddy, are one lucky big brother."

I intercepted them, elbowed him into the kitchen. "Give them some privacy."

"I was going to," he wrangled, but a grin covered his whole face. He "brr"ed Timmy's forehead. "If we save up a dime or two, maybe we can find out if this pregnancy thing's contagious, Cindy."

Finger on my lips, listening to the living room.

Not a whisper.

We peeked out—Rod and Barb, sitting apart, two fragile porcelain statues.

Steve raised his shoulders, questioning, then smacked his forehead. "What are we standing around here for?"

He flung Timmy to me, hurdled the hall, "Out here, Fortier! Now! A Turk attacked Barb."

Feet skittered away from Fortiers' door.

Steve galloped upstairs, towed the landlord back in, pointed to Barb's bruising bleeding mouth, then, *"Gel!"* dragged the poor Turk—collar yanked over his shoulder—across the hall.

"Get a move on, Fortier." Steve almost rattled the iron gate off its hinges.

The door opened a crack. Steve snatched the coward's hand, yanked it through the bars.

"Easy there, Carmine. I'm coming." The coward unpadlocked the gate and waddled out before Steve did him permanent damage. The little vigilante group raced away. Barb drooped.

I bounced Timmy. Patted pups. The silence grew unbearable.

"The only help Wimp Fortier will be is if he falls on the Turk and squashes him like a water bug. Visualize that." I flattened a throw pillow, snickered.

Barb glanced over, sighed. I refreshed tea. She sipped. "Things were so perfect, Rod playing with Timmy like a real father. I was believing maybe he wouldn't flip out if he knew I'm pregnant." She stirred in some milk. "But this wasn't the way I planned to tell him. Not one of the hundreds of ways, in fact."

"He took it fine." I hugged her hard.

Timmy squealed as the pups slid along waxed tile on bulging bellies. Jeff pounced like a cat from behind the drapes. Mutt crouched under the end table poking a teasing paw out at Jeff, too tall to squeeze under it.

I broke the silence. "Jill says my mystery novels are a waste of time. In real life, people don't escape to tell the story. I'm glad she was wrong about you."

We sipped. This time a cup of hot tea seemed to help a little. Until she said, "I always thought I was safe with a man."

Menacing shadows loomed around us. Timmy crawled over to me, held up his arms, nestled close. I hummed the Irish lullaby from the days of life at the end of the McNeilly-Alden lane. "Me, too," I admitted. "I thought a man could keep me safe, too."

Doubts shook me to the core.

The vigilantes stomped back in, empty handed, then escorted Garzas back home.

***

After post, Rod landed at the Airman's Club. Drank. Gambled. Word spread quickly that the Garzas were expecting. "Kind of a drag, all of it," was Rod's response to congratulations.

And Barb cried, like Sophie, like my sister-in-law Jo, like all women wounded by men who'd vowed to love and protect them 'til death.

Chapter 20

The Last Illusion Shattered

Sophie's and Barb's situations made me question things that I never had before. Like the fact that even Grandpa and Dad, a couple of the best men I knew, couldn't save Mama from crazed cells (defective chromosomes, cancer cells) or save Tee from night terrors and seizures. And I admitted to myself, *Maybe men only protect women in fairy tales.*

I think that's what started the nightmares. Images of:

Tee convulsing alone, "Dee! Dee!"

Mama, violin bow slipping, slicing off her breast, blood spouting like from Pompey's statue in *Julius Caesar.* "Princess, help me!"

Pam, box-pleated cheerleader's skirt splayed, tumbling from the top of a pyramid. "Steve, Grandpa, Cin."

Me running, running. Inches from Tee, inches from Mama, inches from Pam's outstretched hand ... falling, falling, falling ... Grandpa piping, "Danny Boy." The whisper of raven's wings.

And I'd wake in Steve's arms. "It's okay, Cindy. We're short. Just a few months and we'll all be together on the farm. We'll be building our own houses and ..."

He just didn't know. Nightmares can become reality—

The envelope in Steve's hand trembled. "I didn't open it. I figured it must be important"—Mama's handwriting, not Nana's. As ominous as a midnight phone call.

The postmark's ten days ago. I ripped it open. Ordered my eyes to focus:

"We agonized how to tell you. Thought we'd send a Red Cross telegram. Faster. Didn't want you to find out after the fact. But we figured it might remind you of Uncle's horrible singing-telegram jokes. Ha ha. We settled on a letter. So I'm writing this in the hospital, hoping you'll never get it. If your dad mailed it, it's cancer."

Cancer. That taboo word splattering my brain like the VC's bullet in the AP photo ... *falling ... falling ...*

I buckled. Mama's letter slid to the floor. *How could I have not sensed she was in trouble?* It seemed so wrong—Mama alone, her second breast gone, lying with drainage tubes, hemovacs, IVs, while I laughed with Steve and Timmy and....

Steve picked the letter up and read the beginning. "Damn!" He hugged me tight several minutes. His whole body tremored.

When we both got still, he started reading aloud: "It was canning season when I found the lump. Dr. Sherman said not to worry. It was probably just a cyst and would disappear. Anyway, Mother and I got sweet corn up, fall got really busy, then Christmas, and the lump was still there."

Of course it was still there. How could I've been so stupid to think, even for a minute, that it'd ever be over?

"Dr. Sherman said the lump is definitely larger now, so a biopsy is required. I said if he finds even one bad cell, take the whole thing. I know what to expect this time. I can handle it."

But I can't!... Nightmare images of Devil-eyed surgeons. Sharpening scalpels on leather straps. Systematically cutting away Mama's nose, freckles, eyebrow, body parts, one by one. "It's essential to eradicate all cancer cells." Mama dismembered like the Venus de Milo ... *falling ... falling ...*

Steve read faster. "So I'm not lopsided anymore. And I'll never have to worry about another breast surgery. Ever."

A pretty radical worry-prevention measure.

"Write me funny stories, Princess. Laughter's good for me. But the best medicine of all is the hope of another grandbaby. Yours and Steve's this time. Ha ha!"

Falling ... The Jesus with power to hush storms, walk on water, heal the blind and lame, and raise the dead hadn't used His power to stop one tiny berserk cell. I practically screamed. "Does God hear any of my prayers?"

Steve shied back, pointed at Dad's P.S: "The cyst was nothing. But on the chest wall was a cancer, the size of a grape. Good thing they went in now or it would've spread before she felt it."

Steve leaned close. "Sounds like God's protecting her to me. Doesn't it to you?"

I yanked away. "You're grasping at straws." I shook in white fury. "This is all Sean's fault. Heading for a divorce. Joking about the Irishman's seven-course meal." A six pack and a potato. "Dr. Sherman said stress could cause metastasis. And Sean's nothing but stress."

I flopped on our bed. "No, I'm kidding myself. We both know whose fault it is. Mine"—after Mama's first mastectomy, Grandpa said, "Love saved God's Angel, [Tee]. Love will save Mae"—"I left Mama when she needed my love."

Bow slipping, slicing Mama ... falling, falling ... "Princess."

Steve wiped my nose with his shirt sleeve. "It's not Sean's fault and it's not your fault. She's surrounded by love. Your dad and Tee, Nana and Grandpa, Jill, Pammy, the people from church."

I stiffened. "But no one understands her like I do. Remember how she fought coming out of anesthesia until I got in her room? No one else knew to take the sheet off her foot." Mama always sleeps with one foot out of the covers.

"No one else knew room-temperature 7-Up helps her nausea. No one else shared caramel corn and a Late Nite movie with her when she had insomnia." My voice grew shrill. Ants raced around my skull. "I should never have left her. I have to get home. Now!"

The pups licked my salty tears. Steve's blue eyes swam. "She's more a mother to me than my own, Cindy," he said. "I'll find a way."

On paper, we had the money for a plane ticket. The captain had mandated proof of passage home for wives (a $500 cash deposit or bank statement or letter of responsibility stamped by a bank). So Grandpa sent a letter of responsibility and a copy of the bank statement after he deposited the milk check. But we all knew those milk checks paid for farm and living expenses, not plane tickets.

"Princess, help me."

Steve ran his hand through his curls. "I'll ask the chaplain. Maybe he'll come up with something." Then he bolted out, returning with Barb and Timmy. "Thought our little buddy might help," he said, hesitantly.

I eked out an insincere smile. *"Princess."*

Timmy offered me his bunny. "Ma-ma" My smile flickered sincere. *"Princess."*

Steve evacuated the apartment a second time.

Barb settled on the bed beside me. "I've been thinking. There isn't time for you to sell this furniture for a plane ticket. Your only option is black-market. It'd take too many ration cards to sell enough cigarettes and toilet paper, but Timmy's outgrown lots of stuff Turks can't get over here. They'd pay top dollar." She started listing: a baby swing, bathtub, infant carrier, barely-used toys.

Surely this time the end justifies the means. I grew excited. "And I quit taking birth control pills a bit ago. I still have three month's supply in the drawer." Our belly dancing tutor had hinted she'd buy them.

"Princess" ... falling ... falling ... I'm coming home, Mama.

"We can do this." Barb said like a cheerleader and hugged me.

But before Steve spoke with the chaplain, before Barb arranged the black-market deal, Jill squelched it all with a letter typed as a Red Cross telegram (ala the Supremes): "Stop in the name of love. You'll break her heart. Think it o-o-ver."

I could see Jill swinging those orange love beads of hers in a backup-singer's move.

"Don't even consider coming home."

Steve grinned. "Can Jill read your mind or not?"

Jill summarized the surgeon's report: The position of the lump (against the chest wall). A bad thing. But the quadrant and size, (inner, upper and small) and no sign of spread. Really good things.

"Your mama's fine," Jill said. "And all she talks about is you two making her a grandma again. She'd be devastated if you flew home." I knew Jill was right.

Mama and I understood each other without words—like in my Rapunzel stage. Nana had to cut Tee's gum out of my hair. By the time she was done, my pigtails were as short as toothpicks. Mama styled my hair with Dippity Doo, really kind of cute. But the next day after waitressing, she brought me a gold brush and said, "Brush one hundred strokes every night and the prince will be climbing up in no time." Mama understood my Rapunzel dream like I now understood her "daughter with a happy marriage and babies" dream.

I need to be home with Mama. I need to help her. But Mama needed to pretend. If I returned home without Steve, it'd be an in-the-face reminder that this cancer could be serious. She'd have difficulty pretending everything was normal and "it" was over. And Mama needed that dream to heal.

I was so conflicted. I'd never ignored Mama's needs before. Jill knew that, too. "Think of your mama, not yourself."

She knew that'd get to me. I'd been taught selfishness is no part of love. If I loved Mama, no matter how much it killed me, I had to wait to go home with Steve at the end of August as planned.

The waiting shortened my fuse. And Steve's.

The pups' antics helped relieve some of the tension. Some days—"Come see this, Cindy." Two pups routing like baby pigs in mud puddles from winter rains. An inch of dirt caked their noses.... "They're playing tug of war," Steve hollered. Come see." The puppies tussled over Tee's hooked rug. I substituted my treasure with a dirty towel.... "Come see this, Cindy." Mutt and Jeff running an obstacle course of piles of laundry on the floor. And we laughed.

Unfortunately, housetraining them also added to the tension some days. Mutt trained easily, but not Jeff. He knew the concept, whined and veered down the hall to be let out, but he always puddled the floor or watered the door before I got there.

Steve blamed me. "You're too soft. Rub his nose harder and he won't dribble all over."

I blamed Steve. "Jeff's not a sentry dog. You make him nervous. Besides, he's growing tall. His insides haven't matured."

He bristled. "You're making excuses. Let him know who's boss. My dad would—"

I wielded the ultimate weapon. "I thought you weren't going to be like your dad."

"Think that's funny, smarty pants?" He dealt out a game of solitaire.

One day, wound tight because the mail was backed up in Istanbul, I opened the door to let the pups out just as Fortier said,

"Way I see it, Carmine, you finally got even with ole Sarge. Nailed him good." He smirked. "You're one lucky son Sarge ain't dead."

Steve slammed the door shut, so hard the glass rattled.

My stomach churned. The pups scrambled for their basket, Jeff dribbling all the way. I discreetly wiped the trail with a rag under my foot and asked, "What'd Ray mean by that?"

Steve was as ambiguous as the Delphi Oracle. "Simply put, we don't need to worry anymore about me getting promoted next board." His lunch pail clanked in the sink. "Now we better pray I don't get busted to E1."

I stiffened. "Why? What happened?"

"Don't bother asking."

I didn't.

He pulled out collars and leashes. "The gypsies are due. Don't want you outside alone. I'll get these little guys collar trained, so you can hook them to a run."

I didn't criticize his logic. How could I hook pups on a run outside unless I went outside? I just said, "I hate leashes. Laddie runs free."

Steve *did* criticize my logic. "Laddie lives in America. We don't."

The pups wagged and jostled for attention.

"Here, buddy." Steve sat on a chair by the hall and cinched a collar on Mutt. "Your pudgy little neck barely fits, buddy." Steve adjusted it. Mutt twisted uncertainly, then, futilely pawing to get it off his neck, fled to the basket.

"Okay, you're next, Jeff." Jeff proudly wagged his whole body and posed as if on sentry duty. Until the collar constricted.

Jeff shrunk back. Which pulled the collar tighter. The tighter it got, the more Jeff battled. Frantic, he nipped at Steve.

"Enough of that, boy." Like a rodeo cowboy wrestling a calf, in one leap Steve grabbed Jeff between his knees and cinched the collar.

Jeff went berserk. Pawing. Snapping.

"Down, boy." Steve's knees pinched tighter. "Sit."

"Give him a minute. Be gentle."

Just then, in an unlucky move, Jeff grabbed hold of the meaty part of Steve's palm, directly under the thumb.

Steve turned Carmine purple and yanked, choking off Jeff's air. "Bad dog! No more of that!"

Steve rubbed Jeff's nose in it. "Outside!"

Jeff lost control and scooted a butterscotch volcano against the kitchen wall. Feces oozed onto the tile.

And that's when Steve lost control, too. Cherubim cheeks swelled into bellows, shot flames. "Outside!" He heaved Jeff, yip-yip-yipping, at the door. Mutt wedged between my legs.

Everything happened so quickly. I didn't have time to react.

He stomped back in. "Have fun cleaning up *your* dog's mess."

"*My* dog?" I planted my hands on my hips, immovable. "Jeff's *our* dog. And what happened to patience and kindness?"

His forehead furrowed. "Patient and kind?" He sounded like he was talking to a space alien. "We're talking about a dog here, aren't we? A dog that attacked your husband?"

"Attacked? He barely scratched you."

"Not for lack of trying."

I glared daggers. "I suppose when your kids make a mess, you'll beat them, too."

He winced, then spun around and whistled out the door. "Jeff! *Gel*, come, *Gel*."

But no patter on the stairs.

He huffed his lungs full. Shrieked, "Jeff!"

"He'd be crazy to come to you." As crazy as I was to come over here with you.

"Then it's *his* hard luck. This country isn't exactly known for its love of strays." He stomped out.

I should've figured it out after Cali—my favorite kitten climbed the pole, hit the transformer, the whole neighborhood went dark. Steve threw her stiff body into the manure spreader. "Why're you so upset? It's a cat"—*Why did I leave Mama for this monster?*

He stormed back in. Flopped down at the table.

"You're just going to leave him out there?" I accused him, simmering.

"So, you have a better answer, smarty pants?" He cracked his knuckles.

"You don't have to be a brain surgeon to figure it out. Stay out 'til you find him."

"You already said he won't come to *me*. If you care so much, why don't you go get him yourself?"

"I will." The top of my head felt about to blow. "And I won't come back." *Ever!*

His chair clanked over as he jumped up. "Where do you think you're going? Get back in the house where you belong." He blocked the hallway. *Why did I leave Mama for this?*

"I'm not Grandma Carmine! I don't march to your orders. I'll go out if I want to." But a vision of the bite mark on Barb's mouth stopped me. I flounced to the kitchen instead. Grabbed a pan.

He pursued me. "I suppose you think this is all my fault, don't you?"

I glared silence, drew water to boil.

"You can't let a dog get away with biting. Don't you have any common sense?"

"Common sense? Common sense says you terrified him. What did you expect him to do?" I banged a pan onto the burner. *I need to see Mama.* "Get away. I never want to look at your face again."

He recoiled. "You don't mean that."

"Don't tell me what I mean." I grabbed the scouring pad and yanked off those rings that broadcast my biggest mistake.

"Don't! You're going to hurt yourself." His voice softened. His shoulder brushed mine. He almost whispered. "Cindy, please." He slid his hand between the Brillo pad and my finger.

I scrubbed harder. My cheeks blazed hotter. Those ants raced in my skull. Scrubbing harder to rid myself of that lying ring-finger promise. "Get out of here. And take your face with you!"

He stiffened. "You don't want to see this face?" He dropped my hand, grasped both of my cheeks, turned me toward him. "You don't want to see this face?" *No, I want to see Mama's.*

"Let go of me now." *I hate him!* I writhed to free myself. "Get out of here or—!"

He heard my vague-but-serious threat.

But he didn't get out. He shadowed me like a depraved mime, contorting his face an inch from mine, turning each time I turned.

I almost vomited. I squeezed my eyes tight shut.

"Someday you'll have to open them. And guess whose face you'll see?" His voice stalked me.... a lull ... I peeked ... directly into his smirk. "I'm still here," he sing-songed.

The safety valve of the pressure cooker of my emotions blew. "Then I'm gone." *Forever.*

"Where to?" He goaded me. "Fortier's *bush bush?*"

I spun around. "I'd rather have my throat slit than stay another minute with you."

He shoved past. "You might as well stay 'cause I'm leaving."
He almost splintered the door on his way out. *Good riddance!*
I flopped down, squaw-like. And covered my face.
Grandpa would've puffed on his cigar and gone to the barn. Julian would've smiled and concocted a reasonable solution. But Steve? His eyes bulged. His temple pulsed. Mr. Hyde popped out. "I'll never be anything like my old man," he'd promised. And I'd believed him. *But he's a liar, a heartless liar. Carmine to the core.*
He clomped back in, put Mutt on a leash. "C'mon, little buddy. Let's go get your pal."
I got up. *Mama, I'm sorry I ever left you. Mama ...*
Through the bars, I could see Jeff crouching in the cotton field, Steve straining under the barbed wire, Mutt proudly tethered.
"Here, buddy," he cajoled.
Jeff inched sideways. He knew monsters can't be trusted.
"C'mon. Your buddy misses you."
Jeff crouched, just a few feet out of reach.
Smart puppy.
He released the leash. Mutt ran into the field, sniffed and pawed at Jeff's head. Jeff, like a Sphinx, never budged.
He stomped back in. Tossed Mutt a bone. Gave him a pat on the head, and a "Good boy." Then left without a word to me.
Don't let the door hit you on the way out.
I grabbed a bucket, scrubbed feces, fumed.
Why did I think he's any different than Ed and Michael? Why did I leave Mama for this creature when I knew "it" could come back? Why...?

Then, voices outside the kitchen window. I looked to see that monstrous Carmine standing back. Rod holding Timmy, kicking and squealing, "Da! Da!" and Jeff edging closer to the baby.
Timmy swatted Mr. Fluffy. "Da! Da!" Jeff slinked closer, closer, close enough to lick at Timmy's nose. *At least Jeff's smarter than me. He knows who's trustworthy and who's not.*

Rod's hand, speed of an athletic slug, inched closer ... closer ... then "snap," clasped Jeff's cowering neck. "Got 'em, Carmine." Timmy whacked happily as the guys talked, then went their separate ways home.

That Carmine creature clomped back in and set Jeff down in our hall. Jeff's paws touched down on the tile and scrambled straight for his basket. Whimpering sympathy, Mutt followed into the spare room. So did that Carmine.

It shocked me to hear him crooning, "Did I hurt you? I didn't mean to. But you can't bite your daddy." He caught me watching him. "Had to check the pups' water bowl," he mumbled, not even capable of admitting to a guilty conscience.

That day the sun went down on my wrath. *I wouldn't have his baby to save the population. I'd never be a party to polluting the world with such savagery, such insensitivity.* My rigid back religiously avoided his side of the bed.

"Oh, to be back home driving the tractor for Grandpa to collect sap. To be in the sugarhouse with Mama, pouring boiled maple syrup in folds onto a tray for the perfect candy ... "Princess" ... "Dee. Dee."

I dozed. *"Princess, help me!"* Running, running, inches from Mama's outstretched hand ... falling ... "Crack!" Ed's fist against Steve's jaw ... I bolted straight up, clammy with sweat.

The bed bounced. Carmine, wide-eyed, was leaning over the bed, craning back and forth, rubbing his thumb against his index finger, repeating, "Here, doggy-doggy," in a strange robot-like voice.

Talking in his sleep again.

"Here, doggy-doggy," he coaxed, then made a great sweeping motion under the bed and in K-9-handler timbre, ordered, "Come!"

Both pups clambered from the spare room onto our bed. I shooed them down and tried to reason. "Steve, Steve, your dog's been located. Jeff is secured in his basket."

"Doggy-doggy. Doggy-doggy." A silly toddler voice. Nothing had penetrated his sleeping brain. "Doggy-doggy." Then he slumped back and laid still. *At last!*

But he popped up again, leaned over and started stroking the air in a Jack Benny-Red Skelton-combo motion.

"Oh, your dog came back." My voice dripped sarcasm.

"He did not!" He pouted and continued calling, "Here, doggy-doggy."

The crazy Carmine can't even let me sleep in peace! I pulled the sheet over my head.

At some point I dozed—Julian patted the seat of his Falcon, "Scoot over, Kitten." One by one, daisy petals fell, "Loves me, loves me not." ... *Mama, falling ... Grandpa's Irish pipe ...*

The second call to prayer. He leapt up. "Want me to get Garzas for pancakes?"

I shrugged. Nothing mattered anymore.

He tossed Timmy and bunny into the air, then burred heads. Before devouring two stacks of pancakes and a pile of eggs. He never let loose of Timmy. Until time for a diaper change, of course.

I reached out and Timmy said, "Mama," Clearly. Distinctly. Not just "ma-ma-ma-ma" syllables. Timmy said it like a word. "Mama." I squealed. "Did you hear that? He called me Mama!" I danced Timmy around the room.

Barb, mute to that point, wrapped me in a rare hug. "There's no one in this world I'd rather have him call Mama, Cin," she said. "He wouldn't be here today if it weren't for you and Steve. You two saved his life."

Instinctively, I clasped Timmy. "What're you talking about?"

Instinctively, he chose escape. "Hey Garza, want to run for some *ekmek*?" On their way out, Steve yelled back over his shoulder, "Fill her in, Barb." The door slammed.

... Barb started haltingly. "Last night I got a craving for chestnuts, so we took off for the boulevard." She twisted a strand of hair. "Timmy was asleep."

I interrupted. "But you promised not to leave him anymore. You said you'd let us watch him."

"I know. But it was only for a few minutes. And Rod—"

I silenced. Understanding her situation made it hard to criticize. Having left Timmy myself made it even harder. I kissed Timmy's velvety cheek.

"Steve came along, really upset about Jeff running away. Wanted to see if Timmy could get him to come. So I went back and opened the door ... to this wheezing sound."

Barb coiled and uncoiled her blond mane. "By the time the guys came to find me, Timmy and I were both hysterical. It was horrible."

I didn't get it. Hand on her shoulder, I asked, softly, "What was horrible?"

"The Venetian blind cord ... was tangled around Timmy's neck."

How could that have happened? I'd wrapped the cord over the rod and slid the crib away from the window. *Who moved it back? He could be dead.* I rocked frenetically. *"Ma-ma." "Dee. Dee."*

Abruptly, Barb snatched Timmy away from me, placed a stiff hand on his back, as firmly as a witness placing her hand on the Bible, and locked her eyes on mine. "Never again! I'll never leave him alone again. No matter what Rod does."

We sat quiet for some time. Barb broke the silence. "Last night was a nightmare, all the way around—Timmy almost hanging. Lux attacking Sarge—"

I gasped, "Lux attacked Cole?" Barb caught me as I buckled.

"I thought you knew." She kept repeating. "I thought you knew."

Black dots floated past my eyes. *Court-martialed, the missing dog in Steve's dream, Lux, not Jeff?*

"It wasn't Steve's fault. Sarge, wasted like usual, was agitating the dogs"—agitation drills were to keep the dogs mean. Mock intruders dressed in protective suits. Dogs snarling and ripping until pulled off— "Stupid Sarge didn't bother to put the suit on. The dogs went crazy. He tripped right in front of Lux. Rod said with a different handler, Lux would've ground Sarge into mincemeat. Steve's lightning-fast reactions saved a death."

Goosebumps covered me from my toes to the tip of my ponytail. *"A dog bites with 750 pounds of force per inch." "Sentry dogs are trained to kill. They're classified as lethal weapons." "Weapons must be secured at all times."*

I said, "Lux's biting Sarge is the same as if Steve shot him."

"Don't worry. Steve got Lux pulled off in time. Rod says Sarge has had worse cuts from beer bottles." She handed Timmy back to me. "Besides, Sarge was drunk on duty. Steve shouldn't be in trouble."

The way things should be isn't the way things are in the Air Force, I knew. I cuddled Timmy. "Steve will be court-martialed."

"It'll be fine. You'll see. Let me make you a cup of tea for a change." We sipped, and Barb added, almost casually, "I'm spotting a little."

I flinched. *This is all too much.*

Our husbands returned, and the story came out, bit by bit. Steve shook his head. "Why me? Right when Lux lunged, Sarge stumbled. On flat ground. Not even a stone in the way."

Lux's lower canines grazed Cole's head and sank into his unprotected arm. "I couldn't get Lux choked off. He passed out before he'd let loose. Taste of blood, you know. With my luck, they'll have to amputate." *No more!*

"Still can't believe those dispensary fools sewed it up, man. Everyone knows to leave dog bites open or they get infected. The relieving shift said Cole's arm was already oozing pus." *No more!*

Steve thumped the tabletop. "Next stop, the brig." *No more!*

"But Barb told me Sarge was drunk and didn't put the suit on like he's supposed to," I said. "You reported that, right?"

Steve sighed. "I've learned the system a little. They didn't ask. I didn't tell. I just said Cole stumbled. Cole reported I had my dog under control, and he tripped. A simple accident. Our stories jived."

When the door closed behind Garzas, I pounced. "And what's this about what Barb told me? About Timmy getting tangled in the Venetian blind cord."

"Yeah." Steve clammed up, then said, "Timmy was just hanging there." He played with his curl. "I looked at him with that blond hair, and all I could see was Pammy." *No more!*

Several games of solitaire later, he said, "You know, Cindy, I used to think if I was out of Ed's house, I wouldn't get so mad. Guess that house came with me." His deck of cards smacked the table. "And poor Jeff got the brunt of it."

I scuffed my toe on the tile, avoiding the cracks. "Worrying about Mama is making me pretty short tempered myself," I confessed. *No more!*

The next day, Steve whistled and Mutt came running. Jeff huddled in the corner.

Steve went to Jeff and picked him up, holding him until his quivering subsided, then pulled out a pill bottle.

"I stopped by the vet's." he said quietly. "Doc's a pretty good guy. Said it sounded like a urinary problem, not an obedience problem. He slipped me these pills. I sure hope he's right."

He balled up raw hamburger and shoved a pill into it. Jeff gobbled it whole. "Didn't want to force it down his throat. Didn't feel like cleaning the floor tonight." He grinned.

The vet was right. Within days, Jeff's accidents ended.

And Steve was right about the system, too. A week after he neglected to report Sarge was drunk when Lux tore up his arm, Sarge assigned Steve back to B Flight with the married guys. Amazingly, Sarge also "found" the "lost" papers that'd kept Steve off the promotion roster.

Fortier grumbled, "Goody-Goody here falls in shit, comes out smelling like a rose."

I wrestled to understand. When Steve told the truth, he was punished. When he lied, he was rewarded.

Maybe Jill was right when she said Cassius Clay had good reasons to refuse the draft. And maybe the Domino Theory *was* the propaganda of Hawks. Maybe the fight for democracy wasn't as pure as the news presented it. Maybe authorities abuse their power more often than I realized. Maybe ...

Chapter 21

"It is more blessed to give than to receive"

Conflicting reports weren't just in military records. The letters that flew back and forth from the States were full of them.

First, doctors said Mama would need follow-up radiation and chemo like the first time. Then, they said the pathology results— lymph nodes clean, second lump independent of the first— precluded further treatment. Then, upon review of her case, the Tumor Board recommended prophylactic radiation. Mama refused it. "It's a waste of Daddy's time to drive me every day for five weeks to prevent something that might never happen anyway."

All those details came from Jill. Mama's only reference to losing her second breast was, "I'm really fine, Princess. It's over."

"It's over." Those hollow words repeated from two years before. *"God, please save Mama."*

Jill insisted, "Don't worry about things here. Pam and I are outta sight exercise coaches. Stick to your own project. Make your mama another grandchild."

Fat chance! Barb uses everything but a spermicide body shield and can't stop conception while I use every tip in that marriage manual and still fail Mama.

But ironically, Barb's difficult pregnancy, sad for her, was what saved me—

That spotting Barb had so casually mentioned became heavy, scaring Rod enough that he got Fortier to drive them to the infirmary (to spare Barb the rough ride on the TUSLOG bus).

"No, no cramping," Barb told the doctor and, "Yes, it's probably time for my usual period."

"Early spotting isn't uncommon," the doctor said, "but for precautionary measures, don't overdo until the bleeding stops." He suggested hiring a Turkish maid while nature took its course.

Barb paused in her report to me, then blurted out, "But I told Rod I didn't want a stranger in our house. I kind of volunteered you instead, Cin, Rod says it's okay with him if you take care of us. If it's okay with you."

Of course, I said yes. She wouldn't miscarry if I could help it.

I almost chained Barb to the couch. Cooked, baked, cleaned, did laundry, chased Timmy. (My letters home brimmed with Timmy stories.) I was so busy that time between letters about Mama passed more quickly.

Barb's spotting eventually stopped. But not her worries.

Rod's resentment of Barb's pregnancy was something you couldn't directly see, but like mold growing in a warm dark place, it was there.

He made huge *bush-bush* deals, "Need dough for the new rug rat," and dropped whole paychecks in the slots at the Club. "Never lost that much before. It's this second-kid stuff."

He ordered daily deliveries of Turkish pastries. "Barbie's eating for two." Then chowed them all down himself while Barb nibbled on plain noodles and dry toast and sipped boiled water. She was afraid he'd hate her if she got too big. (She stayed so small, in fact, that Sophie concluded, "No baby in that scrawny body of hers. She's lying for attention.")

Rod partied, then staggered home, saying, "Got tied up, Barbie doll." His big dashing smile almost hid his lies.

Barb made excuses for him. "Rod's having it rough. He never wanted to be a father the first time. Or a husband. He just brought me over because the Pound's so disgusting. Now the 'dogs' at the Pound look better than me." A tear fell into her tea. "Do you think Steve would talk to Rod for me? About staying home more ... about playing with Timmy some ... about ...?"

I said I'd ask him, but I knew the answer. Steve would never get involved in "domestic issues." He was raised a Carmine.

"Rod has to get used to playing with Timmy and taking care of him or it'll be disaster. I can't take Timmy to Ankara when I go. I can't imagine how Rod will manage."

"I told you I'd babysit Timmy while Rod's on duty."

"I know, but I'm afraid he won't come home after work. He's avoided our apartment since the day he knew I was pregnant. And I'm to think he'll come home to take care of Timmy by himself day after day?"

"It's okay," I promised her. "Don't worry. I'll make sure Timmy is taken care of, no matter how long Rod is gone." After all, it'd take my lifetime to pay Timmy back for leaving him alone pavilion night.

"You're such a good friend." She twisted a rubber band in her hair. "But to be honest, there's more to it. I'm afraid I'll lose Rod while I'm in Ankara."

I joked, "No problem. The U.S. government will keep track of him for you."

She scowled. "Don't try to soften it. Let's face it. When I have this one, Rod will be out of here. And where do I go with two kids? I've never had a real job in my life. My stepmother hates me, and Dad hasn't forgiven me yet for getting pregnant with Timmy."

Tracing Timmy's blond hairline, I searched for words. "You just have the baby blues. Rod'll come around." I thought a minute. "But if I'm wrong, there's always room at our farm"—at the end of the lane that wends itself to love and prayers, my lifelong solution—"You'll have to learn to ice skate instead of surf, though, if you come to PA."

She didn't smile. She hung her head, silent.

I tried to cheer her up, chattering aimlessly about the first thing I thought of, Pam's plans for prom. "She's going with her physics partner. Just as friends. She won't get involved with *anyone*. Wants to travel the world first." No response. "They voted her junior prom attendant. Next year as a senior she'll be prom queen. Everyone loves her, and she's the prettiest in the class."

Barb stirred. "Rod's brother took me to my senior prom. He's a great dancer." She sighed. "But I couldn't love him, no matter how hard I tried." *Well, that certainly didn't cheer her up.*

I switched to the story of Steve's and my senior prom, a Hartstown legend. "I was all dressed"—a long satin sheath Nana sewed me (perfect except for it was pink). Jill did my hair up in a

French bun to go along with the "Evening in Paris" prom theme—"and Julian popped in on some bogus pretense and bet me a dollar Steve'd be late. Steve's never late, so I bet $10 he'd be on time."

That grabber didn't grab Barb. She sat listlessly, but I forged on:

"What I didn't know was Julian had seen Steve's car in the ditch." At the last minute, Ed forced Steve to grease the semi before he left for prom, so Steve, as bribery, told Michael he could drive that spit-shined '55 Ford if he'd pick up our flowers. "Michael was horsing around with the overdrive and ditched Steve's Ford."

Barb never lifted her eyes.

"Ready to hear how I won the bet? It's nuts." I went on as if I didn't notice she hadn't responded. "Steve borrowed his neighbor's utility van"—orange with black primer spots, a rickety kitchen stool improvising as a passenger's seat. "It looked like a pumpkin rotting on the vine." I acted out Julian smirking, "M'lady," and helping Steve hoist me up onto the stool.

Barb didn't crack a smile. But I refused to be discouraged. *This part will get her. It's hysterical.*

I described us freewheeling down the hill on Route #322, me wobbling like a Weeble, then a siren, me praying it was an ambulance, Steve swerving when he grabbed me to keep me from landing with the tools on the floor, the cop checking out the interior as if expecting to find a keg. Well, at least a six-pack. The cop pegging the name on Steve's license, "Ed Carmine's son, huh?" Steve answering the unspoken accusation, "I never touch the stuff."

Barb didn't react to any of that good stuff.

Then I said, "Typical of small towns, the cop checked me out next. He said, 'Oh, McNeilly's granddaughter, right?' When I said yes, his whole attitude changed. He put his pen back in his pocket and told us to slow down and go have fun."

Strangely, that's where Barb lost it. She got totally hysterical. "I'd like to have a good reputation like that. As if that'd ever happen in my lifetime." She laughed until she was gasping for air.

I panicked. "Stop, stop! You're supposed to be careful. Settle down. You'll hurt the baby."

She grabbed her belly.

"Barb, please stop laughing. Please, Barb."

She snorted. "Think of that. Me with a good reputation."

I was almost crying. "Please Barb. Stop laughing. Please. You'll start bleeding again."

But laughter wasn't what landed Barb in Ankara. It was deep grief. Sophie trekked across the cotton field (the first time ever). Her purpose clear. To make Barb as miserable as herself.

"I've been concerned about you," Sophie said. "I wouldn't be much of a friend if I didn't tell you what's going on." Then she bombarded Barb with a litany of anecdotes about Rod hitting on women at the Airmen's Club and at Sarge's parties, the ones Barb couldn't attend because she was on bed rest.

Sophie wouldn't stop the disgusting gossip. "The worse thing is—"

I wedged in front of Sophie, shoved a teacup in her face, cranked the fan on high, everything I could think of to shut her up.

But as it turned out, Barb didn't need my help. With the expression of the Sphinx, she listened to Sophie's every word. Then when Sophie was finally forced to take a breath, Barb lowered her blue lids in the royal dismissal of the Azure Princess and said, "That new shade of your hair is lovely on you, Sophie. This nail polish should complement it quite nicely." Barb handed it over with a flourish.

The topic had been switched to makeup and hairdos.

When the door closed behind Sophie, though, Barb moaned, "Cramps," and loped for the bathroom.

The doctor took immediate action. "Be on the morning flight for Ankara."

Barb directed me in packing her bags and watched me put Timmy in his highchair and feed him supper, then said, "Cin, you've taught me lots in the last months. I think now it's my turn to give advice. I may not be the best at it, but here it goes."

I popped the lid on a jar of tapioca pudding, scrounged for a baby spoon ... and waited.

"I'm sure your mom is going to be just fine after this surgery. I know you worry and feel bad about not going home to help her." She stopped a long minute. "But from what you say about her, I know she's proud of you and wouldn't want you second-guessing yourself on staying here with Steve. Know what I mean?"

I nodded, wiped pudding off Timmy's chin, set him on the floor, and struggled to find a way to reassure Barb, too.

Barb played with eye makeup. Timmy played with books, trying to blow a red ladybug off a page. "He thinks he can blow the bug away like he blows away the flame on Rod's matches," I said. "He doesn't understand, does he?"

Repeatedly, I ran his finger over the picture. "It's pretend, Timmy." But he persisted, blowing to make it fly away. Unfortunately, his mom and I both understood the impossibility of making pretend real.

Finally, I said, "I have some idea how you must feel, Barb, about leaving Timmy. I could barely make myself leave Tee, and she's not even my child." I hugged her, tentatively. "I hope you trust us with Timmy even half as much as I trust the people back home with Tee."

Barb latched on ... and wouldn't let go.

Surprisingly, the evening after Barb flew to Ankara, Rod did show up. Unfortunately, kind of late and really blitzed. No way would I let Timmy go home with his father in that condition.

"Let him stay the night. It's really no bother."

Steve and I put Timmy in bed between us, and he snuggled in until morning.

That day Rod said to Steve, "Hey man, why don't we move the kid's crib and dresser to your spare room? Cin could use our wringer washer, too. I'll come see the kid when I can."

That was the last time I saw Rod for days.

Steve tried. He told Rod that they needed another ballplayer. "That kid of yours is wearing me out." And Rod said, "I'll give you a break in the morning, dude." But he didn't show.

Steve next tried, "Timmy misses you. He even imitates you." (In a full diaper, Timmy strutted just like Rod.) Rod said, "It'd just confuse him to see me without Barb. But if it'd make you feel better, I'll be over when I'm sober and have time."

I laughed when Steve told me that one. I'd accepted Rod would never be sober. Or make the time to visit Timmy.

Timmy monopolized my every moment, 24/7—bottles, diapers, stuffing cracks for sewer gas to protect his olfactory senses, safety checks for choking hazards and bugs, of course.

"You're getting more like Sophie every day," Steve teased.

But in bug combat, I had allies Sophie didn't. A throaty growl of a dog on alert and "Gotcha!" One dead centipede. A whine of a pup and "Slam!" A pancake-shaped scorpion. (A scorpion could kill a pup or a small child, you know.) "It's okay, Timmy," I'd say, the "T" echoing familiarly off my tongue.

One day I realized that with Timmy bouncing on my hip, my fears for Mama were being held at bay—*I guess that proves Nana's wisdom, "To be happy (or in this case, semi-sane), help others."*

I realized, too, that Cindy Carmine was slowly regaining some of the confidence of Cindy Alden. (Though I didn't realize then that my strength would soon be needed to save Timmy.)

Chapter 22

A Dash of Fear

For weeks, the God of Mercy used my caring for Timmy as a way to protect me from going insane from worry over Mama. Then during the Festival of Sacrifice that ends the annual Hajj to Mecca, thankfully, God protected Timmy through me—

Every year the gypsies set up camp by the river before the feast. In their covered wagons pulled by water buffalo, they packed fear. The landlady warned, "*Eid al-Adha* soon. *Cingene, Chok fina,*" and pantomimed thievery, throat slitting.

Sophie fretted. "Gypsies scare me. Stay with me, Cin. You don't have no iron gate." She'd obviously forgotten the step-up preventing breaking ins.

On Sacrifice Eve, a cluster of those gypsies gathered on the sidewalk with our local peasants. Traditionally, the wealthy perform ritual slaughter of sheep and put back one-third for friends and relatives, one-third for self, and give one-third directly to the poor. *Grandpa would approve*—Grandpa never got over his mother donating pence to their Irish priest when her kids didn't have shoes. "Jesus took care of people," he'd say. "My last penny will go for an extra potato for a friend or a stranger in need, not for some fancy church building."

I held Timmy's face away as the landlord raised up prayers, then stabbed. Blood ran down the sidewalk.

I'd seen cows and pigs butchered, even chopped heads off chickens myself, but something about the landlord's surgical precision triggered images of Mama's mastectomies ... *spouting blood.*

Shivering, I crushed Timmy tight. Steve patted me.

Misunderstanding, the landlord pointed at the blood and said, "No problem. Allah send rain. Allah wash."

I thought, *Interesting superstition.* Winter rains had ended long before. The countryside had dried back to its tedious brown.

The landlord set aside two-thirds of the lamb in choice pieces and threw the other third to the beggars (a liver, heart, intestines, tongue, bony ribs), adhering to the letter of the law like he did with wine—the first time Steve declined a glass of apricot wine and drank *chi* [tea] instead, the landlord called him a "good Muslim boy." (The Koran commands followers to drink no alcohol, not one drop.) The landlord then dipped a finger in his own glass, shook a drop onto the floor, and said, "See? Me good Muslim boy, too." *People of all religions can be such hypocrites.*

But unlike her husband, the landlady clearly followed the spirit of the festival. Without condescension, she chose a rump roast from her portion for the milk lady (dyed red braids hung under her scarf and contrasted with the gray hair around her face), and a steak for each of her maids (they'd scowled resentment at me since I arrived, a childless American, carrying full laundry baskets), then kissed me on both cheeks and handed me a leg of lamb from the friends-and-family portion. Steve and I smiled our thanks.

That night, rocking Timmy with his bottle, I heard it. Rain gushing onto the sidewalk, splattering our windows. During the dry season. *Allah's cleansing rain.* I sensed the landlord upstairs, nodding a silent, "I told you so." And I questioned.

The afternoon stretched long—Steve on base for a softball game before swing shift, the laughing neighbors clicking about upstairs, preparing for their evening feast.

I wish I were with Mama and Nana preparing our Easter feast and helping Pam set up Tee's Easter egg hunt.... I envisioned the Missionary Society's church decorations—*Daffodils, tulips, hyacinth, palms.* And after church, the big meal, ending with Grandpa, Tee on his lap, eating mincemeat pie topped with ice cream. Then, him picking up his spoons or pipe and Mama her fiddle. *I wonder if Mama's arm is strong enough to fiddle yet....*

Finally, the crib rail rattled. "Mama, Mama."

I snatched Timmy up. He was sopping from sweat. *A breeze would be nice. Like at Pymatuning Lake, picnics with Tee. Jill made the best S-mores....* I snapped the final snap on Timmy's fresh outfit. *I know I shouldn't but ...*

"How about a picnic, Timmy? Wouldn't that be fun?"

The pups scratched at the door. We romped up the stairs. I checked—empty stairwell, path vacant (no gypsies, not even a child at play), sidewalk washed clean by Allah's rain.

I took a deep breath, flitted to the picnic table, and stirred rice cereal into a jar of pears. Silky white silt melted into paste.

Timmy waved Mr. Fluffy as a ballast and toddled bow-legged around the table, stopping in his tracks to open his mouth like a baby robin, then waddling off full speed in his loop. *Our little man's already eating fast food.*

My laughter was interrupted by a weird foreboding.... *What's wrong? Mama? Tee? ... No! Gypsies! Why didn't I stay inside?*

I snatched up the diaper bag, whistled for the pups. "*Gel.* Come, Mutt. Come, Jeff. *Gel!*" Timmy called in Timmy language, "Da. Da," his word for "dog."

They weaved under the fence, around the landlord's station wagon, down the walk ... skidded abruptly to a halt at the alcove.

"Grrrr," Jeff's low gurgling growl. The scruff on the back of Mutt's neck stood at attention. I started jogging.

"Thump!" A high-pitched "yelp! yelp!"

My arms tightened their grip on Timmy as Jeff streaked back and paced a circle around us. Mutt cowered against my leg.

Why didn't I listen to the landlady and Sophie? "Gypsies rape, kidnap, kill."

Two figures stepped onto the sidewalk. I slumped in relief. *Not gypsies. Bush bush* loaded down with paper bags.

"*Keupek, chok fina,*" one said and spat. His eyetooth glittered like Fortier's Gold-Tooth's. The second man's steel-toed eyes stepped all over me.

I sheltered Timmy, dropped my gaze, demurely stepped aside.

But they didn't pass. They stopped. I could feel their stares. "*Chok gazelle.* Baby, *lira, gazelle.*"

Spots danced on the sidewalk. *I'm going to faint.*

Then around Steel-Toed Eyes' shoulder, I caught a glimpse of Fortier peering through their iron gate. My head cleared. *Thank you, God.* Keeping my tone conversational, I said, "I need help here, Ray."

A smirk. A mouthed, "Payback." The clank of iron. The slamming of the door.

Nooo, my mind screamed. Goosebumps raced up my rigid arms. Timmy reached for Mutt. "Da. Da."

The *bush bush* bared his gold-tooth. And lunged for Timmy.

The furor of a cornered animal drove me. I struck out. At Gold-Tooth. At Steel-Eyes. The hit-them-at-the-top-and-bottom swat method of the streets.

Giggling, Timmy swatted in our new game.

I edged sideways. *I just have to make it down those steps.* I held onto the image of Steve futilely attempting to break in. I tensed for the dash down the stones.

But if they pull our door open before I bolt it? Timmy ... stakes too high to risk it. My only option, mental warfare. "Husband, *Koca,*" I threatened.

Steel-Eyes and Gold-Tooth shrugged, slithered closer, taunted.

"*Keupek!*" I growled. Timmy roared like the lion in his book. Mutt and Jeff bared tiny fangs. *Bush bush* sneered at us all.

Steel-Eyes charged, "*Git.*" Booted Jeff in the chops, Mutt in the hip.

"Yip!" "Yip!" The pups fled to the field. Paced. Barked.

"Baby, *gel.* Baby, *gel,*" the croon. Bags hitting sidewalk. Thin rope sliding through dark hands. Steel-eyes pinning me against cement wall. Gold-tooth jerking at Timmy. A frightening game of Steal the Bacon.

"Father, help us!" And two floors up, a door slammed. The hard hand on my wrist flinched. *I'm going through.*

With the strength of Hartstown's Red Rover champion, I twisted between the Turks. Broad jumped onto the up staircase. Sprinted to the second-floor landing. "Help me. Help me." I fisted the landlord's door. Pounding ... pounding.

Talons seized my shoulder. Timmy suctioned to my chest.

"Lord, please!" I prayed. And the door, like the Red Sea, parted open. The landlady ordered, "*Dur!*"

The hold on my shoulder loosened, infinitesimally.

Using my last ounce of strength. Wrenching away. Shoving through the door—slam, thud of bolt, clank of chains. The landlady's "Allah, Allah, Allah!"

My legs bent like strands of licorice and thumped me to the floor, Timmy on top of me.

Silence.... The door handle jimmied up and down. I pressed Timmy hard against my pounding heart, keeping him quiet, fearing his slightest noise would inject *bush bush* with Superman strength.

The landlady issued imperious commands through the door, only one word I understood. "*Git!*" A volley of spewed curses and menaces in response. Only one English word, "Later!"

Footsteps skulked down the stairwell.

My heart rate cantered, trotted, settled to a walk. "Thank you, God." I covered Timmy's forehead with hundreds of kisses. "We're safe."

Then I looked around—children interrupted in their play. Landlady's sister with her *chi*. A cousin at the stove. Not much of an army against two *bush bush*, maybe not gun toting, but definitely knife wielding—*Safe ... but for how long?*

My mind replayed visions of Barb's bruised-and-bleeding face from the attack in the lane. Ants skittered around my scalp.

They've probably cased Timmy for weeks. The gypsies in town make a perfect cover. Those spots floated in front of my eyes. *I can't hole up here and hope.*

Steve's instructions whispered in my ear, "Incirlik! If there's ever a problem, have Fortier hightail you to base." But that was before Steve crossed him. Without Fortier's help?

The landlord's car, sitting in the driveway.

I pantomimed my plan to the sisters. "Incirlik ... baby ... Incirlik."

The landlady lit a cigarette, nodded. Her sister stiffened. "Yok!" Negotiations ensued between them.

I bounced Timmy. "Too-Ra-Loo-Ra-Loo-Ral."

In Islam, visitors are viewed as gifts from Allah, surely even more so during the days of the Festival of Sacrifice, but I sensed these two didn't see us as much of a blessing.

"We'll go see Daddy. It's okay, Timmy," I tried to convince myself.

At last. The landlady snuffed out her cigarette in the ashtray, picked keys off the hook over the stove, handed them to me—as a Turkish woman, of course she didn't drive.

"*Otur!* [Sit!]" both mothers ordered. The children obeyed like academy soldiers.

The landlady threw a towel over Timmy's head, slid locks, pushed open the door—not a creak. We crouched on the landing. Her sister disappeared downstairs. Voices rose from the sidewalk.

I stroked Timmy's soft cheek under the towel. *Please, Lord.*

The landlady whispered, "*Gel.* Quickly."

As stealthy as cat burglars, we crept down, one step at a time. Timmy balled against me, as if sensing he must be invisible. The diaper bag over my shoulder even molded tight.

The *bush bush,* backs to us, towered over the sister as the landlady and I slunk past. In perfect sync.

We made it. The car. I nodded to her. We each inched open a car door. *Don't squeak,* I prayed.

We slid in the front seat. The landlady, half over the seat, locked back doors.

A brush of Timmy's velvety cheek. *Please save us, Lord. Please save us.*

The keys squirmed in my sweat. Four to choose from.

Lord, make it the first one.

I chose. It slid easily into the ignition. I almost fainted.

Thank you, God.

A nod to the landlady. Simultaneously, we slammed front doors, hit locks. "Please, God." I thrust Timmy at the landlady, pulled the choke, turned the key. "Please!"

The engine cranked. And cranked. *Please, God.* And ... fired.

The *bush bush* whirled toward us, turned back to shake fists at the landlady's sister, then sprinted toward us.

I threw it into reverse, slipping the clutch, smashing the gas pedal through the floorboard. Car lurching backward, swaying dangerously.

I should've taken time to turn around first. They were gaining.

Please, God. We neared the end of the lane, *God.* My hands slipping on steering wheel. Decelerating to make turn. *Please, God!*

"Allah, Allah, Allah!" ... "Ma-ma-ma."

The station wagon slid backwards into the street. Steel-Eyes latched onto the passenger door. Gold-Tooth drew even with the back bumper.

Me hitting brakes. A jerk. Clutching. Shifting into first. The tires spinning. Steel-Eyes holding on.

Second gear. I punched the gas like a stock car driver.

Steel-Eyes hitting gravel. Turks flipping obscene left-hand gesture at our receding trunk. Timmy keening.

Third gear. Roared down the street onto the boulevard. Screeched to an abrupt halt.

Blocked road. An oncoming horse pulling a wagonload of *ekmek.* Two arabas sitting side-by-side while the *arabaches* waved hands in oblivious conversation. A total of three vehicles across the road. *Trapped!*

"*Git,*" the landlady warned, pointing to two policemen striding down the sidewalk toward us.

Me scrunching down behind steering wheel. Geriatric horse shuffling hooves forward. That wagon of *ekmek* snailing closer.

I can't drive over the horse. Can't slide in between the wagon and the araba.

My toe tapping the brake pedal. Peasants gaping. Men shaking fists at me—a Yankee, a woman. *Please, Lord, not a riot.*

The landlady shoved Timmy—a blond baby boy, prime black-market merchandise—down on the floorboards out of sight of the crowd. He pawed my leg. "Mama. Mama."

Police. A finger's length from the door handle. The landlady muttering, "Allah, Allah," then drawing herself up with an imperial air. Her locking eyes with the police.

They stutter-stepped.

C'mon. C'mon.

The *ekmek* wagon reaching the point that I'd calculated would allow us to squeeze through. Hitting the accelerator.

We took off like an IndyCar. The front bumper tickled the bony nag's rump. A whisker separated us from the araba wheel. *I'll have to pay for any damage they accuse me of.*

Not looking back. Accelerating. Winding through pedestrians and around vehicles.

Timmy tugging on my gas-pedal leg. The landlady grappling to lift him off the floor.

"No, Timmy, no! Please sit, Sweetie." Riveting my eyes on the street, not his red-then-purple face. "Ma-ma-ma."

The landlady crooning a Turkish ditty. Dangling her necklace. "Ma-ma-ma."

The landlady prying little fingers from my leg, restraining Timmy on her lap.

"Ma-ma-ma." His deep inhale—no sniffling, no whimpering, his hands extended to me.

My steering with one hand, patting him with the other. Timmy's stone silence screaming louder than his previous wails.

Driving past a gypsy caravan beside the squatters' village. *Lord never let Timmy see inside a gypsy wagon.* Past the stone prison. *Lord, let me never see inside a cell.* Past acres and acres of fields. *Lord, get me safely back to the farm—* "Dee. Dee."

At last. On the horizon. The tip of Incirlik's guard shack.

A vulture circling overhead, threatening to snatch us to our doom in plain sight of the Turkish flag's moon promise.

But nothing stopped us. Until the American guard who'd always waved the Nova and the TUSLOG bus through before.

"Ma'am, your authorization please."

"Please. Just onto base soil. We need sanctuary." My teeth chattered. "Someone might be chasing us."

"Might be? You don't know?" I must've sounded like an escapee from an insane asylum.

"Please. Please call Sergeant Carmine, Steve. At the AP barracks."

The guard stepped back in, dialed. "Sergeant Carmine."

My breathing slowed.

My hero, wearing green fatigues, rode in on a deuce and a half. Timmy squealed and reached for him. Steve tossed him into the air, "brrr"ed his forehead. "You okay, little buddy?"

"It was horrible. Two *bush bush* in the foyer kicked Mutt and Jeff and—"

"What were you doing outside? Haven't I warned you? And with Timmy?" He looked me square in the face and took a great breath of restraint. "So tell me what happened."

His eyes embraced me as I outlined our race to base. "You did the right thing, Cindy." His calloused index finger tickled Timmy's soft pinky. "You're at your best taking care of people."

He bowed to the landlady. "Thank you. Thank you." His tone defined "sincerity." He kissed her hand, pressed it to his forehead. She beamed, coquettishly.

I rocked Timmy and hummed while the landlady and Steve conferred with the guards. Calls were made. Decisions come to. "Timmy will stay at the barracks with Rod," Steve said.

My mind screamed, *No, I can't leave my baby,* but I said, "He only has one bottle left."

"In all that?" Steve teased. "Looks like you brought the whole apartment." He checked off the contents. "Food, juice, diapers. There's an AFEX and commissary for anything else."

"But Rod doesn't have a clue." *This is the man who left his infant alone in a crib to go party. This is the man who has never changed a diaper or fixed a bottle or .... Timmy!*

"Rod'll do fine."

"Timmy needs me. I'll stay here with him."

"Stay where? A knock-out like you in a barracks of sex-starved GIs?" He chucked my chin. "Rod's his father. Don't you think it's time he acts like it?"

I clutched Timmy. "Too-Ra-Loo.... Hush now. Don't you cry," I hummed to myself.

Rod stumbled up. "Ready to go, kid?"

I buried my face on top of blond wispy hair. "Too-Ra-Loo...."

Steve nudged me, whispered, "It'll be okay."

My mind refused to remember when I'd felt that way before. I sucked in Timmy's sweet scent, slowly relaxed my grip.

He clung to me. "Ma-ma-ma." I untwined his little arms, pecked his soft cheek, and turned away, arms heavy with emptiness.... *"Ma-ma"—"Dee. Dee."*

Steve—dismissed from night fire to escort us back downtown—guided us into the blue TUSLOG bus as Rod grappled to hold onto a squirming Timmy.

"Ma-ma-ma!"

Emptiness crushed me against the vinyl bus seat. And my mind acknowledged it. *This is how I felt in the car when I left Tee.*

Mutt and Jeff scurried out from under the barbed wire. Steve rolled each one over for a belly rub. "Good boys. You're good watch dogs. You tried hard."

At the picnic table the landlord and brother-in-law, arms crossed, glared authoritative disapproval. I shivered.

The landlady, though, held her head high. I didn't understand her words, but her cadence indicated a simple terse listing of facts, including the fact that his station wagon was sitting at Incirlik AFB.

Expressionless, her husband nodded her dismissal and, ignoring us, strutted toward their apartment, the brother-in-law following.

The landlady kissed both of my cheeks. *"Gule gule."* Though she never learned to pronounce English, especially the "th," her soul clearly enunciated respect and friendship.

"Allaha ismarladik." I garbled the appropriate response. We embraced once more before she minced upstairs after the men.

And my knees buckled. My empty hands hit the cold cement.

Steve lifted me. "It's over. It's okay." He helped me down the stairs. "We're short. Five more months, and we'll be safely back home, all of us together."

I wanted to believe him.... I trembled.

Thirty-one hours later, Rod brought Timmy home to me.

"He's not a half-bad kid. Kind of fun, actually. Dudes say he's a chip off the block. A real party animal." He shuffled his feet. "The barracks agreed racing to base probably wasn't necessary." He shifted his weight to the other side and cleared his throat. "But it sure showed you'd do whatever to protect the rug rat. Thanks, Cin."

"We love Timmy. You know that."

"Yeah," Rod shifted again. "I'm not good at this father thing. My old man wasn't either."

Timmy chased 'round and 'round the table, squealing after the pups. Rod squatted down. "Bye, kid," he said and escaped upstairs with cartons of Marlboros for the landlady.

***

Home from base the next day, Steve handed me a box of Lucky Charms. "Thought the leprechauns might make you laugh. A little reminder that yesterday proved Grandpa's lassie surely does have the luck of the Irish."

I eked out a smile.

Chapter 23

The Grass Withers

There'd been warning signs aplenty. In the States, divided by the Vietnam War—the VC siege of Khe Sahn led to Walter Cronkite's statement that the U.S. should "Negotiate as honorable people who lived up to their pledge to do the very best we can." Soon after, Lyndon Johnson announced, "I shall not seek, and I will not accept the nomination of my party for another term as your President." Four days after that, Martin Luther King, Jr. (my fellow dreamer) was assassinated by James Earl Ray.

And in our personal lives—Mama's cancer, Garzas' and Fortiers' marital crises, Steve's problems on base, the *bush bush* attempting to kidnap Timmy.

Through it all Barry McGuire sang that we were on the "Eve of Destruction." Yet, Steve and I naively celebrated our first wedding anniversary, May 13, 1968—

"Timmy's down for the night. Sound asleep," I hinted suggestively, closing his door.

Steve stretched. A dramatic yawn. "I'm a little sleepy myself." He pushed the pups off our bed. "She's all mine now, boys. Down."

They grabbed bones and scampered away.

He gave my butt a smack. "Married twelve months with a fifteen-month-old baby. What do you think the Hartstown gossips would say about that one?"

"A lot, probably." I giggled, imagining Nellie Smith's face hearing that news. "Too bad Heidi Marie wasn't born on time"— her due date was May 13th, but she'd arrived early. Rod had brought us Polaroids and said, "*Chiquita mia* looks like the loser of the Saturday Night Fights." Her rough delivery showed—"Barb and I'd planned to celebrate our special dates together," I said.

"Well, I've got a few special plans for us tonight. Maybe they'll make up for it." Steve patted my butt and grinned.

A firm knock on the door interrupted him. "Sergeant Carmine?" And nothing either of us had ever planned existed after that point—

Steve grabbed his fatigue pants. Mutt and Jeff yapped and scratched at the door. My heart thumped. "Were you supposed to be on base or something?"

"No, silly. It's Cole, trashed." But we both knew better. Drunk, Sarge was Tex Ritter. "Basket," Steve commanded and padded out. The sheet chafed my bare skin.

The bolt clunked, chains clanked, "Come in please," Steve invited.

So formal. Definitely not Sarge.

I strained to catch the occasional muffled word over the buzz of the fan—"Red Cross," "home," "Yes, we're sure."

Mama? Tee? One of our drunk brothers? I felt like a block of ice anticipating the sledgehammer's blow.

A click of the bedroom-door latch. A shaft of light, cracking in, widening. Bare shoulders. Stooped. A voice, "Get dressed." Blue eyes on bare toes. Ravines carving forehead. Earth's gravitational force tripling.

"What's wrong?" In my ears, the ticking of time.

His throat clearing. A pause. His whisper, "Pammy's dead."

Words reverberating on my eardrums. My brain refusing to register them. "Pammy who?"

"My Pammy!" Words spit through clenched teeth.

My mind whirred, then clicked. "Pam dead?"

Sledgehammer crashing. The future shattering into icy shards—no stewardess flying to LA, no babysitting each other's blond babies, no family dinners, no vacations, no …

"Get dressed, Cindy."

Me fumbling a dress over my frozen nakedness. His wooden arms around my shoulders. Our heads touching, then like marionettes we marched out. Facing uniformed strangers.

"You have my deepest sympathies," one said.

"I'm sorry for your loss," the other echoed.

Lines from cheap melodramas. Swallowing lumps of coal. Faces blurred.

"You're entitled to an emergency leave. A military hop will be arranged." *This isn't happening.*

Authorities shifting side to side. "Is there anything else we can do for you?"

Steve's head shaking no, fanning a wildfire of grief. Me engulfed in acrid haze. My eyes smarting, lungs exploding.

"We need to get back to base," one said.

"Thank you for coming. I'm sorry you had to drive to town so late," Steve's lips said.

"No problem. Wish our visit had been under different circumstances."

Boots bolting out. Door slamming. "Bang!"

Like a bullet from a high-powered rifle, Steve exploded down the hall, ricocheted off the bedroom wall, boomeranged back. "Nooo. Nooo." His fists battering the door, beating … beating long after a normal man's strength would've failed. "Nooo. Nooo."

He whirled, blasted back again. Bare feet smacking tile with the force of combat boots. The frenzied beat of grief. Toe stubbing kerosene heater. Blood trailing.

"Why? Why? Why?"

Pups whining. Timmy whimpering.

"Why my baby sister? Why? Where was Grandpa?"— Grandpa had promised, "I'll take care of your girl here 'til you get back"—"Where was your dad?"—Dad had promised, "We'll watch over Charity and Pam for you two"—"Where was God?" His fist shaking at the ceiling. "I'll never forgive You!" Boot heaved. Dog bone hurled.

Alone with a madman.

The pups scrabbling on the tile, huddling against my marble legs. Timmy whimpering, "Ma-ma."

Steve veered off, hurled face-first onto the bed, detonating tears dammed a lifetime behind a joke or a shrug—I'd never seen him cry before. I'd never seen any man cry.

"Why? Why? Why?" Him shaking that fist. "Ed's alive and Pammy's dead? What kind of God are you?"

My caged sobs scratched at my throat. I taped down his bloody toenail.

Oh, Jill. Ants raced over the top of my skull. My forehead thumped. *Jill*—I needed someone who'd seen Pam do front handsprings across the gym floor, catch fastballs, frost a cake, model 4-H outfits in Lead Line. Someone other than her brother, mad from grief. "Yea, though I walk through the shadow of death."

Hour after hour, he wrestled tangled sheets. "Pammy, not Pammy," then vulgarities, then weeping.

I slipped Timmy out of his crib, held his damp body against my smoldering heart.

Blond head. As fair as Pam. "Absent from the body present with the Lord." *Our golden-haired Pam resides with God.* But it wasn't time to give up Pam, not even to God. "Man's time is not God's time," Nana explained from afar. No comfort.

Pam, box-pleated cheerleader's skirt splayed, tumbling from the top of a pyramid. "Steve, Grandpa, Cin." Me running, running, inches from Pam ... falling, falling, falling ...

Timmy's sigh, God's faint whisper, "Child, believe in Me."

Shivering in the humid heat, I doubted.

The cry from the mosque. Dawn burned in the world-changing truth—Pamela Rae Carmine dead. Her charred future flaking like burning fall leaves, precious gold, lifeless.

Steve yanked on dress blues for—*Pam's funeral? Pam dead? Without even a chance to live?*

"No details. No details. What's the secret? Sixteen-year-olds don't just drop over."

"You'll know more when you get home." I straightened his "stupid" tie. He hated ties.

His eyes fixed on the green-black-geometric pattern of the rug. "I avoided Nam to stay alive. Now I wish I were the one dead." His clenched fist. "Or better yet. Someone else."

Please, God, don't let Steve do anything crazy. My cold sweat.

"If Ed hurt Pammy, he'll be taking his last breath." His clenched jaw. "But she promised me she'd run to the farm if Ed or Michael went berserk." Hand through curls.

Blond like Pam's.

"But what if she stepped between Mom and Ed? Sixteen is when I did that. If he—" Slam on wall. Plaster dust. Pups escaping to basket.

I brushed his brow. "You're driving yourself crazy." *He's scaring me.*

He shook his head, as if to clear it. "It was somebody else, don't you think? We'll beat him to a pulp"—the Hartstown Mafia reinforced—Ed lost his index finger beating up the dispatcher for a bad load, threw a referee out of the gym, torched a barn and a car, broke Michael's femur, Steve's nose. ... And Michael? One day Pam wore Michael's favorite Penn State sweatshirt to school. The next morning, she woke to her puppy, hanging by the neck outside her bedroom window.

What will Steve do? Enraged over Pam's death. Trained for hand-to-hand combat.

If Merle doesn't get leave, Grandpa is my hope. "I'd think about what you're doing, son," he'll say. "You don't want to disrespect Pam's memory," he'll say.

"Listen to Grandpa." I kissed Steve. "You can make it through this. I know you can."

My head crushed against Air Force blue. "I wish we had money, Cindy. I can't stand leaving you here. But Timmy and the pups will keep you busy, right?" A brush on my cheek. A sigh. "Two weeks is a long time."

Two weeks if you don't end up in prison and strand me here forever.

"I'll be fine, Steve. Keep your family cooled off." *And yourself, too.* "Check on Mama and Tee for me."

Fortier fired up the car. "Sorry about your sister. Least she ain't no vegetable. Seen that happen."

Job's comforter.

The Nova rumbled out the lane with its load of grief and rage. *This isn't happening.*

My feet dragged over the tile like through sludge. I fed and changed Timmy and settled him on my chest for a nap. Cemented to the sofa, it seemed unlikely I'd budge in the next two weeks. Mutt and Jeff settled on the green-geometric-patterned rug beside us. Standing guard duty.

Pam. Steve's Pammy ... Pedal pushers and white Peter Pan-collared blouse. That cute little pout. "Watch out," Grandpa'd tease. "A rooster's going to land on that bottom lip of yours." ... Her application to Allegheny Air Training School half filled out, waiting for the day she turned 19 ½. "I want to travel like Jill used to. I'll leave having kids to you and Steve. Marriage is too risky. I might get stupid and fall for a handsome Ed Carmine." *But she would've come around. We would've made a bevy of cousins.*

Steve's Pammy ... On her thirteenth birthday, she announced, "I'm grown up now, you know. It's time people quit calling me Pammy." No one else listened, but from that day on, I called her Pam. And she smiled every time.

I dozed off. Floated back across the Dardanelles ... *box-pleated cheerleader's skirt splayed, Pam tumbling from the top of a pyramid. "Cin." Me running, running. Inches from her hand ... falling, falling, falling ... falling ...* "Ashes, ashes, we all fall down."

"Clomp, clomp, clomp."

My eyes jerked open to Timmy's little smile. Pups whining.

Rap-pause-rap. "Let me in."

Not a dream? "Steve?" *How can it be?*

I threw chains and bolts. Like Doubting Thomas, I touched Steve's hands. *Flesh and blood.* Rod trailing in behind.

"It was a mistake, right? Pam's okay!" I felt my smoldering grief cooling.

Steve, eyes to the floor, tossed his duffel bag, kicked off gleaming low quarters. Rod snuffed out his cigarette, reached for Timmy and Mr. Fluffy. "Hey, kid, why don't you and your old man go hang out." Rod barely glancing at me. "Okay with you, Cin?"

It wasn't, but I said, "Of course, he's *your* son."

"Mama, Mama." Timmy squirming, holding onto me. I packed the diaper bag. My heart hammered. I untangled tiny fingers from my hair.

"Mama!" Timmy wailed for me all the way up the stairs.

Empty-handed, I spun around. "What's going on?"

"Want to sit down?" His arm around my waist was rigid.

Him settling me at the table. The black wax stain on the tablecloth from our Christmas rendezvous.

"Cut the stalling. What's wrong?" Me fearing he'd answer.

His throat clearing. "The captain called me in for another message ... for you." Scarred thumb running over edge of innocuous-looking paper.

"Well, what is it?" I asked, not wanting to know.

The words stuck in his throat, then vomited out. "Grandpa McNeilly" He ducked his head. "Dead, too."

And the walls came tumbling down.

My hands clenched to strangle him, to force him to take away those vulgar words. My ears roared like that Thanksgiving heater, pressure building over the limit. And my words exploded, spewing all over him. "Liar! You're a liar!"

He recoiled. Extended proof. Ruled in half-hour increments. Diagonal scrawl—

Mrs. S. Carmine
Charles McNeilly
Passed Away
Fun. Baird F H
Hartstown, PA 12 May Sunday

How dare they reduce Grandpa to scribbles on scrap paper?

I shredded the lie, as methodically as Tee had Nana's Bible— *"The pipes, the pipes are calling"*—grief's white-hot flames. Dried eyes, nose, throat … *Pam and Grandpa?*

Steve withered. "I tried everything to get you home, Cindy." The Air Force would fly him back for Pam's funeral but not me, a private citizen, for Grandpa's.

"I combed the barracks for a loan." We were barely making the payments on our first loan for plane tickets to Turkey as it was.

"And Rod couldn't find a babysitter." He rubbed his forehead, didn't look up.

"The chaplain patched through calls. Jill answered at the farm. There was lots of static, but I heard it all." He paused a long time, then blurted out, "Grandpa McNeilly was driving the pickup. A drunk hit them"—*Them? Pam and Grandpa?*—my heart ripped my blouse.

Steve's echoing voice explaining—Jill and Pam at the farm to show off Pam's prom pictures. Jill carrying canning jars from the cellar for Nana. Pam moving 4-H lambs with Grandpa. Tee stowed in the pickup cab while Pam steadied lambs in the pickup bed— *"The pipes are calling."*

Dawdi Hostetler's buggy stopped for the Candy Man to hand out lollipops. (Grandpa kept stashes in the barn, in the tractor, in his pockets. Ready for every child he met, Amish or Yankee.) The men chewing the fat like farmers do—crops, milk prices—*"The pipes."*

Teens up from Pittsburgh on their way from The Inn to line 'em up on Hartstown Hill with a Corvette. Lost it on gravel on the curve—the curve where the Three Musketeers perfected the three-quarters doughnut-slide into the driveway—freaked out at the sight of Dawdi's buggy. Swerved. Clipped the back of Grandpa's pickup—*"The pipes are calling"*—Pam catapulted onto gravel—*The lane, where Pam drove up and down, hour after hour, practicing for her driver's license*—pickup cab door flew open. Tee landed on Old Miracle instead of gravel. Grandpa yelled, "Martha, get an ambulance, Martha." Jill ran outside as Grandpa ripped off his flannel shirt, covered Pam, and sprinted after Tee who was shrieking down the road. The driver argued, "You guys shouldn't have been parked there."

If I'd been there, Pam would've been in the cab with Tee. I'd have been in the pickup bed. I've heard hundreds/thousands of engines slowing for that curve, I would've known it was revved too high to make it. I would have given a warning bang on the cab roof to Grandpa, jumped into the grass. No problem ... If I'd been there.

At the hospital, Pam was declared dead from head injuries. Grandpa kept mumbling, "Not Pammy. Not Pammy. The old should die first." ... *"The pipes"* ...

Tee only required sedation and two stitches. Grandpa kept repeating the doctor's words, "Pammy expired? Pammy expired? What kind of word is that for our girl?"

Back from the hospital, Grandpa sank into his overstuffed chair, lit a cigar and fell asleep, his hand on his unopened *Readers' Digest.* "He just never woke up." *Grandpa ... Pam ... Grandpa ...*

Since the days when I curled against him at naptime, matching my short breaths with his long even ones, Grandpa's presence in the world had cushioned every pain. *Even yesterday's news of Pam's unfathomable death ... "the pipes" ... Grandpa ... Pam ...*

The doctors said shock and grief overstrained a weak heart. (Grandpa didn't have the pep he used to. He couldn't shovel the snow off the walk to the milk house anymore. But he'd refused to get a checkup. "No reason to waste good money on an old man.")

Steve paused in his story. Shifted back and forth. "At our house, Ed heard my voice on the phone and started screaming that I should've been the dead kid. Uncle Sam would've buried me. But with Pam, he'll have to work his a** off to pay for a funeral 'cause the drunk wasn't insured and that dirt farmer don't have nothing." *How could Ed insult my grandpa even in death? How could he care more about funeral costs than his daughter's life?*

Steve scratched Jeff's ear. "Ed said stupid Barney Fife didn't have the brains to send the punk for blood alcohol levels. He told me to keep my butt in Turkey where it belonged. Michael and him could take care of that moron cop without no help from no Oops."

He twisted a blond curl. "So, my family couldn't care less about seeing me. And I can't get money fast enough to fly you home to your family. And I knew how you'd feel, Cindy. So, I canceled my emergency leave."

I gaped at him. *Knew how I'd feel? Canceled your leave? Not representing us at the memorials? What kind of sense is that?* At last I understood the Turkish reaction as America "continue[d] on our course" without a suitable mourning period for JFK. *This is vile!*

"Don't you think it'd confuse Tee if she saw me without you?" Steve lapsed into a croon. "It's too late to say or do anything for Pammy or Grandpa now. At least they always knew we loved them, right?"

How can you use the past tense? I wanted to claw his eyes out.... *Grandpa and Pam ...*

Death, like a medieval surgeon amputating without an anesthetic, had cut them off from us. *So cold!* "Don't plant until Memorial Day," Grandpa always warned. "Danger of frost." A killer frost had nipped PA of its beauty—*Pammy and Grandpa, too?*

Pam said the McNeilly-Aldens had the luck of the Irish, and she was right. Unfortunately, it was the luck of the Irish in the potato famine. *Coffins with sliding bottoms for the next day's dead.*

The K-9 unit sent flowers. *How many flowers has Grandpa planted for his girls?* Mama's sunflowers, my daisies, Pam's daffodils, Nana's rose bushes. Tee preferred dandelions to them all. The landlady brought baklava and a fruit compote. Food, the international response to grief. *How did she hear the news so quickly?*

I buried under icy sheets in the humid heat. *"Life must go on, though good men die,"* Edna St. Vincent Millay lamented. *But how?*

How will Steve survive without his Pammy? How will Nana survive with a broken heart as old as Grandpa's? How will Mama survive when stress speeds up cancer? How much worse will Tee's seizures get? And what about the Hartstown Mafia? They'd mocked us before. "The retard," "Those Goody Goodies." *Now out for revenge, what will they do?*

Dozing. Dreaming—Grandpa disking up corn ground. Coaxing a calf from the warm womb to be licked clean by its mother. Cranking and cranking his steel-wheeled Farmall H. Its engine kicks, putts on two cylinders. The tin can on the downspout-exhaust rattles. Grandpa telling stories about the Irish cottage with eight children in a smoke-filled loft, thatched roof, damp stone floor. About stowing away on a cargo ship for a new life in America. About working on the Bessemer Railroad, saving every cent for a farm.

"The pipes are calling."

Dreaming—Grandpa in flannel shirt and bibbed overalls. Neighbors gathering, "A short eulogy seems preferable. Charley never liked a lot of fuss." ... "They're talking about your funeral, Grandpa. You aren't dead." ... Massive cracked hands on mine. "Oh, you know people. A man ages and the gossip starts." Cigar jiggling in laughter.

Steve shouting in his sleep. "I'll kill him. I'll kill him." His face twisted into gargoyles. "You #!* punk killed my baby sister." ... "Oops should be dead. Not little Pammy." ... "Pammy, Pammy. Grandpa, you promised. Pammy."

Falling, falling, falling ... whisper of raven's wings, Grandpa's Irish pipe, "Danny Boy" ...

I shook Steve awake. "Get Timmy back here right now. I'm going crazy."

***

Like Elizabeth B.B. said, "The face of all the world is changed, I think."

Chapter 24

As Different as Our Fingerprints

SADD and MADD and such. The passing of decades has changed attitudes toward drinking and driving, something taken almost casually in the '60s. But one thing has remained the same over the decades. Everybody handles grief differently—

Sympathy cards and notes flooded in. Steve tossed them, unopened, on the table. "They mean well, but—"

I read every word.

Jill described the funerals. Steve barely skimmed her letter.

I devoured every detail—a botanical gardens of arrangements, the whole town in attendance, the high school letting out for Pammy's funeral, the Missionary Circle covering the altar in lilacs for Grandpa's. (He loved to stick his head in the blossoms of Nana's lilac bush and suck in the scent.) "No one's sure what Tee understands."

Do any of us understand any of this? "At calling hours, Tee pulled herself up on Grandpa's coffin. It started swaying so your dad lifted her. Everyone held their breaths. Tee just wiggled in, kissed Grandpa on the lips, then wiggled back down."

A true Angel kiss.

"I kept expecting Pammy to leap out of the coffin and say, 'Gotcha'" ... *falling ... falling ...* "And Grandpa to walk in to pay his respects to the man in the casket. Charles McNeilly is bibbed overalls, a cigar, Laddie at his heels, a pocket full of candy, and an Irish pipe. Not a silent stranger in a suit."

"The pipes are calling."

Steve honed in on only one section of Jill's letter. "Before the Pittsburgh guys left the cabin at the lake, someone torched that Vette they bragged was so cherry. Everyone knows Ed and Michael did it, but those Pittsburgh guys have brains. They put the word on the street that the gas tank sprung a leak from the accident, then hightailed it out of town."

Steve cheered, "Way to go, Carmines. Way to take care of it. For now at least. When I get home, those punks will get my two cents." He grabbed his softball gear, reporting later, "Hit the best I ever have. Pretended the ball was that punk's head." The timbre of his voice like Ed Carmine's. His posture like an iron rod.

.... Grandpa ... Pam ...

Grief propelled Steve into perpetual motion—pinochle, softball, demonstrations with Lux.

Depression held me down like out-of-control vines in a garden. "It's the heat," I lied to myself, patting rivulets of perspiration off Timmy's damp hair. *Hair as fair as Pam's.*

Only Timmy got me to move. "Ba-ba." I got up and made a bottle. "Ca. Ca." I changed a diaper. "Whah." I fixed *ekmek* and peanut butter or Kraft macaroni and cheese—simple, economical, mindless—mostly mindless, thinking took too much energy.

"I think I can, I think I can," I read. Timmy giggled as the little engine chugged closer to the top of the mountain.

I don't think I can. I don't think Steve can. I don't think either of us can make it.

Toys littered the floor. "No, Mutt. No, Jeff. Those aren't your bones," I said half-heartedly. Steve hid the blond Fisher Price girl.... *Pammy* ... I stored the Fisher Price farmer.... *Old McNeilly had a farm ...*

We bickered over little things.

Steve shoved his bowl of chili across the table. "How am I supposed to eat this? It's too hot!"

"Use your brain. Blow on it!" I spit the words, and Timmy clawed at my leg, fussed to be held. "He senses problems," I said. "We better act more normal."

"Like this?" Steve smacked my butt. "Is that normal enough?"

"Very funny!" I attempted to laugh.

Steve sat on the floor and rolled a ball to Timmy. Back and forth, back and forth, with the concentration of two World Series players. The pups waddle-raced between them.

I played "Pretend" with Timmy. "If I were a bumblebee, I'd buzz all over you." "If I were a puppy, I'd chew Mutt and Jeff's bones." *If I were an airplane, I'd fly home and never fly away again.*

I craved conversation—

"I wonder why butterflies always lit in Pam's hair? Think it was something about her hair color. Or the smell?"

"Don't know," Steve said.

"I'll bet the kids really miss the Candy Man."

"Probably."

"Did you pay attention to Jill's last letter. Do you think she's warning us they're talking about selling the farm?"

"I didn't notice anything. I've accepted it's all going to be bad news anyway. No use thinking about it." He turned away.

"Why did I think our lane was so safe?" I traced the scar on my knee from the Christmas I got my first new two-wheeled bike. A frozen rut in the lane from the milk truck flipped me over the handlebars. "You'd think I'd learn from the past like Jill did from her mom's serial relationships?"

That's when he blew. "What's the point of all this talk? Talking won't bring them back!"

That's when I almost clawed out his eyeballs. *Mama hears what I say, even when I don't say it out loud, but you don't even try to hear me.*

"It's not my fault. I didn't force you to come over here." He'd read my thoughts—*I'll never open my eyes to Grandpa or Pam again, just to this sometimes stranger.*

Nana read our thoughts, too. Enclosing two sticks of Black Jack gum as Grandpa had, she wrote, "I know this time is more difficult for you being so far away. But I want you children to remember you won't be betraying Pammy and Charles if you're happy. Good memories and laughter respect their lives. Focus on God and each other and projects and soon September will be here."

Easier said than done, I thought—Mama used to sing, "Catch a falling star and put it in your pocket. Save it for a rainy day." But I couldn't find a single hoarded star wish or moon promise.

I think the scuzz saw us swallowed up by grief and assumed Steve was too distracted to pay attention to Sophie. Or maybe the creep's pre-Memorial Day-three-day-break drunk was worse than usual. Whatever it was, that final scene at Fortiers' further complicated our grieving process—

Iron clanked across the hall. Footsteps scuttled up the stone stairs. And I thought, *Not tonight. I just want to be alone. I can't deal with drama.*

The entryway light clicked on. Footsteps skittered toward the driveway. Clomping, growling, twittering, screeching, slamming, clanging, the crescendo and decrescendo of footsteps and voices.

"Ignore them," Steve said. "We have more important things to worry about." I curled against him. Wiped away a tear.

Another bellow. Another screech. An order boomed down from the landlord's apartment, "Dur! Dur!"

And Steve detonated. "That's about enough of that." He stormed out, got to the top of the stone stairs, and let out a roar. "You nuts, Fortier?"

I snatched up Timmy and bolted up as Steve—jaw clenched, that vein popping out, face contorted like Michael's—yanked the scuzz bucket around, face an inch from his. Sophie, dangling from the buttons on her sleeveless blouse, dropped to the sidewalk.

"Big man are you? Here. Why don't you try this punching bag? I dare you. It punches back." Steve shook the crud so hard I expected to hear a neck snap.

"Steve! Steve! That's enough," I yelled, but Steve was yelling louder, "Never so much as look at your wife wrong again, Fortier. Ever. You understand me?" His intimidation tone terrified innocent bystanders blocks away.

Fortier squinting little beady eyes quivered a faint yes.

"Don't forget, or you'll be dealing with me." A final shake and Steve flung him down.

"You okay, kid?" He eased Sophie up, propped her against the apartment building. "You need anything, kid?"

And the scuzz, still dancing around in an effort to stay upright, bounced back like a Weeble and "Crack!" struck Steve in the temple. "That's for messing in my business."

Steve gave a shake of his head. Set that jaw. Narrowed those eyes.

The scuzz should've known to run when he had the chance, but stupid as he was, he had the nerve to stand there, smirking like the victor. "Hah, Goody Two Shoe's all show, no go."

Steve doubled up his fist, pulled his arm back, the veins on his fist looking like ropes. "Want a fight, Fortier? I'll give you one. Didn't start it, but I sure as **** am gonna finish it."

"No!" Sophie latched onto Steve like a fly onto a bull. "Stephen, stop it!" The pups scratched their ways up my legs. "Don't stoop to his level, Stephen. Stop it this minute." Sophie sounded like a schoolmarm.

Unfortunate for him, the scuzz, squirming to escape, caught Sophie's hoop earring. A spot of blood formed on her earlobe.

Well, that did it for Steve. You've heard of the old windup pitch. Steve was winding up and screaming in the scum's face. "You booze hounds think you can get away with anything. This time you're going to pay."

Timmy was whimpering. And Sophie was screeching, "Stephen! No! Don't hurt him!" But Steve was past all reasoning.

I cried out in desperation, like in a prayer, "I wish Grandpa and Merle were here."

And strangely, wonderfully, at the sound of those two names Steve paused, dropped his aim and landed a sucker punch to the crud's flabby gut. The groady slime, face still intact, folded up like a lawn chair.

Then, in the rhythm practiced on the punching bag in the Carmine basement, Steve drove blow after blow, blows he'd promised to the driver who'd killed his Pammy.

"Steve, that's enough," I begged and begged.

Finally, he took a deep breath. Glanced over at me. And felled Fortier with a chop to the back of the neck. "You're the last drunk to hurt a woman if I have a say about it." Steve gave Fortier's inert body a boot. "That one was for Pammy."

Then he turned to Sophie, hugged her in that protective way of his and said, "Think we better get you to the hospital and have your baby checked out? Don't want to take any chances, right?"

She stiffened away. "I'm not going. Not pregnant. I'll never be pregnant." A formal edict. Not sad. More like resigned.

She marched away. We followed, Timmy called, "Da! Da!!" The pups came.

The scuzz stumbled down after us and flopped across their table—aluminum tubing squeaking, warm can of beer sloshing—ducking skittishly back from Steve.

"Listen up, Fortier." Steve, three inches from the scum's face. "Forget everything I've ever said in the past. Hold on to this. Better think twice before you manhandle Sophie again or you won't be worrying about someone telling secrets. You'll be worrying about taking your next breath."

He grabbed the scum by the scruff of the neck and the seat of the pants and heaved him into the front room. "If I look at this piece of shit another second, I'm going to—"

He slammed the door. Whitewash particles flew. I clutched Timmy away from Carmine furor.

Steve huffed and turned. "Sophie, you need to leave. Right now." To her silence, Steve argued on, "You're not safe here. Stay with us."

Her razor cut shook no. "I'm sleeping in my own bed." A final verdict delivered with not a twitter, not a tremor.

His hands waved at the ceiling. "No one can make you do anything if you're not ready, kid." Steve gritted his teeth. "But one thing I *can* do. *I can* implement safety measures."

She didn't object.

He braced the table against the living room door. Fortified it with intertwined chairs. "Won't stop him, but he'll make enough noise getting out to give you warning. Now, I need your key."

Sophie fidgeted with her elastic wristband, *So docile,* then handed it over to Steve.

"We're not leaving until you're barricaded in."

Water ran in the bathroom for several minutes. Then Sophie marched out and straight into the bedroom.

"Wedge the bed against your door. Don't try to lift it. Slide it. Longways."

Flimsy iron tubing scraped across rough cement. "Is this right?"

Steve jiggled the latch and shoved. The door held. "Good job, kid. Don't let him in for any reason. Promise?"

A firm little affirmation through the door.

"Any problems, scream, then prop your feet against the wall and push with your back against the bed. I'll be here in a flash. Got it, kid?" He twisted that curl, leaned forward. "You can still leave now, you know?"

No answer.

Steve led Timmy and me out as somberly as from a funeral service, slid our last bolt, sighed, "Poor kid."

I ran my finger over his temple. A goose egg already forming. His sheepish grin. "Guess I should've jucked when I jooked."

He "brr"ed Timmy's forehead.

Not a peep filtered across the hall, then or anytime through the night.

The next day, after the Nova rumbled off toward swing shift, I scrubbed diapers in the tub—*Happy memories honor their lives*—I was remembering the time Pam tripped over Miracle and landed in the gutter beside Grandpa's milking stool when, "Yoo hoo." I confronted a grief unassuaged by good memories.

Raccoon-blackened eyes stared zombie-like through iron bars, then lowered. The right side of Sophie's upper lip looked like it was concealing a walnut. Four finger marks radiated upward on her left cheekbone. Her arms were bruising. *He really got her this time.*

"Would it be convenient for me to come over please?"

Coldly calm, she limped in, without her bug annihilation arsenal, and perched on the couch. Timmy in his highchair scooped macaroni and cheese and biscuit bites off the tray. I steeped tea. Sponged off Timmy's face and fingers. Changed his diaper. Played "Itsy Bitsy Spider."

Finally, she spoke. "It's been like this since Raymond's family left. He hits me."

I startled. *Where are her excuses?*

Her words, rapid-fire, machine-gun speed. "It's always the same. I say he drinks too much. I say I can't live like this. He says, 'Ya better learn if ya know what's good for ya.' So, I shut up. It's just been my arms or legs or chest before."

Just?

Timmy clung to my neck as if he understood Sophie's sad story.

She slowed into a drone. "He says partying makes him forget I don't get pregnant. I try to make him proud and party, too. But he says I act like a retard" –that pejorative word used for my Tee—I shifted.

She swirled the tea in her cup. "I hate false teeth." I leaned forward to hear. "My stepfather slugged me in the mouth once."

The impact of that punch echoed through the room.

She spun two gold bangles, filigree—probably dealt for on post, exchanges tossed over Concertina wire. She gulped, sat straight. "I promised myself no one would ever hit me in the face again." Her voice boomed. "And no one has ... until now."

She brushed the rim of her eye socket. Winced. "Raymond knows this time is different. He asked if we could borrow some Kool Aid from you and Steve."

Waving the white flag like Sean. "I'll make it up to you, Jo," he'd say. But Sean never did. Neither would Fortier. *Words aren't enough.*

"Maybe Raymond's right. Maybe I can't survive without him. But I've almost reached my last straw."

Almost? I shook.

Remembering how Sophie responded to Barb's second pregnancy—setting down her shot glass and picking up a rosary— I suggested, "Maybe mass would help you sort things, Sophie."

That Sunday, the simpering scuzz stalked Sophie out. "Get in the car. Don't need to take no stinking bus." She stared straight ahead. "Some slimy Turk's gonna steal you. You're gonna end up in the Pound."

Her hand shook when she grabbed my arm. She kept walking.

At chapel, Steve leaned against the back wall, stiffly telegraphing his anger to God—once Grandpa described losing three of their babies to influenza. "Catholic and Protestant, God listened to neither of us. That kind of hurt takes time to come to terms with."

I knelt beside Sophie. The priest's chant echoed the cadence of Grandpa's blessings: "May your neighbor respect you, /Trouble neglect you, /The Angels protect you/And Heaven accept you."

Will I ever accept Grandpa and Pam being part of Heaven and not here on earth with me?—my slacks had started to bag even though I was carrying around 200 pounds of depression.

I crumbled. *Lord, save us all in our brokenness—Nana, Mama and Dad, Tee, Steve and me, Garzas, even Fortiers.*

After Communion, Sophie slid back into the pew and whispered, "My head's clear now."

I nodded encouragement.

"Six years ago, I promised myself no one would hit my face ever again. 'No one' means even Raymond."

The couple in the pew ahead of us turned and glared for Sophie to be quiet.

Sophie pulled shoulders straight and continued whispering. "I'm leaving. I'll wire Raymond's family tomorrow to warn them. I owe them that." Her pixie cut made her look sophisticated at that moment. Not vulnerable like when we first met.

"Raymond's sister, Marie, said she'd be there for me if I needed her. I think she knew this would happen." Sophie ran her finger over her swollen cheek. "Will you guys help me?"

Her bruises implored me. I mumbled back, so as not to further disturb the congregation, "Are you sure, Sophie? Steve said we couldn't help you until you were ready."

"I'm sure," she said as an oath. "I need for you two to escort me to the chaplain's office tomorrow."

I nodded yes but didn't believe Sophie would leave. After all, I'd heard Jo's hollow threats for years—"Keep drinking, Sean, and I'm out of here."

The blow to Sophie's face, though, had galvanized her. Turned "ditzy" into "determined." "Flaky" into "fortified." Her brain-dead husband even noticed the change.

The next morning, he crashed across the hall. "Listen, Carmine, that brat sister gets it all if you don't talk sense into the broad. You gotta do something."

He's groveling!

"I don't speak for other people," Steve said. "Talk to your own wife."

"If my old man hears about this, I'm outta the will. You better talk to the broad, or you're gonna regret it." The scuzz raised his fist.

Steve shot him his intimidation glare.

The scuzz lowered his fist and snarled what I thought was a pathetically weak, "Better watch your back tonight, Carmine."

***

We'd thought life couldn't get worse. But the next morning. Rod popped in. "Had to see how the rug rat's doing." He pinched Timmy's pudgy leg, "Hey, kid," then wolfed down a plate of eggs.

Since up to then, Rod had ignored his son and satisfied his hunger without my short-order-cook skills, I should've been more suspicious.

Rod lit a cigarette. "Don't believe Fortier had the guts to face you after post, man."

Steve did the Carmine glare. "Drop it, Garza. Not one word."

"About what happened in the transport?"

"I said drop it. Cindy knows it was a bad night. That's all she needs to know."

"Man, you don't tell your wife anything. Cin better hear it from you, Carmine, before the grapevine gets to her."

My hand trembled. Timmy, waiting for a bite, held his mouth open like a little bird.

Steve clenched his jaw. "It was no big deal."

"No big deal?" Rod slapped his forehead, mocking Steve's Moe slap from the Three Stooges. "Guess you're right if you consider almost getting shot dead-in-the-head no big deal."

Dead? Steve? Every one of my internal organs trembled. *Another knock at the door?*

"Not another word." Steve's eyes shot darts. "Want to ruin Cindy's day?"

"Me? That's a laugh. Fortier almost ruined her life." Rod plunged into the story: Fortier was so blitzed going to post that it took two guys to haul him and his dog into the transport. The guys were "bs'ing about Bobby Kennedy's assassination, another Kennedy dead," and Steve remarked, "Who's next?"

Rod took a long drag on his cigarette, building to a dramatic climax, then said, "And that looney Fortier stuck the barrel of his revolver against your old man's head and said, 'You, Carmine, if you don't talk some sense into the broad.' Not even a dog moved."

I couldn't move either. *Pam. Grandpa. It could've been Steve.*

Rod tapped the ash off his cigarette. "Your old man twisted Fortier's arm almost off and told him to quit fooling around, And that pansy reholstered his weapon like nothing happened."

Rod blew a smoke ring. "Fortier's crazy enough sober, let alone stoned. We thought it was going down for sure."

I quivered.

The brevity of life—Pam. Grandpa ... Could've been Steve.

"Whatever." Steve cleaned his plate with a slab of ekmek. "A little booze and Fortier's meaner than that dog of his. And that's not very mean. If you lived with my old man, you'd know Fortier's all mouth."

I'd seen Steve facing down his father's fist and wasn't surprised by his reaction. But my hand shook as I wiped Timmy's face. *Life is so fragile ... at every age.*

The instant the door slammed behind Rod, I got in Steve's face. "So, when were you going to tell me about the gun to your head?"

He shrugged. "Probably never. Nothing happened."

This attitude's getting old. Not trusting me to handle things. I didn't know then that we carry some issues with us to the grave.

I ran my finger around the indentation on his temple. "He could've shot you."

He pulled back. "You worry too much. I was never in any danger. The armory issues those 1917 Navy Reject '38 pistols. Even if it was loaded, it probably didn't have a firing pin."

"Why do you say that?"

"In the winter there's so much mud, it jams up our guns, Regular security gets the ones with working firing pins. K-9 gets the rejects."

"It's spring now."

"Yeah, but we're using the same weapons."

How can he act so casual? Haven't Pam and Grandpa taught him that only one breath stands between life and death?

Later, Steve hammered on Fortiers' door. "Ready to go, Sophie?"

In the background, the creep spewed threats. "Better keep your *** in here, broad, if you know what's good for you."

Sophie threw the door open, "You don't have to get involved if you don't want to, Stephen. I'm leaving with or without you."

"I'm here, aren't I? Ready when you are."

"Go ahead and go then," the scuzz ranted. "I don't need you for nothing. I got houseboys for my laundry and boots. I got the Airman's Club for grub. And I got the Pound."

I cringed. I couldn't believe he said that word right out loud.

Sophie never reacted. She collected her ID, inventoried her purse and, as erect as Mrs. Cole in her Statue-of-Liberty pose, limped out the gate. The bruises on her face had deepened. Clearly, the scum didn't care about them or the ones he'd left deep in her heart.

Steve shifted Timmy to his other hip and grabbed her arm. "Don't worry, Sophie. We'll do whatever it takes to keep you safe." We flanked her on the street to the bus stop.

And she did it. With the help of the chaplain, she booked a flight and sent a wire to her sister-in-law: "Raymond hits me STOP Flying home STOP Need place to stay STOP."

On the way back, Steve insisted, "Stay with us until your flight, Sophie. You don't know what Ray will do now that he knows you're serious."

One curt nod of that pixie cut. "It would be wise. The decision has been made." Her voice had a professional ring.

Desperate, the scuzz switched manipulation tactics, resorting to the "I can't live without you" method that'd always worked in the past. Whining like a toddler, he stalked her out their gate.

Erect, unflinching, she kept her eyes straight ahead, dropped her luggage in our hall and collapsed on our coach.

She settled into nervous chatter—about her four brothers in Quebec, one a priest working with Indians. (We'd say Native Americans today.) About each of her five sisters, all married with children. Then, "I did fine on my own for four years before I met Raymond." Worked two jobs to pay for beauty school. "Everyone warned me Americans propose quick to get out of the draft, but I wasn't worried because Raymond was already in the Air Force."

She took a breath.

"Now I think it had to do with his family. Raymond mentioned he did something, and now he has to prove to Papa Fortier that he's responsible enough to run the potato farm, or Maria will get it."

Must be quite the "something" the spoiled son did.

She tapped her dentures. "I think he married me just 'cause I was the first one he got to say yes. And it helped that Papa Fortier liked me. I was so nervous when I met him that I called him Monsieur Fortier instead of Mr. Fortier. He liked it that I spoke French."

Her French accent grew stronger, her voice steadier. "No one in Canada cares what happens to me. Raymond's parents and sister act more interested in me than my family ever did."

I hope they're sincere and don't have an ulterior motive. I'd learned by then that not all family love was unconditional.

"So I'll go to Maine. I can support myself hairdressing. Or work at a grocery store. Even clean houses."

The perfect job with her bug fetish.

Rod actually showed up, so we didn't have to risk taking his blond baby son with us on the bus to the airport with Sophie.

She's flying back to yellow buttercups, white daisies, orange Devil's Paintbrushes. Far away from the Big Bad Wolf.

As she boarded the plane, Steve shook his head in wonderment. "I didn't think she'd really go."

I swelled in pride for her. "She set her limit and meant it." I hoped it was the beginning of Sophie's own "happily ever after."

A few days later, Rod made the off-hand remark to Steve, "Wish you guys lived in our building. Barb will need Cin's help with the kids when she gets back," and Steve said, "Your apartment is much nicer than Fortier's. Maybe he'd like yours for a change."

The scuzz bucket had no attachment to the home he shared with his *beloved* wife. In fact, he had wasted no tears on her since she flew out. Never mentioned her name. So when Rod sounded him out about an apartment switch, the creep jumped at the idea. "Need outta this dump."

The "dump" was good enough for the broad. I wanted to spit.

"That balcony be a great place to hang out with chicks." His weaseling little glances dared me to report that back to Sophie. He didn't know I'd never tell Sophie anything. I wanted her to forget he existed.

The K-9 unit pitched in to switch the apartments, guy-style. Flipping dressers with clothes still in drawers, grabbing clothes still on hangers and marching them across the cotton field at which point Fortier (finally moving a muscle) waved everyone to a stop.

"Too much sweat involved here." I could see a little sweat on his upper lip, but it was from the 100-degree temperature, not from exertion. "One couch same as the next to crash with babes. Garza's old lady ain't gonna care what pan she boils water in. I sure ain't washing no clothes. Don't move nothing more."

That got a "Hear, hear. The Club's calling."

I blocked their bolt for a beer. "Just a few things? Please?"

Lots of groans, but I got them to trade Fortiers' shaky aluminum table for Barb's mahogany veneered one and bring me several of Barb's floor-length sheet-curtains.

***

In the middle of stitching curtains for Barb to replace Sophie's tattered ones, I had a stunning revelation. *Nana's right about projects.* Moments at a time, distracted by Timmy or sewing, my mind forgot to mourn.... *Grandpa ... Pammy ...*

Chapter 25

Clinging to the Lifeboat

If you've ever tried to keep up with two tiny humans, two dogs, two husbands, and two households—laundry, ironing, cooking pre-microwaves and convenience foods—you know how time is a blur. That blur was a great gift to me. I don't think I would have survived those three months before flying home without it. My memories of the summer are that blur, interspersed by just a few scenes—

Grandpa ... Pam ... Grieving. The first week of June, time for their traditional summer holiday in Istanbul, the landlady brought me a bowl of homemade Turkish Delight and said, "I stay. You sad."

"No. Hot," I fanned. "Go." Though I knew I'd miss them.

We kissed cheeks. Faint scent of yogurt and *chi*. Her kids kissed my hands and pressed them to their foreheads, patted the pups and Timmy, and scampered into the station wagon, leaving me alone. I picked up Timmy and sang Grandpa's, *"Cockles and mussels, alive, alive, oh,"* about Molly wheeling her fish cart through Dublin. Grandpa would say, "That, Baby Girl, is where I'd like to be some days. Back with my people." I understood him now.

Ten days later, Barb, the closest I had to "my people" in Turkey, flew back from Ankara. Rod carried her luggage into the apartment across the hall. Steve carried *Chiquita Mia.* (Rod was afraid of Heidi. "I might break that scrawny thing.")

I grabbed Barb and didn't let go. *Her ribs. She's thinner than before she got pregnant.* I leaned back and looked closely. *No makeup?* No blue lids. No feline-lined eyes. No lipstick. Hair in a ponytail. *Like a PA farmgirl, not a CA surfer.*

Barb and Heidi both looked so feeble. *Please, Father, don't take anyone else I love.*

"Mommy's home," I said. Timmy clung to my leg and chewed Mr. Fluffy's ear. "She missed you. Show her what a big boy you are now." He whined and raised his arms to me to be held.

"You've got a big job now, little buddy." Steve lifted Timmy to touch Heidi's tiny fingers. "Big brothers have to take care of baby sisters for the rest of their life." He twisted that curl and added, "If you can."

When Timmy started his need-a-nap whining, Steve said, "How about a hand of cards while your kid sleeps, Garza?" They headed across the hall, and I uncorked all the words I'd bottled up.

As I made Barb lunch (which she barely nibbled), then fixed a bottle (which Barb couldn't get Heidi to suck on), I told Barb about the blow that led to Sophie's leaving and about her letter saying she'd made it back to the States okay. "She's bunking in with Ray's sister, Maria, while she cleans houses in Caribou and makes fresh-cut French fries at Spud Speedway to save up for her cosmetology license for Maine. She sounds so confident. Nothing like we knew her."

I told Barb the details of the accident and Grandpa's heart attack and about my fears for Mama and Tee and Nana and Dad, and that Jill said Dad was having trouble keeping up with both the steel mill and the farm—haying, combining, milking the cows twice a day. The neighbors were helping out, but I was worried about long-term. "Steve won't talk about any of it. He says there's no use talking about things. Says he's accepted all the news will be bad."

I thrashed a diaper up and down in the toilet to rinse it before tossing it into the diaper pail.

"I about went nuts in Ankara with no one to talk to, too." Barb said, then gave a short report on the facilities and staff, ending with, "They said Heidi has failure to thrive. She just sleeps and never wants to eat. Maybe she'd eat for you."

"I'll try," I said and massaged Heidi awake, teased the nipple around her bowed lip, swayed and sang, "When Irish Eyes Are Smiling," snuggled, seduced down ounce after ounce as I made up her signature song, "H-E-I-D-I, H-E-I-D-I," to the tune of "Bingo was his name, oh."

Curled around her pillow, Barb said, "I heard Steve say something to Rod about moving Timmy's things over here." She lowered her eyelids. "I know this is selfish with all your losses, but I don't think I can handle Timmy and an infant, too, right now. Could you keep him a little longer? Just until I get used to Heidi?"

Inside, I did backflips. I'd calculated that it'd be seventy-five more days before we flew home. I needed Timmy to occupy me until I was safely back at the farm, tucked in with my people.

That night not a peep floated across the hall from the home with a newborn. In the morning—Timmy dressed, fed, and playing with a truck—I heard the first sounds. The thumps of exercising.

"Let's go see Mommy." I darted with Timmy across the hall and plucked Heidi from her bassinet to give her a quick rinse in the kitchen sink—the welcome blur of activity.

Barb watched, listless, and did side stretches. Until a blast of sewer gas hit. We both ducked. "Welcome to life in the basement," I said. "Sewer gas and views of walls and ankles." I'd always envied her grand windows and her balcony.

"The downgrade is worth it to be near you guys," she answered, though her mind was obviously far away.

She did several more stretches as I chatted, then straightened and declared, "I should never have married Rod. I could've found a way to support Timmy."

That shocked me into temporary silence. Then I said, "But if you hadn't married Rod, you wouldn't have had this beautiful little girl." *Grandpa would've loved a little blond granddaughter. Steve promised Pam a blond niece or nephew.* "Your mom would've been so proud of her granddaughter and—"

She interrupted me. "Maybe I should have just married Rod's brother. He asked me, you know. I didn't love him, but he would've loved me like Steve does you."

"All marriages appear better from the outside, Barb." I didn't know what else to say.

She popped down in a toe touch, then looked me straight in the eye. "I didn't tell Rod this. It'd cause more problems." A pause. "The doctor said I have postpartum depression."

The death of hope. The worst death of all. I tried to lighten the moment. "Well, what did the quack think? That you'd be out dancing? You just had a baby all alone. You need rest and food. You need to laugh"—I sounded like Mama and Nana combined.

She did stomach crunches. I cut her favorite custard pie and entertained with the story about the first time Steve brought Pam to the farm—Grandpa showed her how to milk a cow, then sent her with me to muck out Old Blue's stall. "Always equal opportunity on a farm," he teased. "No woman need fight me for a milk stool or a pitchfork."

Barb gave a little Mona Lisa smile between crunches.

From then on, I plied Barb with stories and food and nudged her to interact with her babies. "Ask Mommy to sing with us, Timmy." He swayed in his Timmy Dance as I sang, "Heidi Garza came to town to live with Timmy Andrew. H-E-I-D-I, H-E-I-D-I...and Heidi was her name, Oh!"

Barb's lips smiled, did another sit up.

"Hold Heidi while I mix up some goulash with this leftover sauce." Barb propped her between two pillows. "Take Heidi while I fold these diapers." Mother and daughter stared unblinking at each other.

"Read Timmy "Go, Dog, Go" while I iron these fatigues, okay?" She set her son on the floor with the pups and did squats.

But I didn't give up. One day I said, "Watch the kids for me while I run these clothes through the wringer," and half through the load of diapers, I heard her kind of giggle. I ran back to check. Barb was holding Heidi, and Timmy was brushing Barb's hair with the dog brush. I giggled, too. *Hope at last.*

"You three look so cute together. Let me take a picture." I got the Polaroid camera Rod's mom had bought for such moments.

Barb managed a half smile for the picture, then slumped back. "Rod's mother calls me the gold digger. It's true I never had much, except my looks. Now I don't even have those. I'm fat."

I didn't see any fat, but I suspected her mirror lied when she asked it, "Mirror, mirror, on the wall. Am I fair enough to keep Rod at all?"

Later, while I was ironing fatigues and Timmy was climbing chair to chair, Barb started again.

"I spent six weeks at my stepmom's after I had Timmy. I think she tried, but she's like Mrs. Cole, know what I mean? She made me nervous. There was no one to talk to about anything serious. My girlfriends were out dancing and never visited. And Rod's brother? Well, that was awkward." She paused as if to say more, then picked up a magazine.

Later still, watching me put Heidi in her bassinet, Barb said, "My daughter has to learn young. She can't always depend on me being there for her."

Unsure where she was coming from, I weighed my response. "A mama is more important to a daughter than anyone else in the world."

"It's worse if you get close to someone, then lose them." Barb was adamant. "Look at how miserable you two are now. If you hadn't been so close to your grandpa and Pammy, you'd be okay. I don't want Heidi to ever go through what you are because of me."

Later, she sighed and repeated, "I wouldn't want Heidi to grieve like you two are over Pammy and your grandpa. I wouldn't want her as scared as you are about your mama."

Something finally clicked with me. "You don't have a lump in your breast, do you?"

She twisted her ponytail. "I found it in Ankara." *The forbidden "it!"* "You know how scary it is." *Quite the understatement.*

She shifted. "There's something I never told you before. I don't like to talk about it." She shifted again. "My mother had a mastectomy, too."

"And you're just mentioning it now? After all my moaning about Mama's first surgery and how scared I was it'd come back? And how upset I've been that I can't be there now as she heals from her second? I can't believe it."

"I didn't want to upset you. Mother's wasn't a good ending. My dad couldn't handle it, so he took off with the next-door neighbor. A real floozy. Didn't even tell me good-bye. Then Mother died. On my fourth birthday. He was forced to take me in." She stirred her tea several minutes. "When I was little, Mother was my only playmate. I even slept in her bed. Like you and Tee. Then she was gone."

My heart fluttered. *Raven's wings.... Mama* ... "You and your mother are two separate people. You can't assume you'll die from a simple lump," I said. "It could be nothing. Most of them are. I think it's eight out of ten lumps are nothing."

"You sound like the obstetrician in Ankara. He said it's mastitis, quite normal after delivering a baby. But I didn't trust him. He might be a quack. Or an ophthalmologist."

That running joke about military medicine did it. We laughed and laughed, the first time since she'd got back.

Catching my breath, I squeaked out, "Risk believing he's right, Barb. Risk believing you'll be here to raise your kids."

Grandpa ... Pam ... I can't bear to lose anyone else.

"I'll try," she hesitated, "if *you* try to believe your mother's going to be okay."

She got me there. At Mama's three months' checkup, the oncologist had found "no lumps or bumps, nothing out of the ordinary," but Barb knew I couldn't make myself believe Mama's cancer treatment had really ended, not with all the other bad news.

"So, it's a deal?" she asked.

I nodded with all the truth I could muster, then teased, "So what's next. Are you hiding a terrible story about a sister killed in an accident?"

"No, I'm truly an only child." She smiled, then said, "But on the serious side—" She averted her eyes. "I think about Rod and what Sophie said before I left for Ankara all the time. I wonder who Rod was with when I was gone the past two months." She paused again. "And who he's with now."

I averted *my* eyes, changed Heidi's diaper.

"I knew Rod wouldn't be able to handle two kids. He says one is like a pet—you can still go out, doesn't cramp your style—but with two, life is over."

She reached out for Heidi, bounced her a few times. "In case you're wondering, Cin, I'm going to do everything I can to make this marriage work. For me and for the kids." She rocked a little. "I don't know how much I should forgive, though."

I told her the truth. "I've asked that more than once myself."

Jo with Sean, Sophie with Ray ... us—once I told Nana I'd never forgive Steve if he cheated on me, and she said, "You don't know that, dear." I was adamant, "Oh, yes, I do." She was adamant, too, "Things happen, dear. You have to keep an open mind." Nana's tone had hinted at much more, though I knew Grandpa could never have cheated on her. Not Grandpa. "Things like what?" I insisted, and she listed, "Like depression. Like separation. Like wars." The master of pushing aside unpleasant thoughts—Mama had taught me well—I refused to connect Nana's lecture to Grandpa's random comment to me: "In France, I thought I'd never make it home. Be careful of chasing excitement, Baby Girl. It can be dangerous."

Was Grandpa protecting Steve from temptation by co-signing for a loan he couldn't afford to fly me to Turkey?

And that was when Steve brought home a final life-changing letter. From Nana. "Charles poured his life into the farm, and it served its purpose well. It kept us together and raised our children and three grandchildren. Now it has new purposes. The farm is too much for your parents and the Millers need another farm for their oldest boy, so we're selling it to them. I would have liked to give you time to get used to the idea, but the Miller boy needs to move before their next baby is due, and I want to be settled before you get home. I pray you can accept this, dear."

I can't accept this. I stood catatonic.

Steve threw a dog bone against the wall. "Is there anything else that can go wrong?" The pups went yipping to their basket.

On the back of Nana's letter, Mama had written, "Don't worry. The place we found in town is like a little dollhouse. When we went to look at it, there was a cardinal perched on a rose bush in the yard. I think it was Daddy telling us it was the place for us." *My dreamer mama.*

I stomped to the kitchen, mixed up bread dough, and pounded it smooth. *The farm, too? No more! I can't do it!*

At that, Grandpa's words echoed, "You can do it, Baby Girl. My people survived the potato famine. You can make it through anything if you set your mind to it."

So I set my mind (though Grandpa wouldn't have approved on what)—*Wherever that dollhouse/shack is with the cardinal, I'll move in with my people and build new memories. And I'll never set my eyes on the farm again. Steve and I will sell our ten acres.*

I immersed myself in the blur of activity—a diaper, a bottle, a load of laundry, a floor to scrub.

Similarly, Steve paced fretfully. "What's Barb going to do when we leave? And what if Rod gets radical and deserts them for Nam?" Rod had made a joke about Nam looking better than the home front. A joke that sounded too serious. "It's about time Rod and I had a little chat." The rule about not getting in the middle of domestic disputes apparently had been revoked. "How about rigatoni and some of your cloverleaf rolls tonight?" One of Rod's favorite menus.

At supper, Rod feasted. I oversaw Timmy's shoveling attempts. So independent. "Me, me," he'd say when I tried to feed him. Steve got Heidi to take a bottle. Barb even nibbled.

After a bowl of cobbler (the vegetable cart had had peaches that morning), Rod slid back and stretched. "Think I'll hop the bus for a little time at the Club, okay?"

"Whatever you want." Barb said. *She has her makeup on today,* I noticed.

"Want to tag along, Carmine?"

Steve wiped Timmy's face. "I've got a better idea." He yanked Timmy out of the highchair and tossed him to Rod. "Why don't you and your kid here have a little male-bonding time?"

"The rug rat motors around by himself just fine now. Doesn't need me. And don't be on me about *Chiquita mia.* I'm no good with her." Rod defended himself against the silent accusations. "You heard Barbie say she didn't care."

"Forget the one-armed bandit." Steve glared. "A walk would do us all good." Timmy, so grown up, waddle-ran around Mutt and Jeff, standing quietly for Steve to put their collars on. Rod huffed.

I could hear Steve lecture all the way up the stairs. "Can't you tell what your wife needs just by looking at her, Garza? Barb's got her pride. She won't say to stay home. Get your head out of your butt. You get one chance. You going to be like your old man? You and me know what it's like not to have a dad." My guess was Steve had stored up a wagon load of tidbits to unload on poor Rod.

Barb acted like she didn't hear a thing.

At our ten days and a wakeup, Rod popped over and said, "Well, man, I just extended my tour in·this armpit." The Captain had jumped at the chance to extend him because Nam made replacement personnel scarce. "I was looking at a tour in Nam to get me out of this mess at home, but after your talk I'm trading a Claymore and a Gook for puke and poopy diapers."

Steve landed a light punch. "You just made two babies happy, buddy. Maybe even a wife."

"For Barbie, the 'happy' might be just some days," Rod acknowledged.

At seven days and a wakeup, Steve asked me, "Don't you think it's time Timmy moves back with his parents?"

I didn't answer—a diaper, a sippy cup.

"Cindy." He held me. "They have to get used to taking care of two kids or they won't stand a chance of making it."

I picked up Timmy and *The Little Engine that Could.* I seemed to hear Grandpa remind me, "You can do anything you set your mind to."

Rod and Steve moved Timmy's things behind the iron gate, leaving our place as quiet as a morgue. That night, the nightmares kept waking me—*Running, running. Inches from Pam, inches from Grandpa, inches from the disappearing farm ...*

In the morning, I examined myself in the mirror—the same mousy flip, the same brown eyes, the same pyramid-shaped body, the same crescent-moon birthmark under the wedding band. I couldn't believe the pain didn't show. *Grandpa ... Pammy ... the farm ... "The pipes" ... Timmy ... Heidi ...*

At the first cry from across the hall, I bounded over and lifted Timmy and Mr. Fluffy out of the crib. Heidi cried for a bottle, her pathetic whimper now a lusty demanding wail. I tucked her in the crook of one arm and Timmy in the other and rocked with the pups on my feet. I felt so torn.

Leaving my new family is going to be as hard as leaving Tee was.

Two days and a wakeup, Barb bouncing Heidi—*Could Heidi be a bit plumper?*—"She's kind of cute, isn't she?" Barb said, shyly, sounding for the first time like a real new mother.

Rod put down his cigarette and reached out, "Come here, *Chiquita mia.*" I hadn't seen Rod hold his daughter before that.

That night, we made the excuse, "We need to pack," and left Garzas to eat their hamburger casserole alone, as a family.

Our apartment was so silent—*Grandpa ... Pam ... the farm ... falling, falling, falling ... "Oh, Danny Boy, the pipes are calling."*

***

August 29, 1968, the "wake up," the last dawn call of the muezzin.

Steve's nose pressed against mine like a child's against a frosted windowpane. "Homeward bound. Home where the—" He stopped and held me close. *Home where two are missing ... Home where the farm is gone....*

He sighed. "How about some doughnuts for our sendoff?"

His replacement (the captain pulled strings with the commander of the sentry dog school in Wiesbaden to get one) had bought our furniture and contents at a good price and was moving in "as is," so our kitchen was still intact.

I mixed up dough. Steve poured oil, then disappeared, returning with the landlord's kids, just home from Istanbul. "This is more fun with kids, right?"

In some ways Steve knew me well.

Zu-Zu and her brothers and cousins bounced in and handed me a bronze etching of Mutt and Jeff. "Keupek! Keupek!" I grabbed their hands and thanked them profusely in my Turkish-American gibberish.

Then I tossed dough onto a floured board and handed the oldest the doughnut cutter. Zu-Zu made eye patches out of two doughnut holes. I deep fried. Steve patted off grease. The little ones rolled them in sugar, Steve did a handspring. The pups yipped. Next batch.

A happy memory of us two Yankees, I thought. Like Mama. *Maybe they'll be part of the minority in the Middle East who tolerate Americans.*

Steve puffed a cloud of confectioners' sugar at me. "Snow!" The children squealed, *Like Tee.* Laughter, *Like Pam.*

"I'll make Ovaltine," I said. *Like Nana.*

We delivered the children and a heaping plate of warm doughnuts upstairs, a second plate to Garzas, just rousing.

I bathed the babies. Steve dressed Timmy and planted him on his knee for "motorboat, motorboat, go so fast." I rocked "little sister" and sang, "H-E-I-D-I. H-E-I-D-I ... and Heidi was her name. Oh," over and over until Steve looked up at me and sighed. "Guess it's time, Cindy." *No more procrastinating.*

We handed the babies to their parents and crossed the hall to get Mutt's and Jeff's basket and toys. "After all the cold nights we shared on post, it's hard to leave my 'alarm clock'"—Steve rested his head on Lux for naps on post. If anyone came near, Lux would jump up, and Steve woke when his head hit the ground—"But leaving the pups is harder. With Lux, it was no choice—"

I interrupted. "We still have no choice." We had no money to fly the pups, so Garzas agreed to take them. "Timmy'll keep them so busy they won't even miss us." I almost choked on the thought.

The landlady and her sister arrived to babysit while Rod and Barb rode the bus with us to the airport. Formal kisses, "Gule. Gule." Informal love. Damp-eyed, they shooed us out.

We dragged bags down the hall. Mutt and Jeff licked our ankles. Heidi cooed. Timmy waved Mr. Fluffy good-bye. *He doesn't understand this good-bye is different. None of them do.*

The white and purple daisy-shaped flowers sentrying the shanties at the end of the lane waved good-bye, too. *I'll always plant flowers, no matter how little money we have.*

A Turkish couple by the *lyceum* glowered and spit, "Yankee go home." Steve laughed. "Will do. On our way." *How can it be home without Grandpa ... Pam ... the farm?*

At the airport, our clothes damp from sweat, faces damp from tears, Rod said, "Do you have it, Barbie?" She opened her purse, extended a silver pin decorated with turquoise. "It's not exactly a maple tree like you talk about, but it's a leaf." She attached it to my suit.

"Those four stones looked to us like the Garzas hanging on for dear life. You two held us together this year." Rod tapped out a Marlboro, rolled the pack back up in his sleeve. "We have the pups as part of you two, man. Thought the pin would remind you you'll always be part of us."

Rod sentimental? Can't believe it.

I mumbled into Barb's shoulder, "I couldn't bear it if Timmy grew up and didn't know me."

I'd shared his firsts—rolling over (on our bed), sitting up (on the tile floor as Barb and I drank tea), his first wave of 'bye-bye' to me ("Ma-Ma"), his first steps (between Steve and me). Heidi would do those things without me. "We'll stay in touch, won't we?"

"I promise," Barb vowed, as somberly as a witness under oath. Rod nodded, "Me, too."

I pushed away black whispers of doubt.

"Don't start craving ice cream without me." Barb winked.

Our pavilion secret, kept for almost a year now. "No wonder lifers' wives drink," I said. *Making friends just to suffer the hurt of leaving them again.*

"Don't forget what I said, bud, about taking good care of the rug rat and *Chiquita mia*." Steve's final punch to Rod's bicep.

Barb whispered, "I know all the changes are going to be hard. I'll light candles for you."

I whispered back, the first time I said it aloud, "I've decided wherever the family is living, we're moving in with them and never leaving again." Steve didn't know my plan. "And no matter where that is, there will always be room for you and the kids if you have a crisis."

Barb and I hugged one last time. *The world we've shared is more familiar now than the one I'm returning to.*

Then off we went, back through the airport of scarves and black eyes, lugging heavy bags and heavier hearts toward PA.

What if Tee doesn't recognize me? What if ...?

Chapter 26

Slivers of Hope

The Chicago Democratic Convention, Black Power, Mayor Daley's thug cops ... *A drunk driver's choices ... falling, falling, falling ... The whisper of raven's wings. The dirge of an Irish pipe* ... PA soil uncharted since Grandpa and Pam were ripped out of our lives. *Good memories and laughter respect their lives, Nana said.* I failed in honoring them that day —

My teeth chattered uncontrollably. My baggy pink seersucker skirt quivered. Steve's arms clutched me. "Colder than Turkey, even in August, right?"
Married over a year and still misinterpreting me.
Him nudging me off the tarmac. Through the terminal door. My thoughts and vision fragmented.
Our welcoming party like a gym class along the line, waiting to count off. Two members absent, permanently.
Grandpa ... Pam ...
My moon-promise birthmark mocked me from under my wedding band. "One child born in this world to carry on."
I'm like a guest arriving at the party empty handed.
Hanging back. Biting my cheek. A loose thread waving from my jacket hem.
Grandpa ... Pam ...
"My little princess!" Mama leaping forward like in one of Pam's bucket jumps. Mama drawing me tight against her little shirt.

Body of a preteen.

"Mama, I wanted so much to be here with you."

She chews her thumb like Grandpa chewed cigars.

Nana. Gentle wrinkles dancing over linen face. Her patting Steve's cheek. Then mine.

Vanilla. Not mingled with tobacco and Old Spice.

"I knew God would bring you two safely home, even if He had to resort to Jonah's whale for the crossing. He would never allow us to suffer more than we could bear."

As if the simultaneous deaths of Grandpa and Pammy are bearable.

Jill whispering, "You can do this, Cin." Dad swooping us all up. His gangly arms. Tear falling on my forehead. Me mumbling into his shoulder, "Where's Tee?" Everyone parting.

Beside a row of orange chairs, *Tee.* Spotless Oxfords scuffing tile. *Tee. The other part of me. The part Steve never could fill.*

Me kneeling in reverence. Tee shying away, ducking her little Dutch boy haircut, strangling Raggedy Ann. My tears stinging.

"I'm home now, Tee. I told you Steve would bring me back." *Alfalfa sprout.* "I missed you, Tee. I love you." Me extending a shiny turquoise button. "I brought you a treasure for your collection."

Tee pulling further back.

She doesn't remember me. Squeezing eyes shut. *I promised myself I wouldn't cry.*

Me singing, "I love you a bushel and a peck." Tee crushing Nana's skirt. *Moon eyes.*

"Tee." Steve kneeling. "I'm sorry I took Dee away from you for a long time. I promise I'll never take her a long time again."

Him flipping into his never-fail headstand, making upside-down face. Tee gawking. Silent. Travelers making wide detour around them.

"Okay, so my headstand's a little rusty. But I can still spot a Coke for our girl here."

Him reconnoitering the area, dashing back with his offering.

No snort. No grunt. No giggle. I can't have lost my Tee, too.

Tee slurping sweet syrup. "Charity, don't drink too fast, dear."

I can't stand this.

Jill wrapping me tight. "She doesn't talk to anyone anymore, Cin." My face smothered by sunset-kissed hair. "You can get used to it, Cin." Jill's love dabbing Bag Balm on my jagged grief.

Luggage claimed. Heading to exit. Cluster of students chanting, "Make love, not war."

Political rocks hurled at Steve's Air Force blue. Like Turks threw gravel.

"Make love, not war."

Inscrutable, Steve stared back. Walked away.

"Baby killer!"

Stop shouting.

"Baby killer!"

Steve's face flushing. His jaw setting. Him dropping Tee's hand.

There's going to be trouble. My feet freezing in place.

Jill skewered his arm. "Wait, Steve. Things are different around here since you left. Let it go."

Him jerking away. Striding toward protesters.

Tee let out a squeaky-frightened cry. Steve stopped in his tracks. His gaze locked back on Tee—oval eyes wide, crouched in aisle way.

His fists relaxed. He strode back. Lifted her. Mumbled something in her ear. No flicker of response on her china doll face.

Jill flipping the protesters a peace sign and saying, "To me, the sign represents Merle's Special Forces' motto, but they don't have to know that." Her adding, "To tell the truth, if it weren't for you guys, I'd be chanting right beside them. War, in general, doesn't make sense. Nam's more insane than most."

Steve slumping along.

Parking deck. A whoop. "G" forces lifting from his shoulders. He ruffled Tee's cowlick. "I love surprises, don't you?"

How can Tee not respond?

Merle's '52 Chevy. Under rear window, a caricature, ala Jill— Merle and Denny in Army green. Caption, "Congratulations! You beat us back!"

"We had to move his car out of the storage shed anyway when the farm ..." Jill trailing off. "Merle thought the old buggy might help a little, even if it's not a Ford."

Still unfathomable, Steve's selling his Ford to pay down our bills. I'd always suspected he'd choose his beloved Ford over me.

Steve dragging Tee along. "Isn't Merle's car beautiful, Tee?" Him caressing the fender. Tee scuffing her Oxford instead of studiously imitating him like before. "Ready to go for a ride, Tee?"

Tee's eyes fixed on the ground. *After our hundreds of "dates," she has to understand him.* Another nail pounded in the coffin of the past. "Please get in, Tee. Let's go for a ride with Steve."

In the backseat, Nana reaching. "Sit with me then, Charity." Slight puff. Tee on Nana's lap.

"No, Mother," Mama insisting. "She's too heavy. It's a two-hour trip." Mama sliding onto Dad's lap, settling Tee next to Nana. *Tee didn't even grunt.*

Me hesitating, hand on car door, hearing Pam's *"Shotgun."* Jill saying, "Scoot in." Rustle of Necco Wafers' roll.

Me not crying ... *Grandpa ... Pam.* ...

Route 19. Crowded together. Familiar smells. *Shampoo. Deodorant. Black Jack gum.* Jill leaning over me, updating Steve on Merle and Denny's strategy in the Army to stay Stateside rather than be shipped to Nam. Dad inserting remarks from the back. Mama's soft murmur to Nana, "I can't believe our princess is finally home," then both of them asking us about Lux and Timmy and Heidi and if we'd heard from Sophie since she left. Tee absolutely silent.

"Slug bug," Jill and Steve yelling in unison. I ducked in time. They walloped each other.

"You're slipping, Cindy. You usually spot VWs first. Especially a Yukon Yellow one."

Jill impaled me with a look, whispered, "Don't bottle things up, Cin. You get yourself into trouble that way."

New Castle. Redeeming myself, I shouted, "And the winner of the U.S.A. Worst-dressed Woman pageant? Reverse boobs"—halter-topped woman, bulges obscenely peering from under shoulder blades—tension snorting out my nose. "Keep laughing." Jill squeezing me.

From behind me, Mama saying, "You girls are so silly."

Tasseled corn, third-cutting hay, Amish shocks of wheat, roadside stands of fresh vegetables, maple trees, chlorophyll, grass. Familiar chatter. *People who know me.*

Feeling myself relaxing a little.

Steve slowed for the Hartstown Village limits. I twitched.

"It'll be okay," he mouthed, his eyes showing doubt.

"Good fair this year," Dad said.

Traffic inched along, stopped at the crosswalk by the school parking lot for Grandpa's coffee shop crony, Lester, work pants hiked halfway up his chest. His smile of thanks—white-powdered sugar-framed-toothless mouth.

"Mmm, an elephant ear would taste good about now." Steve rolled down the window. "And smell that grease."

Tee sniffed. We all smiled.

She still understands some words at least.

"Want to stop for fair food?"—hot sausage sandwiches, greasy French fries …

"Not tonight," I begged. "I can't." I couldn't face a dairy barn without Grandpa currying a prize Holstein. "Rotate corn with good alfalfa, and you've got winners every time," biggest ear, tallest stalk. I couldn't think about the 4-H barn without Pam's and Tee's lambs…. I could think of nothing else.

Jill squeezed my elbow. "Let's do it for Merle and Denny, Cin. They'd trade a little grease for those cold C-rations in a heartbeat."

"Candied apples, Cindy. And cotton candy, right, Tee?"

Tee stared straight ahead.

"We have to face it eventually, Cindy, right?" Steve's eyes challenged me, then turned to the carny rides spinning in a dizzying vortex of color, and focused on the Ferris wheel—Pam always shouted to her friends from the top of the Ferris wheel—Steve held a fist to his forehead. "You're right. Not tonight. Tomorrow's soon enough to harden a few arteries."

Jill smiled. "Next year it'll be better. The guys will save up leave time for fair week."

Yes, next year. If grief doesn't kill us before then.

"Turn left at the next street," Dad directed from the back. "It's a little gray house." Steve braked for a semi to rumble past, then coasted into a back alley.

Grandpa accused me of wearing rose-colored glasses, but there's nothing rosy in this picture—no treehouse escape, no barn or milk house cooling cream to whip, no flower garden, no pasture with livestock. Only Laddie forlornly tethered to a clothesline outside a lead-gray frame house.

Steve whistled. "C'mon, buddy."

Laddie pointed his ears, but the collie who'd stood watch in the pickup bed outside the Diner while the "good ole boys" ran the affairs of the world didn't even lift his head off his paws.

"Laddie went off his feed when we left the farm. He should adjust but—"

Mama interrupted Dad, "He'll be just fine." She grabbed my hand. "I'm so glad you're home."

"You got the key, Cindy?" Steve joked.

Everyone laughed. *They remember the laundry day key fiasco I wrote them about.* I felt somehow reassured.

"Come show me your new room, Tee." She hung back.

I can't cry!

Any shack is home if the ones you love are there. Ten-foot ceilings of the farmhouse shrunk to eight. Familiar furniture cramped the living room. *Too small even for the loveseat and the overstuffed chair and.... I can't stand this.*

Tee crouched with Raggedy Ann on a little wood stool in the corner. *"Any shack is home if the ones you love are there."*

"It's not what you're used to, dear," Nana said, "but God always provides everything we need."

Then why didn't He provide me with a grandpa and sister-in-law to return home to? My ears rang.

The Women's Missionary Circle swarmed out of the kitchen. Familiar smiles. Familiar hugs. Behind them, a small table bulging with meat-and-cheese tray, fresh tomatoes and peppers, cantaloupe and watermelon, cookies, and lemonade. *Staples of fellowship dinners. Stability.*

Mrs. Minnow saying, "I made you your own personal Sugar Pie, Steve, in case the one for tomorrow's luncheon is gone before you get through the line." Her shooing everyone toward the door. "We'll take our leave, so you children can get settled. Visitors will be dropping in the minute they see the car home."

Steve helping the church ladies out, bringing Laddie in. Me burying my face in fur. Laddie shying away. Steve holding a slice of chicken breast. Laddie licking around it … *Mutt. Jeff …*

Maybe Laddie will dance like he used to. Grabbing Tee's hands, humming our Dancing Bear number. Ancient collie ears perking up. Steve lifting front paws. Laddie struggling to prance our staid two-step. His arthritic back legs failing him.

"That's okay boy." Steve scratching under Laddie's collar. "We all age … if we're lucky."

"Whack" Front door against wall. "Sis!" Sean's arms crushing me. *Not a whiff of Stout or whiskey. Sober. At least for the moment.* "Smack" on Steve's back. "Brother!"

Nieces huddling against Jo's legs. "Kiss Aunt Dee and Uncle Steve." *Sticky with pink and yellow cotton candy. All three fitting in my hug—Heidi … Timmy*—"Glad you're home. It's been rough around here without you guys."

My eyebrows rising. *Jo sounds sincere. Softer*—I always criticized Jo's fiery temperament as not ladylike. But Jill defended her. "Sometimes if you don't declare war, you'll get taken over by a hostile party." *Sophie and Barb proved that.*

Jo, glancing at the guys, whispered, "Wanted to tell you straight up. I'm pregnant again. Didn't want it to be true. Thought it had to be another Immaculate Conception. Guess your brother hangs his pants on the bedpost, and there's another Alden baby on the way."

Forcing my lips to smile, I felt as inadequate as a hen brooding over a nest of tennis balls. Sean, not me, having the child to carry on for Grandpa. *All my prim, proper, little virginal eggs refuse to drop their defenses in spite of all our wooing—Heidi … Timmy.*

The screen door squeaked. "Sean, Steve, a pleasure to see you both again." That suave voice.

No, not today! Ants racing in my head.

"Julian!" Jill jumped up, squeezed her brother. "What're you doing here?"

Him pecking her cheek, then mine. "Looking good, Cin."

Me ramrod straight for his hug.

"I can't believe I was stupid enough to let you get away. Steve's one lucky guy!"

Those old lines make me melt every time. Jill rolling her eyes. Him leading a dance of perfect conversation topics— memories of the treehouse view. (I'd stared at it for days after he dumped me.) Events in the Middle East. (He acted as if my opinion, on whether our alliance with Turkey would stand up in a war against their Muslim brothers, carried great weight.) "I knew I shouldn't interrupt your long-awaited reunion. And you would certainly be exhausted from your trip. But I had to see you."

Him hugging me again, then saying, "Jill," and motioning to the porch. "A moment in private please?"

His eyes reminded me of the beggar girl's at Adana Airport.

I could hear him schmoozing—a little short of cash, their mother out of town. Jill put him off. "Julian, you need to be more responsible." Minutes later, her writing a check. Him promising, "I'll pay you back promptly, of course."

Grandpa called Julian's talk blarney. Why do I fall for it every time?

Julian popping back in. "Cin, you know I'm always here for you."

Like you've been in the past? Wondering if Julian said all the right words when he sent his first fiancée off alone to New York for that abortion. *Maybe I should give Steve a break. Maybe his actions should count for something.*

Mama saying, "It was so nice of Julian to stop by."

Michael shoved into the house. "Damn, look what the cat drug in." He faked a punch to Steve, "Hey, bro," then fished out a cigarette. Gwen, still a wisp of a thing, springing over with a lighter. *Like Sophie and the scuzz.*

"Well, Cin, Turkey certainly didn't do you no harm."

He looks like a swarthy gypsy—stud earring and beard a shade darker than his ponytail. An inch shorter than me, he could've still pinned me at a whim.

He turned back to Steve. "Don't ask nothing about the old man. Ain't seen him since he threw me off the roof. Didn't lap the tarpaper to his satisfaction. All I know's they packed up and moved to Texas."

Good riddance.

"Not interested in them." Steve's jaw clenched. "Just Pammy."

Michael shrugged as if Pam's silver bell laughter had silenced without a mark on him.

"What were those Pittsburgh guys doing on Grandpa McNeilly's road anyway?"

Gwen darted into the kitchen, away from Steve's raised voice. Jill and I followed as Michael said, "Cutting across to the back Greenville Road to line 'em up with their Vette. Herrick was talking trash at the Inn and laid down a challenge with his GTO."

Gwen's knee bounced up and down. "Steve's getting Michael stirred up," she said. "He's a little crazy since your grandpa isn't here to keep him steady. Grandpa McNeilly made Michael feel he could be something"—*Like by forbidding the guys to call him Mickey for Mickey Mouse,* Ed's nickname to disparage Michael's height. Grandpa said, "Michael, a man's height is measured in character, not inches."

Nana handed Gwen a plate, "Eat something, dear."

My ears glued to the conversation in the other room. "I can't believe you two let that drunk get out of town alive. Not very Carmine-like." Steve was really agitated.

"Old man couldn't afford no felony with his Chauffeur's License." Michael sounded defensive. "Said a punk's not worth his job."

When did Ed get so logical? A referee's bad call was worth risking his job. A waitress messing up his order was worth risking his job. Evidently, a dead daughter wasn't.

"Good thing I wasn't here. I wouldn't have listened to the old man. But I'm home now, and that killer's going to pay."

Steve sounds like Ed.

"The kid's a cracker. Don't own nothing except that torched Vette. Don't have two nickels to scrape together."

"Money's not what I'm talking about, and you know it." Steve shouting. *Merle could calm him down.*

Jill slipped into the living room in Merle's place. "That's enough, Steve. Nana and Mama are going to hear you." If I could hear Jill's stage whisper, certainly Nana and Mama could, too. "Everyone in this house has been through enough without talk like that."

The screen door squeaking. "Get a move on, woman." Gwen skittering out after Michael. The old frame house vibrating silence … breathing ... breathing ...

Steve dropped onto the rug beside Tee. Jill and I curled together on the company sofa, and she opened Necco Wafers and Good and Plenty like she did after botched math exams and disastrous haircuts.

I'm never going to leave my people again. We can all fit in this house.

Dad talked about the weather, the Presidential campaign, Nixon and the "silent majority," of which Dad considered himself a part. Law and order and all that stuff.

Jill teasingly disagreed. "If the majority hadn't been silent, they'd have had a voice. Either McGovern or McCarthy. But both Humphrey and Nixon mean status quo." She'd been a "Clean Gene" for Eugene McCarthy, clean cut so as not to scare voters. "It's time for change. Any country that'd put a racist like George Wallace on the ballot has to be totally messed up."

She whirled on me. "And what happened to you getting political, Cin? The Middle East is the biggest world crisis since WWII, and all you write about is bad marriages and wild parties."

I grinned.... *falling, falling, falling ... the whisper of raven's wings, Grandpa's Irish pipe, "Danny Boy." ... Pam ... Grandpa ... At least I'm with my people.* I twisted Tee's alfalfa sprout.

Nana, like a wise nurse, probed the painful wound we were protecting. "If you kids are to have any peace, you need to ask your questions about the accident."

I winced.

Mama untucked her tiny feet, grabbed a handful of candies, kissed us, and rushed upstairs. The word "accident," obviously the new "it." ... *falling ... falling ...*

I wanted to run after Mama. To play a grownup game of "pretend." *But not even a wish on a diamond in the sky can change this reality....* "*The pipes*" ...

Nana ran her finger around my chin. "Charles and Pammy would want you to come to terms with the accident and not just grieve. Life must go on, dear."

Falling ... falling ... Tee plopping Raggedy Ann on the wood stool. My festering question exploded—"How could you sell our home?" The instant those words escaped, my mouth snapped shut in shame.

Neither Nana nor Dad flinched.

"We knew it'd be hard for you, dear." Nana's eyes stroked me. "But we didn't have a choice. The mortgage was twice its original amount."

Nana's voice lowered more. "Charles never worried about money if someone he loved wanted something. And I never questioned him. I excused myself as being submissive, but a true helpmate wouldn't have left him to handle financial burdens alone."

Dad said, "We didn't talk money. I assumed we were making it. Guess I should have known better. April 15th meant nothing to us. Never made enough to pay income tax."

Dad chuckled, then lowered his eyes. "There wasn't money to pay the mortgage, let alone a hired hand. And I couldn't keep up with two jobs. The farm had to go. GM has Charity's insurance."

We all looked at Tee, curled around a throw pillow and her Raggedy Ann. *The peaceful rest of the innocent.*

"Charles and I avoided unpleasant things," Nana said. "It was one of our biggest mistakes."

I remembered Grandpa telling me, "The Emerald Isle has all the fighting Irish. The biggest hurdle Martha and I have had is learning to have a good fight." It made no sense then, but now— *The price of peace ... The farm. My sanity.*

Nana and Dad talked about the accident and Grandpa's heart condition. Though Jill's letters had covered most of the details. they added tidbits, especially about the bidders, Yankee and Amish, at the auction of farm equipment.

"Charles had it all, from our New Holland baler to Old Blue and his wagon. You know his philosophy." We repeated it with Nana like a chorus. "Never throw away the old just because there's something new."

"He had to have been the only man in the state who kept the outhouse painted even after we got indoor plumbing," Dad said.

We all laughed. It felt good to laugh.

He said the Millers' barn-raising crew moved the contents of the farmhouse while Merle's mother and sisters helped unpack and arrange things. "We were as busy as a fox in a henhouse that day."

We laughed, recognizing another of Grandpa's old sayings. Tee whimpered in her sleep. I wrapped my finger in her cowlick.

Nana praised the Lord for "heaping his blessings on us by sending the Millers to buy the place and the stock and the crops in the field." I wasn't honest enough to say, "It sounds like God blessed the Millers, not us. I just said, "Why, Nana? How can you forgive God for letting everyone we love die?"

Crepe arms encircled me. *Warm vanilla.* "I don't understand. I may never. But I trust God. For some reason, Pammy's and Charles' purposes were over." Her hairnet scratched my forehead. "Remember how Charles said an egg with a broken yolk looks different, but it's still delicious and useful? That's our life now. Different but delicious still."
I don't care about delicious. I want unchanged.
Jill's understanding green eyes caught mine. Nana hummed, "Great Is Thy Faithfulness." Steve fiddled with Tee's pearl button. "You haven't said anything, dear." Nana patted Steve's curls.
"There's nothing to say" Steve set the pearl button on top of Tee's button tower.
"We're learning talking helps, son." *Grandpa used to call the guys "son" when he was serious. Now Dad is.* "You said dog bites fester if they're stitched up. I think it's the same way with grief."
Nana held Steve's cheeks. "We're so sorry about Pammy, dear. Charles kept going over how he should have foreseen those events. We love your sister so."
Steve stared at the wall. Jill plucked out the Eagles' "Turn, Turn, Turn." *The "season to mourn."*
Nana probed gently. "Charles couldn't save our babies from influenza, so when Charity and Cindy came along, he was so afraid he'd lose them, too, he couldn't call them by name. They became Angel and Baby Girl. But he called your sister Pammy from the very beginning. He was confident he could protect her." She kissed Steve's cheek. "God promises never to give us more than we can bear. I think God took Charles because he couldn't bear to live with Pammy dead."
Dad agreed. "If he said it once, he said it a hundred times. 'I promised Steve.' Then, 'How can it be? Pammy went to the hospital in an ambulance and left in a hearse.'" (Osborne Funeral Home was also our ambulance service. The cot the same for the living and the dead. A simple matter of switching signage and a yellow light on top for a red one and "scoop and run.")
"Your folks said Pammy spending time with us was nothing but trouble waiting to happen. After the accident, Charles said they

were right. They should never have let Pammy hang around a killer."

I gasped at that word.

Steve exploded. "Grandpa's not a speck at fault. Sitting in his own pickup on his own property minding his own business. Dawdi Hostetler's buggy in the lane. I could've driven a semi past that buggy." His face turned purple. "The drunk's at fault. And he'll pay for it!"

Jill settled close against my trembling. Nana against Steve.

"He's only a boy, dear. He deserves forgiveness. If you'd seen his face.... I pray for the child every day."

"Well, I don't."

"He was with his friends, dear. Like you boys doing your brody thing. Driving fast like you boys do." *Steve in his Ford, glass packs rumbling. All of us laughing.* "Young men drink." *Michael in the ditch. Sean and the mailbox*—Sean'd had too much Stout, took the curve too fast, smashed the mailbox, scraped a strip of paint off the "McNeilly" on the milk co-op sign. Grandpa never fixed it. "That white scrape's a reminder, son. Stay out of the hooch."

"We've all made mistakes, dear. Accidents happen." Nana touched Steve's cheek.

"Accidents?" Steve's body tensed. "Murder happens!"

Don't say another word, I silently pleaded. *Please.*

Dad intervened. "It's been a long day, son. Let's get some rest." Dad handed me a Payday and shook Steve's hand. "Nothing will bring them back, son. Make choices that honor them."

Dad lifted Tee from the floor and carried her up to Nana's bed. *Not mine.*

Steve, looking like a prisoner contemplating a jailbreak, sidled toward the stairs. "Looks like it's turning into a girls' night."

Nana stopped him en route. "You will be going to church with us, won't you, dear?" I held my breath. God was on Steve's hit list, right above "that murdering drunk."

"Even Sean's going in the morning." Sean hadn't attended church since he started drinking after high school. "I've prayed for the day we could all be together."

I didn't have Nana's faith in answered prayer. *Steve's going to break her heart.* He had lashed out to me, "What kind of God would take my baby sister and your grandpa? I'll tell you what kind. An Ed-Carmine-God. A cruel power wielder."

But facing Nana, he took a deep breath, let it out slowly, and said, "Sure, I'm going, Nana." The words, "for you," silently and clearly understood by all.

"And, dear, it'd make me very happy if you'd take Charles's pickup." The insurance had repaired it. "I can't drive it. Cindy's folks don't need it. Charles would want you two to have it. We can transfer the title this week."

Steve swallowed, nodded okay, and stomped upstairs. A door thwacked shut. Music from the fair filtered through the silence.

After a few minutes, Nana turned to me. "I noticed you didn't ask one logical question. Why we didn't wait for Steve to come home to work on the farm with your dad."

I didn't respond.

"We discussed that possibility, dear, and decided against it. First, it would strap you with a debt you didn't create. And your father felt strongly that you kids should choose your own lives without obligation. I agreed. Charles chose his life. He would want you to choose yours. Besides, I believe farming is too confining for your young man. He likes action and there's none of that in the barn or the field."

I couldn't argue that they were wrong, though I wished they were.

Her hairnet on my forehead. "We have many tomorrows to talk later. If God grants them." *That warm vanilla scent.* "Don't leave Steve alone now. Help him with his grief, dear, and your load will be lighter, too."

Jill said, "Nana's right." *That familiar crooked smile. That auburn hair. My forever friend.* "We better take care of our guys every chance we get."

So, I climbed the stairs to a strange room in a strange house and crawled into a strange bed, Steve was already mumbling in his sleep. Sleep, his typical response to problems.

I can't believe any of this ... Grandpa, Pammy, Tee's silence, the farm gone ... "Baby Girl, any shack is home if ..."

Steve's arms clamped me tight. I stared at a full moon.... Once when I was little, I fell asleep, Tee clutching my nightgown, the moon smiling straight into our window. Later, Tee shook me, "Dee, drink, Dee," and I opened my eyes. The room was dark. I cried out, "The moon's gone." Nana came running. "No, dear, the moon is never gone," she comforted me. "It's hidden from our view sometimes. But it's always there."

Is that the way death is? Are Grandpa and Pam here but just hidden from our view?

I finally drifted off … A fire-breathing dragon chased the fair damsel Pam. Grandpa futilely hacked on it with his shovel. The dragon devoured Pam then whirled…. Grandpa charred—

My brain screamed awake. "Steve!"

He flailed. "Oh, it's you."

We clung together. The dragon receding into the aroma of biscuits and sausage gravy. But Grandpa did not call up the stairs, "Rise and shine, Sleepyheads."

We padded downstairs in bare feet—safe from scorpions and centipedes but so vulnerable—ate in silence, dressed for church, climbed into Grandpa's red Ford pickup.

Cigar smoke, flannel, denim, Old Spice, the truck bed haunted by Pam's silver bell laughter.

Grief, like rat poison, ran through my soul.

Chapter 27

"Death leaves a heartache no one can heal;
Love leaves a memory no one can steal."
(From an Irish headstone)

"Doesn't Rev. Minnow know anything else to preach about? Love your enemy. Forgive. Love. Forgive. Love. What about 'an eye-for-an-eye' for Mr. Murderer?"

Jill, riding shotgun, glowered. "Go ahead, big man. Beat the kid up. Beat them all up. Prove what they say is right. Prove you're a typical Carmine."

He punched the gas. Grandpa's pickup speedometer had never registered that high—

That afternoon the phone rang. "How are you, kid?" Merle and Denny in stereo.

I slumped in relief. "Actually, still plotting revenge for the knotted clothes in the luggage. Had to wear Steve's T-shirt to bed the first night."

"TMI! TMI!" Merle's cheeks would be crinkling. "Enough about the honeymoon night."

Denny chimed in. "How's our buddy, Cin?"

"Mad," I said softly. "Ready to blow. It scares me. ... I don't know—"

"That's what we figured. We'd have been there, Cin, but used up our leave time for the funerals." I must have paused too long. Merle dropped that subject. "Put that husband of yours on the phone, and we'll see what we can do to talk some sense into that Carmine head of his."

They let Steve have it. I heard bits and pieces.

"Don't do anything stupid. Pammy and Grandpa wouldn't want that."

"You said you weren't going to be like your dad."

"Nothing you do will change a thing. Don't mess up everyone's lives."

"Think of Cin, not yourself."

"Don't waste your energy on anger. Stick to what needs done." Work on house blueprints. Price out lumber.

The ending came through loud and clear. "Let's make 'good new days'"—living side-by-side. A passel of Amish-Japanese-hippy babies to play with ours—"Don't let the past destroy today, Steve. Or our futures." (I decided it wasn't the time for me to announce I had changed our future plans.)

Anyway, it must have cost them half a month's check for that long-distance call. But it set Steve on the straight path. At least temporarily. I guess I shouldn't have been surprised. I'd seen Merle calm Steve down time after time.

But I didn't respond so quickly to their advice or to anyone's.

Jill said, "Labor Day's over, Cindy. Didn't you hear the guys? It's time to get on with things. Pammy and Grandpa would want that."

"Denny's dad has a couple of leads on trucking jobs for me," Steve said. (Since he was sixteen, he'd driven the semi while Ed slept in the bunk.) "Buddy of Merle set me up an interview at Wonder Bread. Hours would be better and local runs. It'd be a piece of cake." He laughed at his own reference to Twinkies and Hostess cupcakes, great delicacies to us.

"And at work [the Camp for the Trainable] I heard about a trailer for rent in Edinboro. A cute little place." Jill's green eyes drilled me to the floor. "Come on, Cin," she urged.

For the second time in our friendship (black-market was the first), I wasn't open with her. I didn't tell her I was perfectly content to hole up with my people. Forever.

Steve flashed sad eyes. "Come on, Cindy. It'll be an adventure. A new job and a new place to live."

I balked. *I have a place to live. Right here. Permanently,* I thought but said, "Tee and I need to help Nana and Mama with these elderberries." We canned over fifty quarts a year, and it took a mountain of clusters to shuck enough to fill a quart jar.

Jill tried another approach. "On the way back, we could check out our lots."

Steve agreed. "The guys said our driveway looks amazing. Lined up to Charles McNeilly perfection, of course. He added split-rails along the fencerow of elderberries to dress it up." His blue eyes pierced mine. "But I'm not going there without you, Cindy."

I didn't have the courage to tell them I didn't plan to ever go there. I refused to live on the lot next to the "Miller Farm." I simply shook my head no. "Go on without me."

Steve ruffled Tee's and my head, said, "Nana says putting it off won't make it any easier," and they went on their way.

I nuzzled Tee and whispered, "This is where I belong. I should never have left you." I took her hand, and together we yanked a grapefruit-sized purple clump from the bushel basket, then pulled off berries the size of the beads on Nana's string of pearls.

As our fingers stained wine-colored, my mind flashed back to Rod at the parties with his boda bag, then to Timmy reaching for me, "Mama," and Heidi, silent, listless. *Everything is so complex.*

I guess my not going with Steve and Jill—totally unprecedented—kind of shook Mama up.

With two elderberry pies cooling on the windowsill, Mama took me out on the porch before she left for work. Staring up at the sky, she came the closest I'd ever heard her to facing a problem.

"When you left with Steve, I hid in the pantry. That's always been like my tree house, you know."

I didn't know.

"Your grandpa found me crying there because I couldn't stand it with my little princess gone. He took me outside and held me until I was quiet and said, 'Listen!' But I didn't hear a thing.

"He pointed up at the birds singing on the electric wire and said, 'Those mamas push their babies out of the nest. Those babies flap and squawk, and their mamas just stand by and sing. If those mama birds saw you crying, they'd give you a good shake and tell you it's a wonderful thing to see Baby Girl grow up.'"

Mama stretched her tiny frame. "After the accident, your nana reminded me of that story, and she said Pammy and Grandpa simply grew up into the next world. We should keep singing."

I'll never be able to make myself sing again, I thought as Mama's car backed out and headed for the Diner.

I guess I shook Nana up, too, though she was more direct. She joined Tee and me for Ovaltine and warm cinnamon twirls and said, "We could have done the elderberries without you today, dear. You need to focus on making your future with Steve. It's hard work, not magic." That sounded like Grandpa. "No prince is going to ride up and sweep you away like in your mama's stories. You and Steve have to build your own castle together." Her eyes actually twinkled. "And fill it with babies for me to love on."

I swallowed a sob and blurted out, "I'm like an old dried-up heifer. I've lost faith in believing I'll ever get pregnant."

Nana patted me. "There, there, dear. Faith isn't believing you'll get everything you want. It's believing if the house is taken, there'll be a roof somewhere else to cover your head. If there aren't any beans, there'll be a hunk of bread. If one person leaves, another will come." She kissed my cheek. "If you don't have your own child, He'll give you someone else's to care for."

She'd murmured several more appendices to her "Advice for Marriage" lectures by the time Steve and Jill returned, Steve with the broadest grin I'd seen in months.

He twirled me in his signature pinwheel swing, then gave Tee a gentle twirl. "You missed it Cindy. You missed a super successful mission!"—the trailer by Edinboro State campus, "Still available. His Wonder Bread delivery job out of Erie, "Starting Monday"—"It's going to work out, Cindy," he said, then tugged Tee toward the kitchen. "C'mon, Big Sis, let's go celebrate with a Coke."

Jill tossed me reenrollment papers for Edinboro State. "Thursday is registration. Better get moving. Grandpa bragged to everyone that you'll be the first in the family to graduate college."

I made excuses. "We don't have money."

She had answers. "The Bursar will help get your PA grant reinstated. A BS degree this spring for you. Half through my

Master's at Kent for me. We're right on track to support our guys while they get their degrees."

I avoided her green eyes. "We're trying to get pregnant."

"So? What's that have to do with anything? You won't be the first to go to college pregnant and you won't be the last."

When I didn't answer, she bristled. Her crooked smile straightened out. "You can't keep putting off making decisions."

She paced the tiny living room. "Edinboro classes start Monday, and I'm leaving for Kent"—on quarters, Kent State's classes started later, but she was working orientation for RAs for extra money—"You'd better snap up that trailer. It's choice, walking distance for you from campus."

I stood firm. "I'm not going back to college, and I certainly am not leaving Tee and Mama and Nana ever again."

She could tell I was serious. She shoved me out to the sidewalk. "You promised Steve 'for better or worse,' so you'd better figure things out." She practically hissed. "Don't go running back to sponge off your parents like your mama did."

I stared, shocked. But then, as I've said before, Jill knew my thoughts.

Her green eyes flashed. "Your mama lost her father, you know, but she goes to the Diner and carries trays with both breasts and a chest wall gone. She doesn't make excuses. Nana lost her home and her life's companion, but she's humming around this tiny house. Steve lost his little sister, but even the Carmine's trying. I suppose you think your excuses are better than all of theirs?"

Rhetorical silence. This disagreement was more serious than whether Jill's hair was ugly Ronald McDonald hair or the color of the glow of a sunset's kiss.

"Get on with life. For Grandpa and Pam. For Steve. For yourself.... For me."

But I didn't know how. I dug around in the basement and found an extra dresser to store Steve's and my clothes.

Jill kept hounding me up to the evening before she left for Kent. Nana came out to the porch and said, "I thought you should reread this, Cindy dear. Charles would say, 'Baby Girl, it's time for the sun to shine." She handed me his memorial bulletin opened to its Irish blessing:

Perhaps my time seemed all too brief

Don't shorten yours with undue grief.
Be not burdened with tears of sorrow,
Enjoy the sunshine of the morrow.

Then she handed Jill a pair of scissors. "Are you ready, dear?"
Jill held them as if they were a coiled scorpion. "I'm kind of nervous."

"You have no reason, dear. You always do such a lovely job." Nana slipped off her hairnet and untied her braids. "I wouldn't want anyone else."

Their conversation sounded like gobbledygook.

Nana brushed her hair into a hip-length filmy fan. *An angel's halo.* Jill spritzed it with water, combed it into a low ponytail and lifted the scissors like an executioner lifting his axe.

And I understood. "No!" I screamed.

Nana waved Jill to a stop. "Just a minute, dear."

Cradled in vanilla. Deep firm murmur. "My hair was for Charles, dear. Its purpose is gone now, like the farm's purpose for raising a family is gone now." She brushed my cheek with firefly kisses.

I doubled my fists. "Everything's changed! Even Tee. You can't change, too. It's too much." I was so tired.

"Change builds strength, dear." Familiar lips forming familiar advice in a familiar alto voice. "It's important to move on. I learned that too late. We should have let your mother and father work things out alone after Charity was born. But I was selfish. After losing our babies and your mama got married, the house was empty. I saw Sean and Charity as my chance to fill the house again."

Jill opened the scissors, and I watched in horror as she sawed off Nana's angel halo. *Chin length bob cut. Nana? A pretty radical object lesson.*

But no matter what anyone said or did, my mind was set. I'd never leave the house. It might be a shack, but it was where those I loved lived.

Then a Hatton Florists delivery—a bouquet of daisies with one blue carnation and one pink carnation tucked in the middle. The vase decorated with pictures of dogs. The card signed, Garzas, "We lit candles for you. Love, Your other family."

How did they get these delivered? They've gotten so resourceful. Maybe they can save their family after all.

An hour later, the party line's ring—two short and one long. "Did you get them? Are they fresh?" *Sophie!* "Barb sent me money to order them. She said daisies are your favorite. Did they find a vase that fit Mutt and Jeff? Did you figure out the carnations were from Timmy and Heidi? Instead of wondering, I treated myself to a long-distance call to find out the answers firsthand."

She sounded like a happier version of the Sophie I knew before. She told about Fortiers coming over after mass for chicken and biscuits. "I never thanked you for teaching me to make that recipe. I never thanked Steve and you enough, period. Things could've been bad if you two hadn't stepped in."

"No, you thanked us, Soph."

She went on as if I hadn't said anything. "Marie has told me lots of things I didn't know. Right before we met, Raymond got caught in a bust in the red-light district. But Papa Fortier knows people, so Raymond didn't get arrested like his friends."

Her accent was barely detectable.

"I decided that might be why I didn't get pregnant. Raymond might have a disease or something."

She was right about that one.

"Papa gave him six months to settle down with a respectable girl or he was out of the will. So, no more lies to myself. I had to accept that Raymond never wanted *me*. He just needed a wife."

I had no comment for that truth.

She gave a little sigh and said, "I can't do anything about the past. But I can make my own future." Her cleaning business had really taken off. "I'm really good at cleaning, you know," *An understatement.* She'd received her cosmetology license for Maine, rented a station at Limestone Salon, saving up to buy her own beauty shop, and enrolled in Citizenship classes.

"Raymond and I are forever married in the sight of God, but Raymond could get the government to divorce us, so I'm using my Air Force benefits now while I have them. I went to the dentist at Loring for new dentures, but he said I just needed these tightened up. Did you notice my teeth don't clack?"

It was obvious.

She cut herself off, "Enough about me," she said and started asking questions. "How are Tee's seizures?" "Are your mama and nana getting settled in town?" "Is Jill back to Kent yet?"

I was shocked she remembered my people's names, let alone remembered details about their lives.

"And how are you two? Barb asked me to join them in lighting candles for you guys. Is it working? Are you two okay?"

Sophie had never asked how I was before. At first, I didn't know how to respond. Then I started babbling. And she added the comments. Our roles had reversed.

"Jill's pushing me about everything," I said. "We've never disagreed like this."

"She must really be worried about you."

"Steve was crazy mad about the accident and the farm. Now he acts like I should just get over it and go on with our plans."

"You've got no choice but to go on, Cin. Like me." *You might choose to go on, but I choose not to. I'm not ready.*

"Steve was so excited about your grandpa building your driveway. It must be comforting to have a piece of your grandfather in that land. I bet you go walk that driveway every day."

I didn't answer for a moment, and then I said it. "I'm going to have Steve sell the lot. I haven't told him and Jill and Merle yet, but I can't live next to our farm. It'd be torment."

She hesitated, then said, "I go driving in New Brunswick every time I can. Something nice about familiar scenery and hearing French spoken. I used to think I wanted to get away from the bad memories in Canada, but I realized that would mean I'd give up the good memories, too." *She's mimicking Nana's indirect approach to advice.* "You've got more good memories in that ten acres than I do in all of Canada. Don't give them up. Go build your house and your future. You and Steve are perfect together."

I twisted my wedding band over the Brillo-pad scarred crescent-moon birthmark.

"I know you're doing that look you do when I say something not exactly real." She paused as if thinking how to phrase it. "You *are* perfect together. I know Steve gets mad. Like when you got locked out of your apartment. But I've seen how he looks at you. And talks to you. And you two tell each other the truth."

We hung up, but Sophie's words continued to echo—"No more lies to myself," "truth," "past," "future," "real," "memories," "in the sight of God," "together," "piece of Grandpa"—*Was Grandpa right? Can I do anything if I put my mind to it? Can I go on?*

The screen door squeaked, Steve pecked my cheek.

Nana said. "Before you get out of your work clothes, Steve, dear, could you run to the farm for Charity's milk?" Tee drank gallons of milk but wouldn't touch a drop of store-bought pasteurized milk.

Turning away from the tiny living room with my people to focus on the man I'd promised myself "'til death," I whispered, "We'll both go, Steve. We can stop at our lot."

Steve stood like a monument to Wonder Bread, then crushed me against him. Several minutes later he cleared his throat.

"It's rained quite a bit lately," he said. "Better get your boots."

Leather boots mold to your feet, more comfortable with time. Glass slippers shatter, leave shards deep in your soul.

"Cindy, did you hear me?"

I nodded. "Steve's taking us for a ride, Tee."

She lifted her head slightly.

"C'mon, Big Sis." Beaming like before that knock on our apartment door, Steve held open the door to Grandpa's pickup, and we scrunched Tee between us.

Focus on the moment. Not the past, not the future, I told myself as Steve drove down our road as sedately as if he were driving a hearse. But still, with my eyes scrunched tight, I felt every familiar bump. We coasted around the gravel curve. No brodies into the lane this time. I felt Tee pointing—*Pammy lying on the gravel, Tee on the lamb, Grandpa helpless*—the top of my head pulsed.

The pickup stopped. "The Millers said to tell you the tree house and barn are open to you and Tee any time of day or night. Want to check things out while I go to the milk house?"

Eyes tight closed, I shook my head no. *This was a big mistake! Looking at the lot is one thing. It's the future. But the farm's the past. I'll never drive in from this end of the road again. I'll never look at what we've lost.*

I heard the pickup door open, a jug set by my feet. We backed up, then took off, kicking up stone a minute, turned, then slid to a stop.

"We're here." Steve nuzzled me. "I was afraid you'd never come with me."

I rowed against drowning tears. Ravens' wings whispered at my shoulder. *If I stand up, I'll faint.*

He lifted me out of the truck, held me. *I can do it if I set my mind to it.* I peeked—bowed heads of ancient elderberry bushes, fence row, split rails added by Grandpa, the property line of our ten acres. *The last of the McNeilly farm.* Sean had refused Grandpa's offered land. "No need for it. Jo and I aren't staying married forever like the rest of you."

Steve got Tee out of the passenger's side. Pointed through the trees. "See, Tee? See the tip of your tree house? Remember your castle? Remember Zul?"

I adjusted Tee's hat. Neither of us looked. *Nana used to call the porch Grandpa built, "as wide as a highway, sturdy enough to hold a barn dance." In truth, it was as narrow as a young girl's coffin, as shaky as an old man's heart.*

"I know missing the farm is ripping your heart out, Cindy. But just look at our place." He stooped to Tee. "Help me, Big Sis. Tell Dee she needs to see this."

Tee scuffed her boot in the gravel. I raised my eyes. *Nothing. Probably one of his "gotcha" tricks.*

"There, Cindy, there. By those two really old maples."

And there in the crook of the gnarled arms, *A platform.* Shasta daisies framing steps up to it. *Grandpa's one last gift.*

I clasped Tee. "I see it, Tee? Do you?"

"It's a preview of the future for the Alden girls," Steve said softly. "Nana said in April before planting season, Grandpa and Pammy built the base and a porch, He said you and Jill could design exactly what you want in your very own tree house. We guys will build it now."

Can we build our kingdom again?

I towed Tee off, halting at the base of the tree. *The sign!*—a slab of scrap lumber. The "No grils," printed in blobby black paint, slashed out with Massey Ferguson red touchup paint the day Sean decided I was big enough to scoot up and down with "Injun feathers" from the chicken coop and shelled corn for bullets for his metal cap gun. "Jill thought to ask the Millers for it."

I lifted Tee's boot onto the first railed step, built the perfect width. Tee scrunched into an exaggerated dowager's hump, wouldn't budge. I whispered, "I miss Grandpa, too." She stomped her foot and snorted. Steve and I managed to get her up on the platform with its protective railing.

Steve and I flopped on our bellies and listened to the rustle of wind through the cornstalks now laden with corn—in spring after planting, Grandpa would stoop and dig in the dirt to check germination. "Life's funny, Baby Girl," he'd say. "This seed's the pretty one." He'd hold up a yellow corn seed, hard and intact. "But it's dead." Digging farther down the row, he'd hold up a shriveled kernel with a disgusting white tail. "Now this seed looks awful, but it's life coming."

Grandpa had shriveled and fallen into the ground. So had Pammy. I had to believe they were life coming. Eternally alive.

The fall air smelled green as it blew over my mildewed soul. "Let's plant daffodils on both sides of the driveway to celebrate Pam every spring." I said to Steve. "As you said, life must go on."

His blue eyes held my brown ones. "We can do this, can't we, Cindy?"

And for the first time, it struck me. *Only Steve always calls me Cindy. Everyone else uses pet names for me*—Baby Girl, Dear, Princess, Dee, Cin, Sis—*Steve sees me just as myself.*

I twirled my band over my moon-shaped birthmark. Sarge's wife had questioned how long I'd believe Steve was a "good man." I'd had my own doubts. But now I decided, *He's not Grandpa. He's not a prince on a charger. But he's as good a man as they come on this side of the moon.*

"No more lies," Sophie had said was her first step. So, I faced Steve's ocean blue eyes. "I need to talk to you about a few things that happened in Turkey."

"Later. We need to check out where Jill and Merle put the stakes for our houses."

No more lies!

"Now!" I jumped up before I lost my nerve. (Nana would never have yelled at Grandpa, but then, Nana hadn't married Steve.) "Just listen."

He stood with eyebrows scrunched together.

"We need to talk about that black-market deal."

"That? That's a long time ago." He twisted that curl.

"Listen!" I took a deep breath. "After the *bush bush* left with those Marlboros, I was livid, so mad that I ran to Barb's." ... "*Whatsoever things are true.*"

"By yourself? Didn't you think how dangerous that was?"

"Hush, I've just started!" I guess I was shouting because Steve grinned.

"You're sounding like a real Carmine," he said. "Pammy would be proud of me. It only took me a year to water down that McNeilly-Alden niceness trait of yours. What do you think of that?"

I punched him.

Grandpa and Nana never learned how to fight. On the other hand, the Carmines, experts at fighting, never learned to fight fair. *I guess our challenge is to learn to both fight and fight fair.*

So I began.

My list of topics was long. Thankfully, I'd brought Tee's bag of "pretties" to entertain her.

I was angry I might never get pregnant, and if I did, our baby could be handicapped like Tee. I was angry I'd never be an aunt to Pam's children. I was angry Grandpa left me just when I was old enough to appreciate his wisdom. I was angry Death took my sanctuary, the farm, and our carefully laid plans for the future, and my husband's laughter....

When I'd finished ranting, I could feel Steve's chin quivering against my cheek.

"I thought it was just me you were mad at, you know? For taking you away from your Tee and from your mama when she got cancer again. And for your grandpa dying because *my* sister got killed. You blamed *me*, right?"

"Where would you get that idea?"

"The way you acted. Unhappy. Like everything's my fault."

"No, Steve. I didn't need you to make me happy. I needed you to listen to me."

"I guess I didn't know how." He stepped back. "Do you have a clue how afraid I was?" I had no answer.

I treaded softly. "You can touch me, you know."

He fingered my shoulder. "Think we can ever be happy again? Think we can make it? Think we have what it takes?"

Those serious questions provoked serious thought, and I realized, *We have more to build on than a school friendship now.*

In the last sixteen months, he'd seen me run from "Yankee, go home" boys, scowl at being called "Elly May," shake my head over Sophie, stand in unrighteous indignation as I held dirty lira, swivel belly dances, train puppies, protect Barb and Timmy. He'd wiped my tears at news of Tee's seizures and Mama's breast cancer. Most of all, the two of us, alone, had gone through the crucible of death. Our love had taken on the scent of vanilla.

I leaned against Steve. "Nana would say our solution is God, people, and projects, I think."

He messed up my flip. "I've got a project, Mrs. Carmine." His arms and mouth swallowed me, and automatically, I started humming, "Some Day My Prince Will Come." He gave me a twirl.

"Remember after I gave you your diamond, you took me to your tree house and sang that song and said the prince was me? It didn't turn out that way, did it?"

"Oh, Steve, you'll always be my prince. A good man who loves me and tries hard."

I nestled into his arms and belted out, "One Day My Prince Did Come." And we danced.

Tap-tap-tap. A tug on my jeans. "Dee." My boots froze to the platform.

A little grunt. "Dee. Zul."

I whirled, knelt in reverence. "Tee, I'm listening. Do you want to play Rapunzel? Is that what you mean?"

"Uh!" Her almond eyes glowed yes. Her thick tongue protruded in concentration. "Dee?"

She's talking! My tears fell on Tee's Alfalfa sprout.

"Now that's my Big Sis," Steve said.

She shuffled over the rough sturdy wood floor and lay down again on her back. As tradition demanded, I wiggled over beside her. Steve joined us.

"Rapunzel, Rapunzel, let down your hair," I chanted and shook my brown tresses through the protective railing Grandpa had built us. Steve shook his curls. Tee almost imitated us.

Then Tee, Steve, and I flopped over on our stomachs to survey our new kingdom.

***

That night, upstairs in my parents' and Nana's gray frame house, Steve's tears ran into mine, soaking our shared pillow with our shared sorrow. Then Steve approached the Holy of Holies, the empty spot deep inside me. For the first time in months, I felt a stirring in the void, an uncoiling from my emotional fetal position. At his touch, the first scab over grief's wound began to form.

I sensed Grandpa and Pam smiling down.

> Those we love
> Don't go away,
> They walk beside
> Us every day,
> Unseen, unheard,
> But always near,
> Still loved, still
> Missed and very
> Dear.
> —Irish Blessing

Postlude—2009

Our daughter waited while I quoted that final blessing—she knew how I loved reciting Grandpa's sayings. Then she said, "It took you long enough to make your points."

But her sarcasm had softened, her eyes, too.

I grinned. "In my defense, I had a lot of background to fill in for you. You didn't grow up watching your dad and me like I did Nana and Grandpa."

She was fifteen when Children's Services gave us custody.

"I get that you guys worked through some serious things—black-market, the near explosion, friends with messed up marriages. And death." At that, her face got that wild-eyed fear I recognized so well. "I couldn't survive if something happened to either of you. You are the only ones who've ever cared for me."

"We love you, too, dear." I said simply, not bothering to tell her that, of course, she'd find a way to go on. We all feel how we feel.

"And I get you think I should be honest with Rob about what's really upsetting me. No more secrets." She slid back into her defiant tone. "But you don't get what I'm saying. Admit it. Dad just tried to protect you. He never made you hate him the way I hate Rob."

I didn't give her a lecture about not hating. I just said, "You're right. Probably my feelings were more like disillusionment from life not going as I'd imagined."

She did that eye-roll thing. "At least you had illusions to start with," she said and started ranting again about Rob's flaws.

When she paused a microsecond to gasp in enough air to keep from fainting, I whispered, "I'm so sorry you two have to go through this, dear, but it's worth it. It's worth all of this."

I'd save what else I had to say until after their next marital crisis. I knew there'd be a next one. If they made it through this one. That's the way life is.

Life doesn't come with a manual for happily-ever afters. Each one of us has to make her own happiness, with lots of work—and lots of tears.

Made in the USA
Las Vegas, NV
05 November 2021